THE GREAT DAYS OF THE
SOUTHERN RAILWAY

Patrick Whitehouse & David St John Thomas

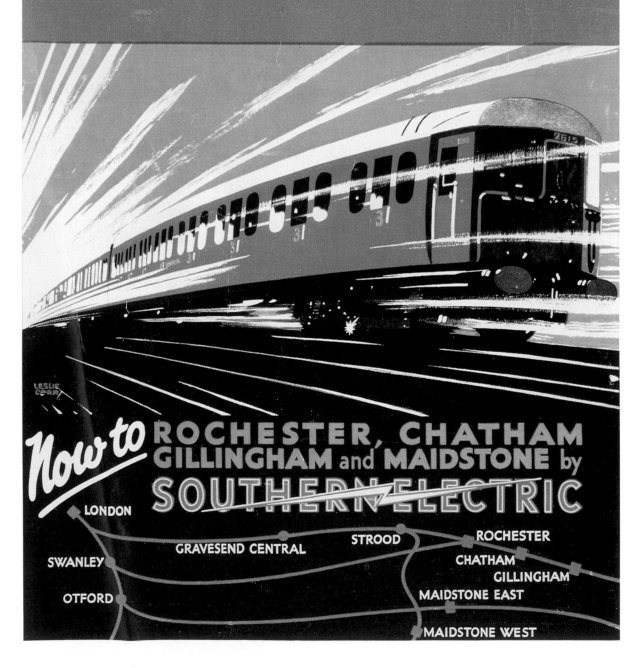

SOUTHERN RAILWAY

Electrification — Extension

ROCHESTER, CHATHAM, GILLINGHAM
AND MAIDSTONE

Now to **ROCHESTER, CHATHAM GILLINGHAM and MAIDSTONE by** SOUTHERN ELECTRIC

LONDON

GRAVESEND CENTRAL   STROOD   ROCHESTER

SWANLEY   CHATHAM   GILLINGHAM

OTFORD   MAIDSTONE EAST

MAIDSTONE WEST

LESLIE CARR

Frontispiece *A poster advertising the new electric services to Rochester, Chatham, Gillingham and Maidstone West, dated 2 July 1939.*

Above *Spirit of the Southern! BR-built West Country class No 34101* Hartland *(February 1950, rebuilt September 1960, withdrawn July 1966) of Stewarts Lane, Battersea depot (73A) leaves Victoria with a Continental boat train to Folkestone or Dover. Stewarts Lane duty 3 was for a Merchant Navy 4–6–2. About this time it was usually the 11.00am Victoria–Dover Marine via Orpington. It usually came back on the 2.30pm Dover Marine to Victoria via Chatham, but there were summer variations. The first coach is a corridor brake second (old second class retaining the figure 2 on the doors) so the date is prior to June 1956. The first (usually Pullman), second and third classes related to the status of the boat passengers where the fares included travel from and to London both on trains in England and on the Continent also the cross channel journeys. There is a further West Country Pacific to the right of the picture carrying the headcode discs for a Kent Coast train.*

First published by
David St John Thomas Publisher
PO Box 4, Nairn, Scotland IV12 4HU

This edition published by
BCA by arrangement with
David St John Thomas Publisher

CN 9378

© Patrick Whitehouse, David St John Thomas, and Millbrook House Ltd 1992

Printed in Great Britain

Book designed by Michael Head
Typeset by XL Publishing Services, Nairn
and printed in Great Britain at The Bath Press
for David St John Thomas Publisher
PO Box 4, Nairn, Scotland IV12 4HU

THE GREAT DAYS OF THE
SOUTHERN RAILWAY

Patrick Whitehouse & David St John Thomas

BCA

LONDON · NEW YORK · SYDNEY · TORONTO

CONTENTS

A view of Merchant Navy class Pacific No 35014 Nederland Line at Salisbury around 1959–60 with a down Waterloo–Exeter working. The professional support crew are hard at work pushing coal forward as it was low, probably due to a modified tender which had an increased water capacity of 6,000 gallons thus making it shallow at the back where the men are standing. Note the old Great Western shed to the left of the engine and the 'W' cut out indicating the position of the water stop.

A Padstow–Exeter local train leaving Yeoford headed by West Country Pacific No 34020 Seaton in 1961. A WR Fruit D van is the leading vehicle followed by Bulleid coaches in Southern Region green.

King Arthur class 4–6–0 No 30789 Sir Guy leaves the New Docks with an up boat train. The stock is mainly red and cream plus a Pullman car. The SR had a policy of constantly revarnishing its coaches so it is no surprise that the picture is dated 1960.

Lord Nelson class 4–6–0 No 30857 Lord Howe waiting to leave the Ocean Terminal with an up Cunard Line boat express made up mostly of Pullman cars. The passengers have almost certainly come from the USA on Queen Mary or Queen Elizabeth.

O.J. Morris's Central Division

One of the best and most prolific recorders of the Southern Railway's ex-LBSCR (Central) section was O.J. Morris, a Brighton man through and through, and a stalwart member of the then very august Stephenson Locomotive Society whose founders leant heavily in the direction of anything once painted in Stroudley's 'improved engine green'. Morris was one of the old brigade who believed, quite rightly, in the adage 'the bigger the negative the better the picture'. He lived in Southern territory at Norwood and was a familiar sight in the 1920s and 1930s especially if the sun was out and the subject was a Brighton one. He was easily spotted with his black suit, trilby hat, spectacles and camera set on a tripod. The following pictures show a cross section of his work, especially his love for Stroudley engines, in the Southern's earlier years.

The Peckham Rye depot, home of the old LBSCR overhead electric suburban units which pioneered the emus of the future. This photograph shows the shops in January 1927 with the four-wheeled petrol electric cars built in 1905 and still lettered LB&SCR. These were originally inspection cars but were also run as railmotors, for example, on the Brighton to Kemp Town branch and were later rebuilt as overhead line inspection cars for the South London line.

Waddon Marsh on the West Croydon-Wimbledon branch in the days when the countryside was closer to London, September 1929. The two coach train is propelled by a class D1 Stroudley 0–4–2T No B627. Note the desk in the wooden hut, the fire buckets, fire hand pump box and ground frame which apparently only controls access to the two sidings.

Brighton in May 1932 with two of O.J. Morris's favourite class of engine, the Stroudley class B1

generally known as the Gladstones after No 214 which is now preserved in the National Railway Museum thanks to members of the Stephenson Locomotive Society's efforts on her withdrawal. In LBSCR days most of the passenger classes, including tank engines, carried names. This photograph shows Nos B172 and B197, smart in their new green livery but with only a short time to go, outside Brighton station. Note the very LBSCR signals with wooden posts carrying arms on each side, some with brackets.

Old Havant station on the LBSCR Portsmouth line probably around 1929–30. There is a main line train behind a B4X class 4–4–0 entering the platform with a full head of steam and the signals are off. Note the high repeater arms enabling the driver to see the state of the road ahead when well to the other side of the station and its footbridge. The left hand bay platform is for the Hayling Island service worked by a Brighton Terrier 0–6–0T. Note the spoked wheel, visible behind the signal box sliding windows, for the level crossing gates with their red warning oil lamp, and the signal in the goods yard pulled off for a shunting movement.

Brighton London Road station in October 1933 with a Brighton-Tunbridge Wells West train behind ex-LBSCR class E5 0–6–2 tank No 2592 (once named Eastergate) made up of a six-wheel van and an ex SEC Birdcage non-corridor set.

Bognor shed on 5 May 1934 with four of Stroudley's class D1 0–4–2 tanks used for local services. All are in Southern olive green livery with Nos 2605, 2299 and 2616 lined out and carrying their new numbering, the 2 prefix indicating ex LBSCR engines and No B615 in the rear, unlined with its original B for Brighton prefix above the number. Nos 2605 and B615 are sitting neatly on the turntable. Note the immaculate state of the track.

Above *Whiter than white. Steam, chalk and spotless ballast are all highlighted here as No 850* Lord Nelson *takes a train of wooden bodied Pullmans along the Channel coast as it leaves Shakespeare's Cliff Tunnel near Dover in 1927. From a coloured painting based on a* Times *photograph.*

Below *King Arthur class 4–6–0 No E764* Sir Gawain *on a Victoria–Dover boat express at Bickley. The coaches are the 1921 SECR Continental stock plus three Pullman cars.*

*A Southern Railway local train
headed by Wainwright H class
0–4–4T passing through Surrey
woodland on a winter's day. The H
class tank engines were built for the
SE&CR between 1904–15 and most
worked through SR days to the
1950's of British Railways. From a
painting by Don Breckon.*

Plymouth Friary station probably in the late 1920s with an LSWR T9 class 4–4–0 heading a train bound for Okehampton and Exeter Queen Street. There is a heterogeneous collection of stock behind the tender with nine coaches in view; the fourth coach is probably an ex LSWR dining car. In the bay on the right is an O4 class 0–4–4T.

East Grinstead on 3 March 1934 with an ex-LBSCR Marsh I1X 4–4–2T No 2002 in olive green heading a London Bridge–Tunbridge Wells West train. The leading coach is a 3rd brake with a wooden destination board slotted in above the compartment windows.

12

1
THIS WAS THE SOUTHERN

THIS is not just a second volume of our volume in the '150' series but, like *Great Days of the GWR* (others will eventually follow on the LMS and LNER to make a second quartet), a portrait of the railway as people actually experienced it and as many indeed remember it. And what a railway it was! Uniquely among the Big Four of the Grouping era, it was made up of three systems, if not equal, at least comparable in size, though of extremely different characters: an aggressive London & South Western which had already pioneered third-rail electrification and gave the GWR a hard time in much of what might have been natural 'Paddington' territory; a gentlemanly London, Brighton & South Coast, whose start on overhead suburban electrification had to be abandoned; and an impoverished South Eastern & Chatham (in fact a management committee of two railways) where daily miracles were performed in keeping the commuter wheels moving on a second-rate system with poor track and bridges and frustrated in its plans for electrification.

Once it was in its stride (a committee of the three general managers each of whom had to sign off every agreement predictably did not last more than a few months) the Southern Railway became one of the world's best-run commercial concerns. It was progressive, especially with electrification, yet much of it was a living museum. It had a consistent policy: to electrify and increase the productivity of its basic output, passenger train miles. Yet it was as pragmatic as a family business in meeting changing times. Above all it was economical (examples of that abound in the following pages) yet the second of its two greatly contrasting locomotive engineers (one of our chapters goes into the differences in theory and practice) was among the most wasteful top railwaymen in Britain.

While there was not that element of worship that seemed to characterise much on the GWR, the Southern's great achievement was that from a bad beginning in terribly depressed times it forged an extremely creditable railway that was generally respected, sometimes even loved, by its customers and its none-too-well-rewarded staff. Again, it demonstrated how the combination of a consistent long-term policy and pragmatic approach to short-term situations brings the best rewards in business. It was indeed the utter opposite of what we have had to experience in more recent times: a wavering policy (largely because the politicians move the goal posts) but dogmatic practice. One dreads to think how less effectively the Blitz, leave alone the great Dunkirk evacuation, would have been handled under latter-day philosophy. Where, incidentally, we return to familiar ground such as the war, we do so with new angles and material, and have again been fortunate in tapping into the experience of many who

---

Milk Traffic Record on SR

In January 1933 for the first time on record the Southern Railway dealt with over a million gallons of milk at Vauxhall in one month. Undoubtedly the steady increase was due to the popularity among the large dairy firms of the bulk transport of milk in the new rail containers.

With the six new glass-lined tank trucks recently completed at their Lancing Works, the SR have now 25 of these vehicles in daily use, many of which are of the road-rail type fitted with rubber-tyred road wheels.

The six new wagons, which have been delivered to the order of the United Dairies Ltd., are six-wheeled trucks of the most up-to-date construction fitted with vacuum brakes. They are attached to passenger or express milk trains, and bring the daily supplies from Somerset and Wiltshire to the firm's depot at Vauxhall.

Each vehicle will hold 3,000 gallons of milk, and as this quantity would require anything up to 300 milk churns, one of these new type containers will displace at least three of the old milk vans. – *Meccano Magazine*, 1933.

Above *An ex-LSWR M7 class 0–4–4 tank propels its pull-push train for Seaton out of Seaton Junction around 1960. The train consists of two corridor coaches converted for auto working in green and a ten-compartment non-corridor 2nd class in red.*

Below *Royal train to the races. Schools class 4–4–0 No 30938 St Olave's runs through East Croydon with four Pullman cars for Tattenham Corner in the early 1950s. The engine is in early BR black livery.*

Right up to the last days of steam the Southern made good use of elderly four coupled tanks engines on their country services, both on the Eastern and Western sections. At Oxted on 4 June 1963 an SECR Wainwright H class 0–4–4 tank is still in regular service having brought in an afternoon train from Tunbridge Wells. The engine, No 31551 is taking water at the column which also serves as a bracket to hold the stop point numbers for the diesel electric multiple units in 6 or 9 car sets.

Waterloo station 30 April 1966 with an RCTS special train bound for Longmoor Military Railway. The locomotives (specially cleaned for the occasion) are U class Moguls Nos 31791 (once 2–6–4T No A791 River Adur) and 31639.

worked on the Southern in its Great Days. Much of the miscellany that makes up this chapter comes from one railwayman's notebook.

What do you remember most about the Southern? Probably its smart timings, especially on electric services but throughout the system; even in the far West its station work disgraced the lethargic GWR. Possibly nowhere in the world were trains divided and put together with such clockwork precision as on the Southern. Seating was, however, seldom luxurious and, while at other London termini you would be welcomed onto the platform twenty minutes before departure time, a last-minute queuing system on the Southern was quite common. Nor did you enter a particularly luxurious world in the restaurant cars, and while the Pulmans had a touch of glamour their food was nothing to write home about. They seemed to share the same slight disinfectant smell that was part of the character of Southern trains. But you still thought yourself someone sitting at a table with its own lampshade.

It was a very seasonal railway… in different ways throughout the system from Padstow and the Isle of Wight to around London. A special characteristic was the number and variety of special trains: for ferries and ocean liners, works, schools and other parties, the hop pickers going to Kent, and their families and friends who visited them at the weekends during the season… and above all extra crowds of trippers going down to the coast for a few hours on Sundays and Bank Holidays. Freight and parcels, including prodigious quantities of milk and fruit, was seasonal in the West Country… and if, in exchanging a few friendly words with station staff, you remarked on it being quiet, they would surely reply that you should

Opposite, above A Newhaven boat train passing Clapham Junction in 1939 with an ex-SECR class B1 4–4–0 No 1443 piloting class H2 Atlantic No 2422 North Foreland . This is a very heavy train for Newhaven, thirteen coaches including one Pullman car plus a four-wheel van, hence the assistant engine.

Opposite, below With the electrification third rail firmly in place H15 class 4–6–0 No 524 takes a Southampton boat train past what was then West Weybridge (now Byfleet & New Haw) in the summer of 1939. Note the single Pullman car as the fifth coach doing duty as a 1st class diner. The line coming in on the right is the burrowing Junction from Chertsey.

Waterloo station around 1932 with H15 class 4–6–0 No 334 complete with Urie chimney awaiting departure for the West of England. On the left is class D15 4–4–0 No 463 with a Portsmouth train.

Victoria station, Chatham side, with an electric multiple unit for Orpington on 5 May 1939. On the left is L class 4–4–0 No 1772 with the 7.33pm train to Ramsgate and Margate via Maidstone East, Ashford and Dover Priory.

Opposite, above Torrington station and yard in August 1946. Two originating trains are at the platforms, on the left the late afternoon through coaches to Waterloo via Barnstaple Junction and Exeter Central behind an M7 class 0–4–4T and on the right a North Devon & Cornwall Junction Light Railway train for Halwill Junction behind E1R class 0–6–2T No 2095. This end on junction station closed to all traffic in 1965 with the Light Railway (already partially closed) going on 1 March and the Barnstaple branch on 4 October.

Opposite, below Midhurst ex LBSC station on 6 March 1948 with an ex-LBSCR class D3 0–4–4T No 2384 in the bay with a Pulborough train. The engine has not yet received any evidence of its BR ownership and is in unkempt, unlined wartime black. Note the Southern totem in green with white lettering on the modern concrete lamp standard. There were originally two stations at Midhurst, Brighton and South Western, the latter was closed on 13 July 1925 and all trains used the Brighton premises.

come back at such-and-such a time. Every last porter and platelayer seemed to have it drummed into him that the railway depended on its traffic receipts, and throughout the system huge efforts were made to ensure that everyone and everything on offer was carried efficiently. It worked, in good times and bad, with remarkably few interruptions.

There were of course many great men on the Southern, but none as important as Sir Herbert Walker, who rejected an invitation to head the much larger LMS when he took over as sole general manager. The coherent policy largely stemmed from him: face problems head on, have a bold policy but be pragmatic. Electrification was the great goal, and between 1923 and 1938 passenger traffic increased by half with Southern trains making around seven orbits of the globe each weekday instead of five. By 1938, the average late arrival of electric trains was .91 of a minute, that of all trains 1.07 minutes. But it was not of course all down to electrification. Much had to be done to improve the track and strengthen bridges on the SE&C, for example.

How about this quote from a Southern official?–

'To improve in efficiency, productivity, reliability, safety and punctuality requires endless energetic, often boring and always thankless drive to produce a) a catalogue of our wares, ie a Time Table that is both popular and within our capacity, free from foul timings and efficient; b) maximise utilisation and availability of all assets by good diagraming of men and machines; c) ensure safety by tight technical discipline in drivers, signalmen, gangers, examiners etc; d) by punctuality (the politeness of princes) keep the promises implicit in the Time Table; e) to sell our services and to safeguard the revenue.'

In 1930 the company was reorganised on a Traffic basis: operational responsibility went with commercial judgement under one head. It was

18

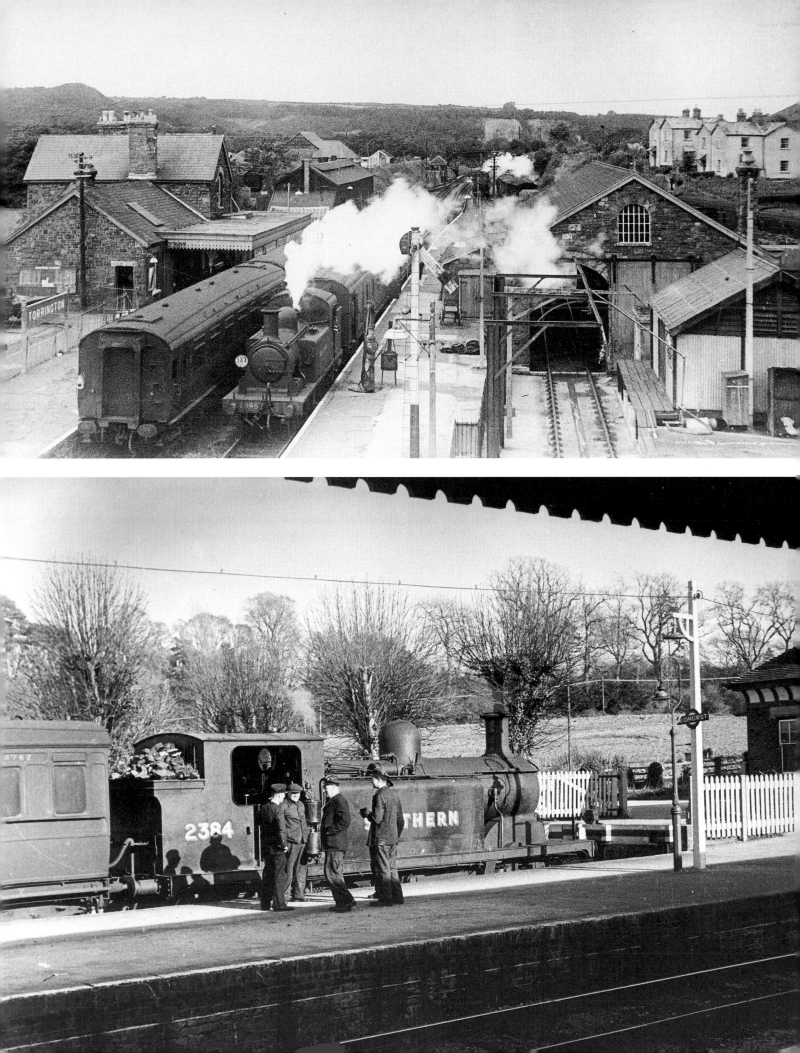

Chichester ex-LBSC about 1953 looking east with a local freight leaving the yard possibly for Bognor as there is a brake van at each end for running round at Barnham. On the left is a class C3 0–6–0 No 32300.

the only major reorganisation after the early days and worked well... and was not disturbed till after nationalisation. The divisions into which the system was split had no budgetary control but were headed up by fine operators who imposed their mark. The London (East) man was highest paid with £1,100 in 1930; London (Central) and Southampton were rated at £1,000 each, Exeter £950 and London (West) at only £900. By comparison, Walker was paid £10,000, his assistant Gilbert Szlumper at £4,000 receiving less than the key traffic manager, E.C. Cox, at £5,000. Again one has the hint of a modern company pay structure rather than that of a conventional railway: a divisional superintendent got four-and-a-half to five times the salary of a class five clerk, the traffic manager five times as much again, and the general manager twice that. Nobody questioned that the top team earned their keep, however.

Certainly clerks in the divisional offices thought they earned theirs! London East, for example, had a minute staff, a dozen dealing with all staff matters relating to 250 busy stations (two of whom issued all the free passes and privilege tickets for the entire division). Head man was one Jimmy Basford, remembered for depopulating booking offices whose staff he habitually referred to as 'glorified tram conductors'.

20

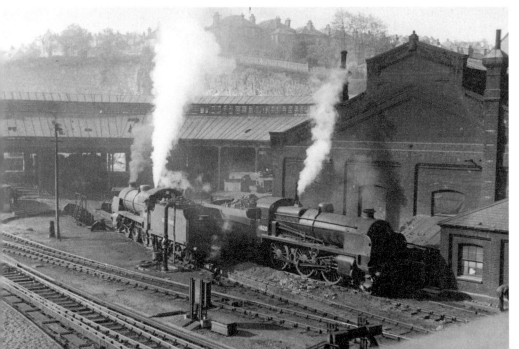

On 3 September 1955 class M7 No 30479 surprisingly fitted with a snowplough, waits to depart with the 11.12 (SO) to Alton over what has now become the preserved Mid Hants Railway.

Guildford shed on 27 April 1948 with two Moguls in SR and BR liveries. On the right is U class No S1620 in black – using the temporary 'S' prefix. On the left, in dirty SR green, is N class No 1817. Guildford was one of the few open roundhouses in Great Britain.

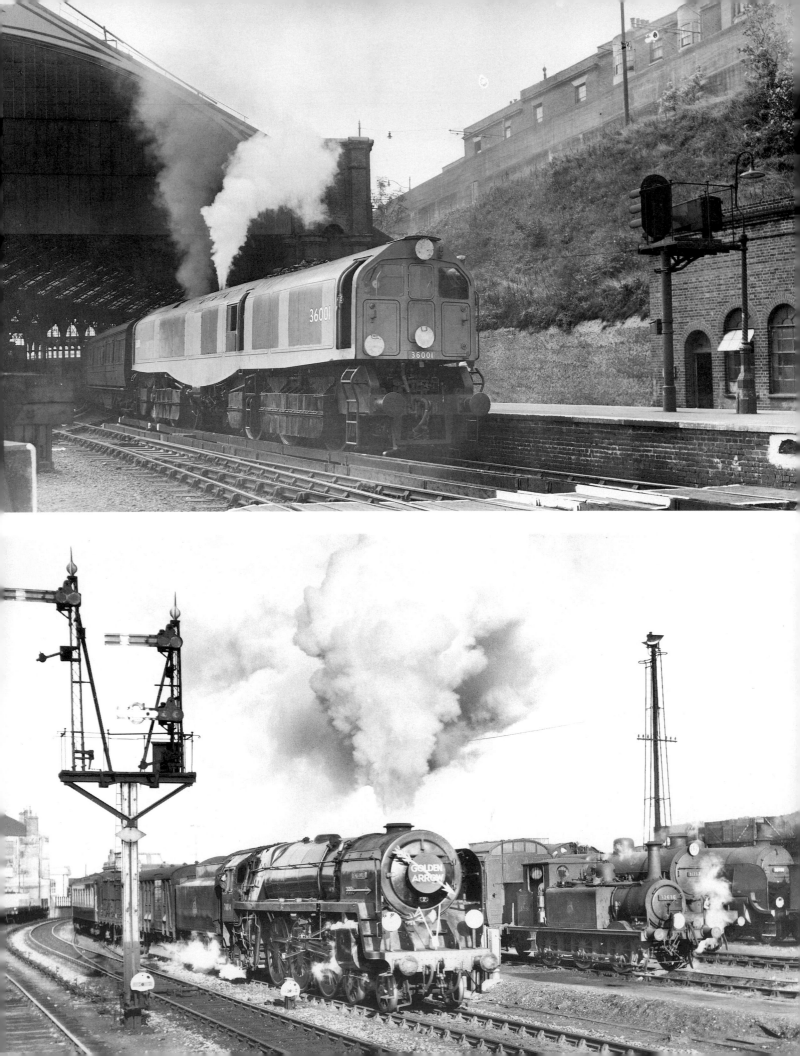

East and Central London shares an excursion office: a single storey, low ceilinged structure frugally built on a small piece of ground made available by curtailing the dumping area for the Post Office and the acceptance area for Billingsgate fish at London Bridge Low Level. Imagine the scene: little air, much noise, considerable smell. Telephones ring, typewriters clatter as Carreras charter five trains for 'Black Cat Cigarette' girls, Mothers' Unions and chapels requested special trains or reserved vehicles, new ranges of excursions for individual travellers are discussed and publicised (a frantic checking of handbill proofs hardly ceases). No overtime and things must be kept up to date. Reward comes in discreet disappearances to mid-week football games when things are quiet in winter, never cricket in the busy summer. And the head man, learning that if he signs the chitties, audit will not question the fares, increases business by judicious cutting of corners: if the spiel about 'unlimited refreshments of your choice and toilet facilities always available,' does not work, a special fare will be invented on the spot. When a firm's outing to Herne Bay was put on a non-stop to Margate, there was no beating about the bush; just a generous offer of free tickets for next year's electric trip to Brighton. But the canvasser who suggested the first educational excursion to Southampton Docks to see the *Queen Mary* was given short shrift when, after dozens of trains had been run, he asked if he might be rewarded. Canvassers were supposed to have ideas.

The Southern's enterprise was endless. For example, booths dispensed publicity material on promenades to save enquirers having to go to the station. Famous people like S.P.B. Mais led massive Sunday afternoon hikes, and just as strenuous efforts were made to retain freight. That declined but less rapidly than on other systems. Though, with more profitable traffics usually the first to switch to road, it was only the coal traffic that justified continuing many of the daily stopping freights that covered almost the entire system.

Coal indeed was saviour, for during the Depression the amount mined in Kent increased to $1\frac{1}{4}$ million tons annually. Dividends and wages were

Opposite, above Bulleid's last fling. *An unusual shot showing the only one of the ill-fated Leader class actually to work. No 36001 stands in Brighton station, blowing off hard, with a test train of empty coaching stock weighing 248 tons for Eastleigh on 18 August 1949. The engine is running bunker first which would relieve the driver of the heat from the smokebox in his cab. The engine was withdrawn in December 1950 after running about 6000 miles, and cut up at Eastleigh works during April and May 1951.*

Opposite, below Dover Marine circa 1952. *Newly commissioned Britannia class Pacific No 70014* Iron Duke *(a Stewarts Lane engine) departs with the up Golden Arrow. This engine plus No 70004* William Shakespeare *was specially allocated to the Southern Region for this service.* Iron Duke *is spotless and carries, in addition to the Golden Arrow motifs, flags of Great Britain and France. On the right is ex-LBSCR 0–6–0 Terrier tank No 32636 for the street tramway to the Eastern Docks. In the background are class L 4–4–0 No 31767 and an unidentified* King Arthur.

Over the hump at Feltham. G16 class 4–8–0T No 30495 shunts a brake van into place sometime around 1952. Note the loco shed in the background, an early example of concrete construction. The four 4–8–0Ts were built in 1921 specially for hump shunting at the new marshalling yard at Feltham.

cut, but thanks to positive points the Southern never lost its nerve, and when the government abolished passenger duty the windfall was immediately seen as financing electrification to Brighton, Britain's first electrified main line. The last Brighton 'Overhead' ran on 21 September 1929. The coaches were later used for dc sets, and some of the driving trailers for steam push-and-pull sets. The motor coaches or 'locomotives' 1934, when they were – typically Southern – reincarnated as the 27 ton 'Queen Mary' bogie brake vans for freight trains.

The Brighton electrification was by far the largest undertaking to date, involving 162 single track miles and replacing 1,971,983 annual steam train miles by 4,921,000 electric. The annual increase in cost was a mere £72,000. The introduction of automatic sub-stations in place of the manned electric sub-stations hitherto needed every few miles on the dc system was important; 18 sub-stations were controlled centrally from Three Bridges. For the first time, rotary coverters were replaced by 2,500kw mercury arc rectifiers. The 36 miles between Coulsdon North and Brighton was the longest section in Britain with continuous electric light signalling, but semaphore signalling was retained elsewhere.

Electrification in Kent had to wait till well into BR days, but big were the improvements when, following reballasting and bridge strengthening works, the Schools were allowed onto the Kent Coast and Dover routes. New classes of locomotive came both early and late in the Southern's history, with a long gap between. At the start, R.E.L. Maunsell insisted on

One of the last haunts of the SECR unsuperheated class D 4–4–0s was the Reading–Redhill service. No 31574 leaves Guildford en route for Redhill on 3 April 1956. No 31574 is one of the members of this class with four spectacles in the cab, two circular and two oblong.

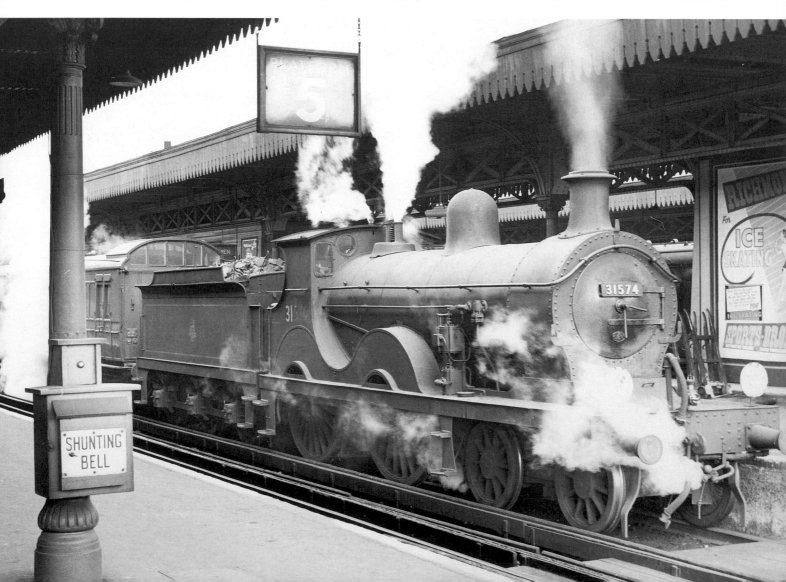

machines that were well ahead of current requirements in power, efficiency, easy of maintenance and had wide route availability. He built few classes and these had standard boilers, cylinders, motion, tyres, axles and so on, all which he intended to be as interchangeable between classes as possible. The first ten Schools class were built in 1930, twenty more in the four following years, and the total finished at forty.

Drivers thought the Schools a wonderful engine, and nowhere more so than when galloping over the undulating countryside between Tunbridge Wells and Hastings. The restrictive gauge had been taken into account, the cab sides being tapered sharply to clear Bopeep tunnel. So close was the height clearance that the whistle was mounted horizontally to save a few inches. Though the total weight had to be kept down to 67 tons and the axle load to 21 tons by the use of round-topped instead of Belpaire fireboxes, spacing of the coupled wheels kept ten feet apart with the installation of an unusually long grate, their Hastings debut still needed the usual bridge strengthenings, completed by July 1931. An enormous amount of paperwork was of course generated by the various track, bridge

A Bournemouth–Eastleigh train running through the New Forest at Woodfidley (between Brockenhurst and Beaulieu Road) on 6 April 1953 behind LSWR built N15 class No 30743 Lyonnesse (7/19–10/55), a Bournemouth locomotive (71B). This was one of the early withdrawals of the class, their duties being taken over by the new Standard Class 5 4–6–0s and the later Southern built Maunsell Arthurs. The passenger accommodation is provided by Bulleid three car set No 981, comprising two corridor brake thirds (six compartments) flanking a composite.

25

Ramsgate shed (74B) in the summer of 1957 with the track gang tidying up the results of a derailment which delayed services by marooning a number of engines. These were the days when the Kent Coast trains were a joy to behold. The locomotive variety was tremendous, including the 4–4–0s. In this picture there is an N15 4–6–0, a West Country Pacific No 34017 Ilfracombe, another Pacific plus a Mogul, a C class 0–6–0 and an N class 2–6–0 No 31411. The structure to the right of the water tower is a water softening plant. No 34017 carries two duty numbers, 430 was Dover's up Night Ferry duty and No 18 was Battersea's assisting turn on the same double-headed train. 73A probably pinched the Pacific for a round trip to the Kent Coast so chaotic did things become on summer Saturdays, but why it displays both duty numbers (neither right for where it was) is unknown. It was typical of conditions on the Eastern Section.

West Country No 34033 Chard *(6/46–12/65) takes the 2.50pm Plymouth Friary–Waterloo over the Western Region line at Mannamead near Plymouth on Sunday 15 July 1956. The train has been diverted onto the up line due to engineering work. Note the flag on the down track. No 34033's home depot was Exmouth Junction and duty 531 on Sundays comprised 10.38am passenger Exeter Central–Plymouth Friary; 2.50pm Plymouth Friary–Exeter Central; light engine to Exmouth Junction shed arrive 4.54pm.*

Opposite page With spark arrester giving it an almost extra-terrestrial look, Stroudley's A1X class 0–6–0 Terrier tank No 32661 leaves Havant for Hayling Island on the afternoon of 7 August 1956. The stand-by locomotive is stabled at the far end of the left hand siding. The train comprises an ex-LSWR non-gangwayed corridor composite and two BR standard non-corridor seconds.

N15X (rebuilt from the LBSC 4–6–4 tank No 2331) 4–6–0 No 32331 Beattie leaves Knights Hill tunnel, Tulse Hill, with a London Bridge–Windsor Ramblers Special on 23 June 1957. Only days prior to withdrawal (7/57) Beattie in lined (LNWR style) black has been well cleaned for the occasion.

strengthening, electrification and signalling schemes, but everyone clearly knew every last detail applicable to their job.

Talking of paperwork, if a guard 'booked time lost' by the locomotive of his train, he had to give the driver a 'lost time ticket' on which the driver had to record his explanation to the depot foreman. Drivers naturally hated it, the more so because some guards did not pass the tickets through them but despatched them straight to the depot foreman.

Then, the Southern had a peculiar system for the production of its permanent timetables. They were all produced at HQ but the actual work was done by two divisional representatives who spent most of their year at Waterloo. The principle was that HQ were responsible for deciding the train service required to attract and carry the traffic but that the divisional superintendent (responsible for the operation) would have to sign it off. So why not have the divisional man's staff do it under HQ supervision? It was one of the frugal beauties of the system that the timetable men came back when the timetable went to Press in early April and remained until October – so that they were available to relieve the senior journal clerks for leave and so see how their work stood up in practice.

During the 1930s, the TP (trains, passengers) section was demoniated by the restless spirit of Reg Martin. His drive and energy were prodigious,

One of the lesser-used crossings to the Isle of Wight ran from Lymington Pier to Yarmouth. The railway connection was from Brockenhurst with the service usually worked by an ex-LSWR M7 class 0–4–4T except on busy summer Saturdays when some trains ran right through from and to Waterloo. M7 No 30028 leaves Lymington Pier's single platform station with the 17.35 for Brockenhurst on 10 July 1957. The signal post is constructed of old rails.

Your Firm's Outing

The Southern Railway offers greatly reduced fare facilities for Firm's Outings, Cricket, Tennis, and Football Clubs, School and Choir Parties, etc. For parties, these cheap fares can be quoted and seating accommodation in the trains reserved.

The favourite resorts within easy reach of London are in the Sunny South, and you will choose one of these for your outing, of course! Club Secretaries and Organisers should write to the *Indoor Commercial Manager, Southern Railway, London Bridge Station, S.E.1.,* as early as possible, stating the stations from, and to which, tickets are required, date of proposed excursion and probable number of passengers. A form may also be obtained at principal SR booking offices. – The July 1927 timetable.

A detailed photograph of Margate pre electrification c1955 looking east. N15 King Arthur No 30794 Sir Ector de Maris (Eastleigh 3/26–8/60) of Stewarts Lane depot (73A) is leaving on a train for Victoria via Chatham. The station pilot to the right of the platforms appears to be an ex SECR H class 0–4–4 tank.

S15 class No 30514 (3/21–7/63) rolls into Portsmouth & Southsea High Level platform with the 12.15pm service to Plymouth on Saturday 8 November 1958. Like many SR trains this was but a portion of the final make up as it linked at Fareham with another section starting from Brighton. No 30514 was on one of Feltham shed's few duties, No 103, which had a passenger element incorporated. Unusually the train is using the High Level station at Portsmouth rather than the Low Level platforms due to engineering work.

No 31902 (7/31–11/62) was one of four U1s transferred from Tonbridge (74D) to Exmouth Junction (72A) in May 1961. They worked mainly on local goods trains and the Padstow services replacing the last of the 72A T9s which were withdrawn in July. It is seen here with an afternoon Padstow–Exeter Central train near Port Isaac Road on 12 July 1961. They were not popular and at the beginning of the winter services (with less work available) all were transferred away (October 1961). No 31902 worked out of Norwood Junction (75C) for the remainder of its career.

even if his assistants did not always quite know what he was trying to do. London area timetable schemes were his speciality, and he normally produced one each year, usually just after Christmas. He would sit for hours in his little glass-fronted cubby-hole, peering through the London area timetables with his nose almost on the pages he was swishing to and fro. Sheets were covered with scribble littered the desk and floor.

Eventually something would click. 'I've got it,' he shouted, bursting out of his office. Next stop George Cheal, the chief clerk and dispenser of Sunday duties. As already hinted, overtime was sparingly given on the Southern, but a scheme to run a few more business trains was worthy of support... and the overtime paid the summer holiday.

Late on Thursday or early Friday morning, young management staff were told who had to take Friday afternoon off, and work all day Saturday, going to strategic signal boxes to assist in traffic regulation or to help keep punctual one of the stopping Kent Coast services by acting as travelling porter, throwing out mails and parcels. Some went to Margate where a local control centre was set up on Saturdays... an unpopular assignment since staff had to travel in their own time.

At Tonbridge West Junction there was little to do as the station master, an ex-signalman, spent the whole day perched on the lockers calling the shots, and thinking half an hour ahead of events. Swanley Junction was very different. The Chatham main and Maidstone East lines diverged here and, with only one up and one down line to St Mary Cray Junction, there was scope for action. The Sole Street and Otford Junction signalmen advised the passing times of all up trains and so it was possible to guide the signalman in making priorities. There was only one signalman, and so no train register was kept and on summer Saturdays he could not even answer the phone. When help was not immediately at hand Swanley Yard signalman would answer for the Junction man on those circuits to which he was connected – and would pass a message to the staff to try to attract the Junction man by one beat on the block bells in the time-honoured and unlawful fashion.

Great was the enthusiasm when the Portsmouth No 1 project was started in October 1935 and the full electric service instituted in July 1937. Its success was instant and gave a tremendous boost to the Isle of Wight. Almost as large, the Portsmouth No 2 project (75 route miles, 162 single track miles, estimated cost £2,775,847) began in 1937 and was finished for a full service next summer, 2,083,898 annual steam miles being replaced by 3,812,544 electric ones for a decreased working cost of £12,818. It only needed a ten per cent revenue increase (quickly exceeded) to cover the cost. They were heady days.

Cannon Street was pressed into use on Friday evenings and on Saturdays in the late 1930s to deal with the ever increasing numbers of 'Agents' specials... the package holiday business which (contrary to popular belief) is not a post war invention but got away in earnest when you could take a break in Switzerland for £20 for a fortnight. The need for relief came when Victoria was handling more than sixty outwards Continental services on summer Saturdays.

The Southern at war, the subject of a separate contribution, was

Steam power was in retreat on most other regions when in October 1961 the Southern scheduled the fastest ever times for the Atlantic Coast Express. The down train was due into Exeter Central (171¾ miles) at 1.56pm (2hr 56min inclusive of stops at Salisbury and Sidmouth Junction). Merchant Navy No 35014 Nederland Line *(Feb 1945, rebuilt July 1956–March 1967) is ready to leave Waterloo with Nine Elms duty No 6 on 7 June 1962.*

Opposite Ventnor, Isle of Wight in the 1960s. Class O4 0–4–4T No 14 Fishbourne *takes water and has its smokebox cleaned out before running round its train for Ryde Pier. As with the mainland, the Island's coaching stock was usually coupled semi-permanently into sets. Set 491 appears to be a mixture of ex-LBSC and SECR coaches.*

surprisingly similar to what it had been in the thirties. Of course the black out, air raids and the rest (especially poor coal) made a huge difference, but the basic philosophy, the fact that the railway was a big business having to serve an extraordinary range of needs, the organisation and in many cases even the staff (those who might have retired working on while younger men were at the front)... in hindsight there was much greater commonality between the thirties and forties, peace and diabolical war, than between the last days of the Southern and reorganised and then reorganised again BR. And how life has changed, not just for the railways. Indeed you would not get anyone working the hours and conditions that tens of thousands did on the Southern, peace, war, and then peace again. Yet the saddest day for Southern men was that they took their uniform off for the last time.

For one thing, there was always something happening. If it was not electrification or bridge strengthening, or running special trains, there was still *something* that put the railway right in the centre of things... and not just to take people to and from work in London as seems to be its real role today. And with things happening, there was always much to talk about. The staff endlessly shared experiences, often with great enjoyment.

To end this miscellany of an introduction before moving into the book proper, many Southern men had especially fond memories of the autumn

32

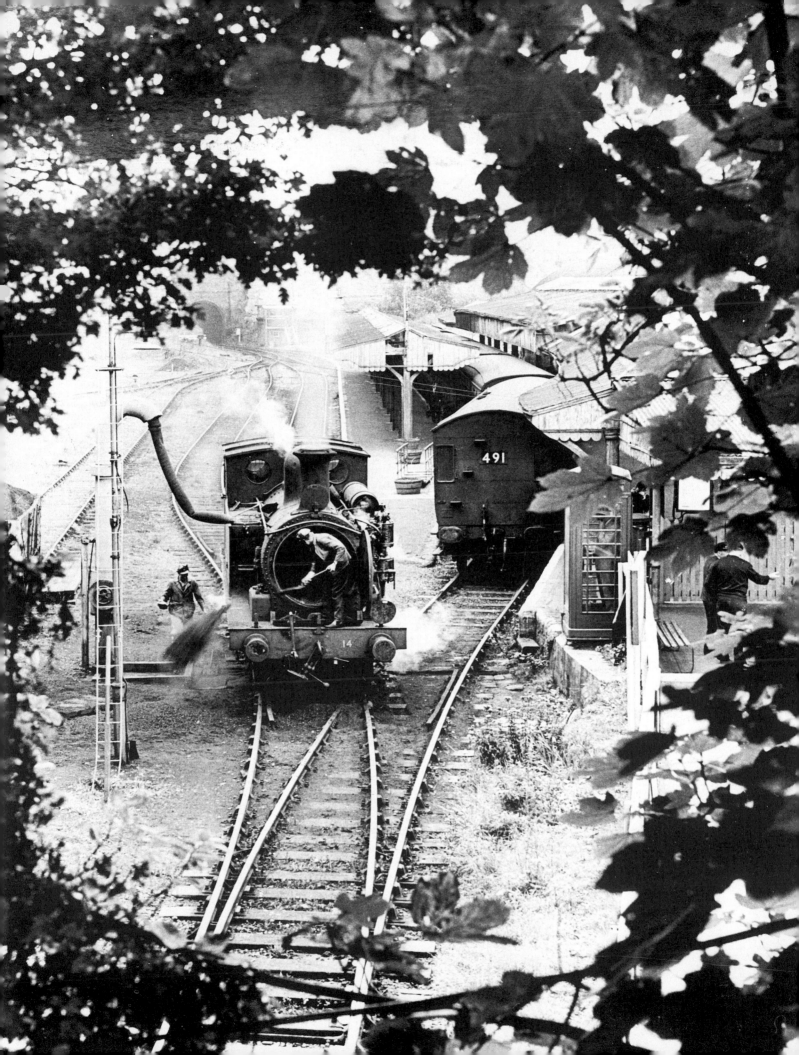

Nearly five hours after leaving Waterloo, the Plymouth portion of the down Atlantic Coast Express leaves Tavistock hauled by class N No 31846 on 4 August 1960. The western edge of Dartmoor forms the background.

of 1943, when the possibility of invasion had virtually disappeared and thousands of London families once more returned to the customary hop picking. Up to twenty daily hop pickers' specials were run. The areas of Bermondsey, Southwark and Greenwich must have been in chaos as mums and such dads as were available, often grandparents standing in, set out with their possessions stowed in boxes, sacks and small baths tied to ancient prams, trolleys made of wooden boxes or old bicycles. Although they were given only 24 hours' notice, they all got to London Bridge.

Trains ran to Hawkhurst, Pluckley or Yalding, but whichever the destination there were always four vans: one for each, plus Paddock Wood. For it was impossible to confine people to the right train. They all knew about changing at Paddock Wood. The ones really in the know found out from staff at London Bridge which route was to be taken and dodged out if they found it was the long way round via Oxted. The first arrivals got the best huts!

The scene at Paddock Wood might have been out of a Dickens novel. Since there were many Artful Dodgers and not a few Fagins about, the detrained passengers were penned behind railings while their possessions were unloaded by the staff and displayed on the platform. When the railings opened, the lot surged forth to make their claims. While this was going on, the vans for the routes not being served by the train were detached, and others from previous trains attached. Each Sunday, the hoppickers were visited by friends, and they had many of them... thirty to forty train loads. It was light relief from military specials, of which the Southern had run 20,000 by 1943. Another 10,000 were run for D Day. Incidentally two trains of super heavy batteries were used to shell the French coast, potting away from time to time in the Ashford-Hastings area, and there were also two 'patrol' trains of armour-plated trucks with machine guns and runner wagons whose occasional excursions from their camouflaged nets were for exercise purposes only.

The smallest of the Big Four the Southern might have been. But who dares say it was uninteresting?

Just one station away from the village after which it was named, West Country class No 34104 Bere Alston *crosses the River Tavy bridge south of Bere Ferrers with the 9am Waterloo to Plymouth Friary on 4 August 1960. This bridge, taking a much shorter route than the road, has enabled this part of the Southern to remain open, for the service from Plymouth to Bere Alston (reverse) and Calstock (the Southern's only remaining station in Cornwall).*

How I Became a Cadet

The cadets were the idea of Gilbert Szlumper, the irresistible assistant general manager, and from 1937 general manager himself. Patrick Stevenson tells how he joined the elite few.

My father had written to Szlumper having seen a newspaper article about the way the Southern was introducing new blood into its management, and we were granted an interview . . . a good start since there were on average only two cadetships every three years.

Szlumper seemed to like us and said to 'keep in touch'. He added that they actively did not want a university degree. 'The Railway will be your university. But you must have London matric. Simply because you need that qualification to attend certain classes towards your AMInstT at the London School of Economics and the Bow & Bromley Institute.' So I worked at school and later at a crammers until I had my matric when I was 17½ and instantly wrote to Szlumper, who again granted me an interview. He told us – my father came too – that there was no cadet entry for eighteen months. 'Meanwhile,' he said, looking at me rather quizzically, 'I suppose you want to start and do *something* on the railway. I'll see what we can fix – maybe even get you a very little money. I'll ring Toby Wheeler!' (H. E. O. Wheeler was superintendent of operation). 'Hell, he's asleep. I'll get Trangmar!' Mr Trangmar was a senior clerk in the general manager's department. Not a personal secretary, whose name then was Bond; more a kind of *eminence grise* who had great scope as regards access to the various Ears of God and who had been deputed by Szlumper to see to the detail of the running of the cadets.

These fortunate individuals – never more than five or six on the railway at the same time – were salaried trainees who went through all departments, usually spending six weeks, two months or even three months in each. They were also expected to pass out in a main line junction signalbox, and a single line country one as well as gain certificates for emergency single-line working from the Croydon signalling school, run by the railway (ex LB&SC). They were attached at one time or another to all the divisional superintendents (London West, Central, London East, Southern and Western), docks (involving trips on the bridge to the Channel Islands), electrical engineer (involving Wimbledon's Durnsford Road Power Station, for the SR generated its own traction electricity), signal and telegraph, civil engineer, general manager's AND loco (which involved an all stations footplate pass – oh, utter glory!)

But I was not yet a cadet. Trangmar came in and discussed the possibility of my semi-employment. In the end, I was sent first to my home station of Fareham, under the stationmaster, to work in the booking office, goods office and both signalboxes. There was also a disastrous slip in the cutting on the Fareham side of Botley station, which involved a very long period of single line working between Knowle Junction and Botley. Knowle came under Fareham, so I was sent out there to learn. Thence I went to the Portsmouth goods for three months. After that I went to the divisional offices at Southampton, Central (Southern Division). Then, the cadet interview came up. It meant everything, but of course I was up against very serious competition, for there were many applicants. The interview took place in a large room, furnished with a long boardroom table and chairs with other items of furniture such as cabinets, ornaments and a mantel clock on the mantel piece and so on. At the table sat a curious interviewing board. One side of it held senior officers of the company – really senior. The solicitor (in person), superintendent of operation, traffic manager, secretary, like that. On the other side of the table sat the same number of people but they were either uniformed staff or fifth class clerks, a signalman, perhaps, a truck driver, a fireman (loco), a railway police constable, an office boy! These all had the same voting power as the very senior other side. At the end of the table sat Gilbert Szlumper.

They were all certainly in cahoots. Somebody would ask a simple question to which there was a simple answer. According to your reply, one side or the other would comment, perhaps dismissively, or perhaps disparagingly; and it did not take much intelligence to realise that it was one's reply to *that* which would be marked. 'Where were you at school?' If you said 'Eton', one of the uniformed staff would make a snide remark about the old school tie network and you had to deal with that with charm and brilliance but firmly. If you gave as your school some little-known grammar school, the solicitor promptly jumped in with a curt 'Never heard of it!' This was my case – to which one replied 'Notwithstanding that, Sir, it is a very fine, upright school with a splendid reputation with those who *have* heard of it!'

Many questions like that. Also lead questions to make you make a fool of yourself like 'What do you think is wrong with the Southern Railway?' The correct answer, in spite of longing to tell them, was on the lines of 'Until I have had the benefit of cadet training and thus know *why* things are done as they are, it would be impertinent to attempt an answer – perhaps when I am a little older and know a little more . . .' The wrong answers were (a) to try and tell them and (b) to say unctuously 'Nothing, Sir!' You really were led and encouraged to proceed right up the garden path.

Finally, you were given a piece of paper. On it was typed something like this: 'Go to the desk on the opposite side of the room by way of the fireplace, putting right anything you find wrong there. In the fourth drawer from the top on the left hand side you will find an ABC timetable. Look up the last train from East Grinstead to Baynards on a Friday in August and return to your place by the same route. Speed is important.' I thought hard. Then I asked, 'May I take this piece of paper on my travels?' Assent. So I went via the mantel-piece, deeply suspecting the clock. Something else was upside down. I turned it right way up. The clock I checked with my watch and it was dead right. I looked up the very tricky timetable question – I would have been far happier with a *Bradshaw* – noted my answer and returned to my place via the fireplace again. There was a curious sensation that something was in the balance. The secretary spoke, 'You looked carefully at the clock. Did you, in fact, see anything wrong with that clock?' I didn't answer but got up and went straight back to the clock. It was hours wrong. They had set it at ten o'clock or short of it. They were watching their own watches which were just coming up to ten to twelve, the correct time. They timed that question exactly so that the clock and the real time would look exactly the same while being, to the *really* careful looker, nearly two hours wrong. By the time I returned to the clock, it was obvious. Six minutes make a lot of difference to a watch like that. I covered my eyes with my hands. 'I've heard of interview nerves making people do stupid things,' I said, 'but I would never have dreamed I would be taken in when I was actually looking for error there. Confound it, you saw me even listen to make sure it was going, in spite of the fact that it appeared to be telling the right time! Well – you win! I'm sorry to be such a fool!'

But they had not won. I passed and was one of the two selected.

There was a Time
Below are a few of the cadet's memories!

There was a time when I was in the electrical engineers' department and travelling down from Victoria to Brighton on the electric Brighton Belle – an evil-riding cheap substitute for the earlier Southern Belle, whose beautiful old Pullman cars spoke of greater space as being one of the principal reasons for travelling first.

The driver was an old Brighton man, brought up on

I3 Atlantic tanks, J 4-6-2 tanks and of course the Baltics. There would also have been the Atlantics themselves, which were astonishingly smooth-riding; but the others, while smooth, ambled from side to side, amiably but worryingly if one was not used to it. Even so, the driver preferred them to the emu which, unpleasantly though it rode, was more comfortable than any engine. 'These jerks and bumps are so sudden, like. It messes up my digestion. Now the tanks – well, yes, I admit that sometimes a Baltic would seem to be at cross-purposes with the track but that only meant that it would settle down for up to a mile pointing north-east when the track was due north and south until you wondered if the leading drivers were off o' the road except it was too quiet, like.'

We were making up time lost and fairly hurtling down the bank towards Haywards Heath – about 82. 'Rides a bit smooth going faster.' Before there was time to consider that, we hit not one but two pheasants, flying across in front of the train. The driver did not hesitate. Hands off everything. The dead man's handle activated and we ground to a savage halt. 'Better go back and examine something hadn't you? Quick, get down. See you in Brighton!'

With this, the train got briskly under way again, incredibly with no audible flats, and I made my way back – quite a way back – and found the two birds, which (hidden under macintosh) had to be carried the long walk to Haywards Heath. A suspicious gamekeeper at a

Lord Nelson class 4–6–0 No 861 Lord Anson hauling an up continental express from Dover past Ashford in April 1939. The engine has Bulleid modifications – multiple-jet exhaust and extended tender sides – and is in well polished condition. Note the SECR signals with mechanical route indicators on the up platform, and Ashford works behind.

footpath crossing had to be given 'good-day' in an obviously headquarters-voice-of-authority.

The driver had one pheasant and I had the other. My landlady roasted it for me. 'Funny the way that bird was shot. When I plucked it, I couldn't see any shot holes but every bone in its body seemed to be broken.' The only case I ever heard of a train being actually stopped for a pheasant, though more than once one has seen the fireman of a King Arthur arriving at Salisbury jump down before the train had quite stopped to beetle round and remove a bird from the front buffer beam.

There was the time, while I was in the Loco Department, they sent me to Brighton to have the experience of riding on one of the great Brighton express tanks. The Baltics had all gone – converted into not very strong (but quite fast) N15X 4-6-0s and there were only two 'big tanks' left – the J class 4-6-2Ts *Abergavenny* and *Bessborough*, now nameless and, since electrification of the Eastbourne and Hastings line, with little to do, so they were rostered to work the Hastings portion of the Sunny South Express on from Brighton to Hastings. Only three coaches and an engine nearly as long as one of them – 2325, once *Abergavenny*, with inside valve gear. She and her sister were legends, supposedly better than the great 4-6-4 Baltics which followed them, they were the most famous express engines on the Brighton. She lumbered up the hill and down into Lewes, the Downs misty and wet, with effortless power, beautiful riding – all no longer necessary with three coaches at 50mph, and shortly to be but a memory.

There was the time when I was on the footplate of my favourite Nelson, *Lord St Vincent*, on an up continental express from Dover Marine by the normal (Tonbridge) route. Also with a footplate pass was a rather uppish pup reporter who usually wrote about motor-racing and clearly thought railways were very small beer. The driver and fireman were wicked men. At Ashford in those days there was a brickwork bridge carrying the road over the London end of the station with a separate arch for each of the five lines. The very slight curve just beyond always made it seem as if an engine would hit it – and a Nelson looked certain to.

As we really started moving down through Smeeth with a lot of power and the speed rose up the seventies, the driver with a puzzled expression shouted to his fireman 'They don't usually route these engines this way, do they?' (The Nelsons were of course built for the route.) 'No!' shouted the fireman. 'Will she go through the bridge?' No more was needed. With whistle open the express fairly thundered through the junction then on the fast road through the platform. It was clearly impossible for it to get through the narrow arch. The reporter, white with fear, teeth visibly chattering, was clutching at the fireman, gibbering. A second later with the usual claustrophobic 'whoof' we were through and on to the 25 mile straight to Tonbridge.

There was the time when I was able to bridge a gap. Fratton Gates was a ground frame on the old East Southsea branch which had long since been abandoned, leaving only half a mile from the old junction at the Portsmouth end of Fratton Station to the back of the loco sheds as a triangle for turning the engines. The 'signalman' or rather, crossing keeper, had a wheel for the gates and bells but no actual signals and when he saw an engine coming, he would ensure the gates were open. They only gave access to wagons in the yard and were seldom needed. This man had tragically lost both legs under a train saving a little child from being run over at Brockenhurst, where he had been a smart, up and coming signalman. After this terrible misfortune, the wheel at Fratton Gates was all they could find by way of 'light duties' and he had become bitter saying that once he had had his bravery medal all the top officers just forget you.

The general manager, Gilbert Szlumper, was a really splendid man: strong, friendly and no stickler for etiquette. As a cadet I accompanied him on some of his inspections. The engine (a I3 Atlantic tank – what a waste of power!) and the single inspection saloon drew to a stop in Fratton station on the loop and I told him of the embittered man at the Fratton Gates Ground Frame, about 60 yards across the tracks. At once he climbed down: 'This can be put right!'

And there he was, drinking signalbox tea with the totally astonished keeper. He stayed all of ten minutes, told him a very questionable joke about balls and made him laugh, recalled his bravery, took some notes, gave him a cigar and left, saying 'We do remember, only sometimes we need reminding. I shall take personal charge of this and we shall find you something much more congenial.' And they did. And the GM stayed in personal touch.

Inherited Grandeur

No London termini were rebuilt during the Grouping era and until Euston was rebuilt in the 1960s, the Waterloo the Southern inherited was the most modern. It was rebuilt in stages from 1909 to 1922 delayed due to World War I. The roof over platforms 16 to 21, dating from 1885, was the only part of the station which is not new, though it blended with the new concourse. After nearly 70 years the north-west side of the station is again being rebuilt to accommodate the Channel Tunnel international trains to Paris and Brussels. The office block between platforms 15 and 16 was demolished to provide space for two platforms and two more were inserted on the site of the cab road – so long a feature of the station – between platforms 11 and 12, all this to compensate for the loss of platforms 16 to 21. The new part of the station will have 5 platforms, separate arrival and departure areas and customs clearance facilities.

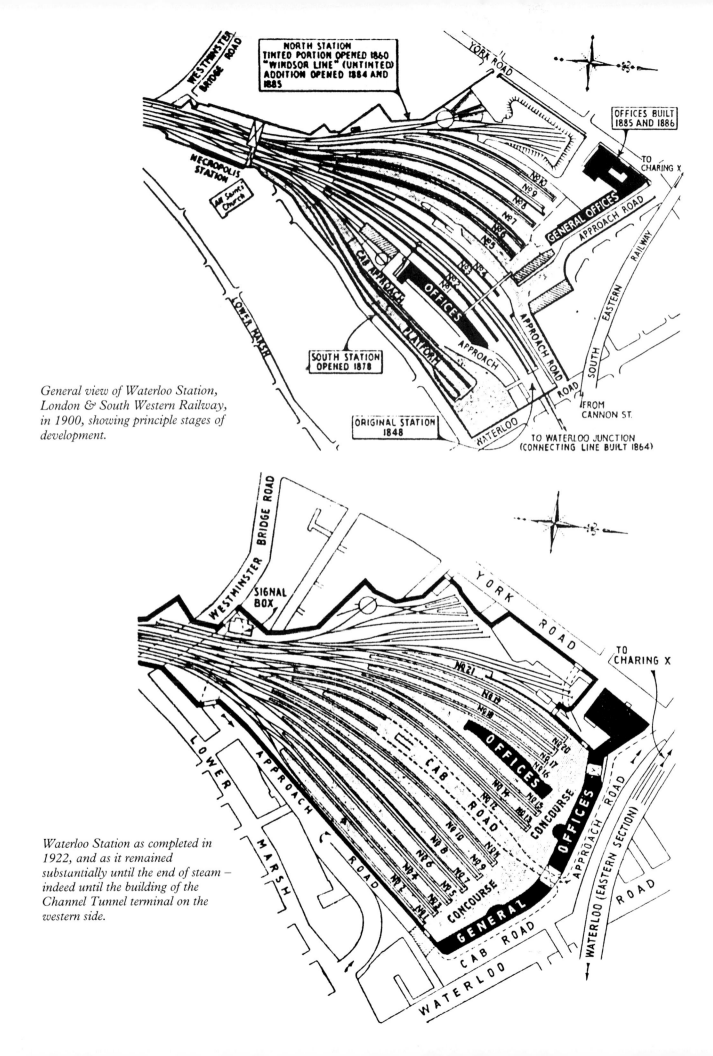

NORTH STATION
TINTED PORTION OPENED 1860
"WINDSOR LINE" (UNTINTED)
ADDITION OPENED 1884 AND
1885

OFFICES BUILT
1885 AND 1886

TO
CHARING X

WESTMINSTER BRIDGE ROAD

YORK ROAD

NECROPOLIS STATION

All Saints Church

GENERAL OFFICES

APPROACH ROAD

No 10
No 9
No 8
No 7
No 6
No 5

LOWER MARSH

CAB APPROACH

OFFICES

PLATFORM

No 4
No 3
No 2
No 1

APPROACH

APPROACH ROAD

SOUTH EASTERN RAILWAY

SOUTH STATION
OPENED 1878

ORIGINAL STATION
1848

WATERLOO
ROAD

FROM
CANNON ST.

TO WATERLOO JUNCTION
(CONNECTING LINE BUILT 1864)

*General view of Waterloo Station,
London & South Western Railway,
in 1900, showing principle stages of
development.*

WESTMINSTER BRIDGE ROAD

SIGNAL
BOX

YORK ROAD

TO
CHARING X

LOWER MARSH

APPROACH ROAD

CAB ROAD

No 21
No 19
No 18
No 20
No 17
No 16
No 15
No 14
No 13
No 12
No 11
No 10
No 9
No 8
No 7
No 6
No 5
No 4
No 3
No 2
No 1

OFFICES

CONCOURSE

CONCOURSE

GENERAL OFFICES

CAB ROAD

APPROACH ROAD

WATERLOO (EASTERN SECTION)

WATERLOO ROAD

*Waterloo Station as completed in
1922, and as it remained
substantially until the end of steam –
indeed until the building of the
Channel Tunnel terminal on the
western side.*

South Eastern Railway Stirling Class F 4–4–0 No A172 had just over two years to live when photographed on Ashford shed on 18 August 1928. Built at Ashford in 1893, it was one of twelve of the class not rebuilt to Class F1 with domed boiler. Along with No 156 it was fitted with the air brake in addition to the standard vacuum brake for handling coaching stock from other railways, and retained this until withdrawn.

2
THE 4–4–0s
AND THEIR WORK

At the century's turn the inside cylindered 4–4–0 was the archetypal express locomotive on Britain's railways. Thanks to a deep firebox between the coupled axles, it was relatively easy for the fireman to support its full potential. At the end of the Edwardian era the 4–4–0 received a superheated shot in the arm. New and rebuilt locomotives started to produce performances the like of which had not been seen before and which (in relation to the size) have seldom been surpassed to this day. Only their limited adhesive weight caused some anxiety on selected duties.

The Southern's three principal constituents contributed 4–4–0 designs in some quantity; no less than 606 of its 2285 locomotives were in this form, a proportion more than double that of any other company. They were overwhelmingly inside cylindered, for both passenger and mixed traffic duties. Some were on the verge of scrapping, others in their prime – as might be expected of machines whose accountancy lives were reckoned as 35 years or so, and which in real life often lasted much longer.

By the 1920s the 4–6–0 had come into its own, after a decidedly shaky start, and taken over the heaviest and fastest duties. This resulted in what would now be described as a progressive cascade of 4–4–0s from top grade work to secondary trains. The highly seasonal nature of the Southern's holiday traffic resulted in numbers of the older and less satisfactory classes being put into store through the winter months, perhaps emerging briefly for Christmas and Easter.

Maunsell, in his pre Grouping days, had produced a mixed traffic locomotive, the N class 2–6–0, which was the natural replacement for many of the elderly 4–4–0s. Indeed, the three-cylinder version with 6ft wheels, the U1 class, had been brought on to the Portsmouth direct line expresses in 1931 in substitution for Drummond D15 4–4–0s – though, it must be conceded, not with huge success, for the boiler was hardly man enough for such a hard task. But no railway, least of all the Southern with its successive electrification schemes demanding capital in large doses, was going to spend money to replace its 4–4–0s. Southern policy was to retain them, many by now fully depreciated, and maintain them in good mechanical fettle as long as they could be gainfully employed until major renewals (such as boilers) were needed.

A total of 29 separate classes of 4–4–0 were handed over in 1923, and their numbers and histories are outlined in the table. Nine of them were already, or in the process of being, superheated. Many had boilers too small for sustained express passenger duties, and were confined to stopping passenger, assisting, local freight or station pilot work. Seven classes were earmarked for early withdrawal, which in some cases had already

Vindicated

Those of us who have agonised that BR's signal engineers have been given freedom to spend too freely feel vindicated when we see what the Southern did. No necessity of clean sweeps then, but pragmatic common sense. The Southern indeed boasted that gantries that had been used for arrays of semaphores now accommodated simpler clusters of colour light signals, and that new electronic signalling was frequently inserted into manual signal boxes while they were still in use. Where the old cabin was unsuitable, a new one might still be erected beside it on the same bridge, as it was over the tracks at North Kent East Junction.

The railway was *adapted*, not rebuilt, for electrification and the value for money was far greater than in nationalised days. Nothing of course gives a better indication of this than the famous London to Brighton in four minutes film; look out for the surviving aspects of the traditional railway next time you have a chance to see it.

Opposite, below *Ex-LBSC class B4 4–4–0 No B54 at the top end of Brighton loco yard circa 1928. This shows the Maunsell dark green livery with orange/yellow lettering and the section prefix, B=Brighton, to the number. No 54 was built at Brighton in May 1900 and named* Empress, *being renamed* Princess Royal *in August 1906. It was one of the last four B4s in service and was withdrawn in May 1951 although none had worked for some years.*

*L.B. Billinton's rebuild of the
original B4 class was fairly drastic,
involving new frames, cylinders,
boiler and cab. Maunsell did further
work on them to comply with the
Southern's composite loading gauge:
cut down chimney and dome, altered
cab roof, hinged glass windscreens
fitted and other details. No 2043,
seen here in Brighton station, had
been so modified in September 1935.*

started; some were already in store and never turned a wheel for their new owners.

Just occasionally one might be called on in emergency in its old role. There is a graphic account in the companion volume *SR 150* of the last days of No 595, an X2, standing station pilot at Woking when a Lord Nelson failed while working the thirteen coach down ACE. The little Highflyer took over the train and struggled with it single-handed to Salisbury. It dropped a lot of time and arrived with rather less white metal in the bearings than when it started!

The smaller Drummond engines, too, were limited in what they could do. Bert Hooker recalls that Hoppers had quite a turn of speed, despite their 5ft 7in wheels, though the larger L11s were more popular with enginemen because their larger fireboxes gave better steaming. The vacuum brake lacked power, requiring great care when working loose-coupled freight trains. On straight track they were firm on their feet but pointwork quickly had them dancing. Drummond's sanding arrangement for tender-first working was crude – a sandbox in the cab on the fireman's side only, with a funnel-mouthed pipe in its centre, down which the fireman had to *scoop up the sand by hand* and feed it to the rail.

Of all the inherited 4–4–0s the ones that really *mattered* to the Southern and earned their keep were the Drummond T9s, S11s, L12s and D15s, the Maunsell D1 and E1 rebuilds of Wainwright's Ds and Es, and Wainwright's Ls (which appeared during Maunsell's reign). Robert

Billinton's handsome rebuilds of the Brighton B4s also generated hope, the programme being completed in Southern days, though that hope proved distinctly forlorn.

The superheated Drummonds were imposing-looking engines; the S11s and L12s had the same boiler but the S11s were 6in smaller in the wheel. Bert Hooker, who both fired and drove them, comments:

'They did not appear to thrive on a thrashing but I can disprove that. I was with Charlie Hardy ('Big Cosh') on the 5.09pm Waterloo to Basingstoke one day, a heavy commuter train calling at Woking and then all stations. He really thrashed the S11 but the boiler stood up to the demand well (and I *had* to!). I started the driver's side injector before Clapham Junction and it wasn't shut off until arrival at Basingstoke. I worked my own side feed as required when the regulator was closed to top up the boiler to ⅔ glass and to lay the dust on the tender – there wasn't an overwhelming amount of water left in the tank after *that* trip!'

That would not be the only thrashing meted out to an S11. When first superheated they had been allocated to the Waterloo–Portsmouth

Drummond D15 class No 30465 in BR lined black livery, wheels the 1.00pm Southampton–Bournemouth stopper away from Lyndhurst Road on 4 April 1953. In the summer of that year No 30465 was one of three D15s regularly working the Waterloo–Lymington ten-coach services. By this time all these splendid engines had been disfigured by fitting a fabricated Urie-style stovepipe chimney. No 30465 lasted until January 1956, and was the last to be withdrawn.

Test Runs

In 1953, early in my reporting career, the *Western Morning News* sent me out to find news in a pretty empty North Devon. I naturally tapped into the railway network, the day's first discovery being the launch of the new Ambrosia milk puddings made at the factory beside Lapford station with its staggered platforms. Then to Halwill Junction where I was able to report a new Crewe-built BR standard 2-6-2T which had just arrived from Torrington on trial on the Southern's most rural byway, the North Devon & Cornwall Junction Railway.

'Though there are only two passenger and one goods trains a day running on the Light Railway, drivers have sometimes found the old tank engines of the London, Brighton & South Coast Railway insufficient to pull the loads up steep gradients,' explained the report.

'The train left Torrington with 19 trucks, picking up an additional six wagons of clay at Marland. Gradients are so steep and curves so sharp that loads have to be kept to a minimum, and considerable difficulty has been experienced in the working of some cattle specials.' Said driver M.T. Johns: 'It was the best trip I have ever made over the line, which is one of the most difficult in all Britain. No 41313 really mastered its job.'

The next time I travelled that way my editor was invited on a trip on the engineer's saloon given me by way of thanks for support for the new but alas short-lived Plymouth Division, which put some common sense into the running of the West Country's railways. We took the first diesel over the Light line but alas had to leave it at Torrington as the driver could not restart it after lunch. – D St J T

expresses, where summer loadings demanded very hard work. In the summer of 1925, also, ten L12s had been transferred to the Eastern Section at Bricklayers Arms and Dover at a time of acute power shortage caused by scrapping and a backlog of heavy repairs at Ashford Works. They had been set to work the Charing Cross–Dover trains with their fast 80 minute non-stop timing to Folkestone, and handled them with great success. They could show the local Ls a clean pair of heels on the straight and level Tonbridge–Ashford section. Their only serious weakness was a propensity to run hot boxes.

The superheated T9s soon earned a fine reputation. They could be driven with wide open regulator and shortish cutoffs. In the twenties they were to be found all over the Western Section, hauling Southampton boat trains and far-flung portions of the Atlantic Coast Express, sharing the working of the fast Waterloo–Portsmouth expresses (which could load up to eleven coaches) over a road with lengthy gradients as steep as 1 in 80, and a host of semifast and stopping trains. The 1925 power shortage on the Eastern Section saw ten of them transferred to Battersea, whence they worked Margate expresses and some Dover boat trains. The local men took to them well, while naturally not admitting them to be the equal of the splendid D1s and E1s, and hung on to them until after the outbreak of World War II. In 1928 six more went to Brighton, working to London and along the coast to Southampton and Salisbury. They were accepted happily, for they showed themselves able to lift a twelve-coach train, including heavy Pullmans, unaided out of Victoria and up the 1 in 64 of Grosvenor Road bank.

All these Drummond 4-4-0s were fitted with his pattern of steam reverser, and had slide valves in a vertical steamchest between the cylinders, even after superheating. The valve gear was Stephenson's. As Hooker remembers:

'Woe betide the driver who attempted to reverse one with a steam chest full of steam; the lever would stop in the middle and refuse to go either way until the steam had dissipated. Crews have even shut off entirely the hydrostatic lubricator to help ease the position, whilst the fireman has used the heavy dart as a lever inserted between the driving wheel spokes and under the reversing links. A regulator 'blowing through' wasn't a sight to gladden the heart; this would mean opening the cylinder drain cocks at every station in case reversing was needed.'

Of the oldsters from the South Eastern & Chatham, perhaps the rather dated-looking Stirling F1s led the most varied lives. Hooker again:

'As on all big-wheeled 4-4-0s the unwary crew could be thumped on the legs when the engine lurched, especially when due for shops! But they were reliable, free-steaming engines… New Cross Gate men called them 'Chaffcutters' because of the 'stair rods' emitted from the chimney… at Nine Elms they were colloquially known as 'Flying Bedsteads'… the ex-SE&CR engines all appeared to be draughted to

A very grubby E class 4–4–0 No 1275 is in charge of a van train between Sevenoaks and Tonbridge. This engine was one of two fitted with superheaters and piston valves in 1912.

T9 class 4–4–0 No 30732 passes Cosham Junction on 1 November 1951 with the 8.54am Romsey–Portsmouth stopping train. Note the fine tall lattice LSWR bracket signal.

Something Up His Sleeve

During the middle sixties there was a running shift foreman at Nine Elms named Bert Hulbert, colloquially known as 'The Galloping Major'. I booked on one morning at 8am 'spare' and was immediately instructed to prepare a West Country No 34009 *Lyme Regis* and place her in the stores sidings right outside the foreman's office, a main line engine 'ready for the road' once the fire had been levelled and the trimmings put in. The preparation was completed, tender topped up with coal and water, footplate wiped round and everything in order. By about 9.30 my mate and I were in the cabin, a can of tea was made and we were about to enjoy a cup.

Shortly afterwards the cabin door burst open, the foreman came in shouting orders 'you and you' to half a dozen men, myself included. 'Go out and prepare a Merchant Navy – the 10.30 Bournemouth engine has failed'. It should have been 10.00 off the shed. I ventured to ask 'why not use that engine I've just put in the stores siding?' Bert Hulbert roared: 'I can't use that one, that's my spare engine!'

So there were several of us endeavouring to prepare a rebuilt MN, getting in each other's way. The loco went out fifteen minutes late off the shed with a fire leaving a lot to be desired. Happy days? – A.E. Hooker

burn coal of indifferent quality and provided the 'stair rods' were going up the chimney, steam would be forthcoming. The F1s were no exception.'

The Eastern Section demanded hard work from its Ls, D1s and E1s. The Ls, built with short-lap piston valves above the cylinders (a detrimental last-minute change to Wainwright's design by Maunsell in his early days at Ashford) were very strong on the banks but decidedly sluggish on the flat. They largely settled in the early 30s at Bricklayers Arms and Hastings to work the Charing Cross–Hastings expresses via Tonbridge, which suited them well; they seemed to thrive on the 1 in 100 gradients.

The D1s and E1s were nearly new at Grouping – in fact more D1 rebuilds appeared in 1927. They were a brilliant answer to the special needs of the Chatham line, where bridges still imposed a $17\frac{1}{2}$ ton axleload limit and prohibited the Ls. Rebuilds they might be classified, but in fact there was not much of the original Ds and Es in them, particularly in the case of the E1s. The boilers, essentially the same on both, were well proportioned, with a good sized grate, and the front end with long lap valves was excellent. They proved capable of being driven very hard, even flogged, and provided the fire was kept thick under the door and tapered off well towards the front, they would steam their heads off. Working mainly from Battersea, Dover and Margate they were soon handling boat trains to Dover via Chatham, and Margate expresses, with great *elan*. Loads of 300–350 tons on Kent Coast services were quite acceptable to their enthusiastic crews. But the frames of the D1s, which were those of the original Ds, did not stand up well to this treatment, fracturing and needing extensive patching. Some were given stronger frames in the 1930s.

Blowing off hard, L1 class No 31758 of Ramsgate shed is in charge of a Margate via Canterbury East–Birkenhead through train approaching Dumpton Park in April 1957. The stock comprises six Maunsell corridors in blood-and-custard livery.

The spirit of these two remarkable classes was well summed up by Richard Hardy, 2½ years shedmaster at Stewarts Lane, writing evocatively of 1952:

'a little 4–4–0 roaring over the Battersea arches, the white feather showing and Driver Alf Murray whistling to the Shed Foreman down below that all was well with the world; ten corridor coaches bound for Ramsgate, to be restarted at Bromley on 1 in 95 on a curve and 1 in 100 at Whitstable, Herne Bay and Birchington, never without noise but always without distress.'

Bert Hooker paints a fascinating picture of a D1 in the difficult days of World War 2:

Nominally a rebuild, D1 No 735 was turned out by Beyer Peacock in July 1921. In the late 1950s, now No 31735 and shedded at Bricklayers Arms, she emerges from Chislehurst Tunnel while hauling a Dover via Tonbridge train.

German built class L 4-4-0 No 31780 climbs through urban Chatham and approaches Darland Tunnel with a Victoria to Dover train via Chatham on 26 March 1956.

'One unforgettable night I was with a passed fireman, Charlie Sutton, on... No 1145. We were booked to work a troop train from Canonbury to Fleet via Willesden, Kensington, Clapham Junction and the East Putney line. When the train arrived from the LNER the load was fourteen coaches filled with soldiers and their equipment! The train locomotive, an LNER V2, gave us a push start along the length of the platform. Up the heavy gradient to Hampstead Heath the D1 was worked 'flat out', full regulator and full travel of the... valves, but she marched them along without a falter, with the boiler pressure maintained at 180 psi and the... safety valves ready to lift. It was an extraordinary experience under the wartime blackout sheets'.

What higher praise could be bestowed on these splendidly willing little engines?

Disparaging comment has been made about the Brighton B4X 4-4-0s, which were choked by undersized piston valves below the cylinders and rarely exceeded 70mph even on long falling gradients. And yet the design was not wholly unsatisfactory. Hooker recalls that the rebuilds:

'were fitted with the finest drop grate and ashpan I have ever seen on a locomotive. The firebar section under the tubeplate dropped away when the controlling lever was operated and a section of the ashpan immediately under could be dropped also, allowing the fire and clinker to be pushed directly out into the pit... The remainder of the ash in the pan (was) then raked out, well damped down with the ashpan cock in use, a useful feature... unhappily not perpetuated on some subsequent larger locomotives in SR days and later BR ones.'

Perhaps Maunsell produced his biggest surprise when, in 1926, North British Locomotive Co turned out fifteen brand new inside cylindered 4-4-0s – the L1s – not, as on other railways, for secondary duties but to replace the hard-pressed Ls on the Folkestone and Dover expresses. With a greatly improved front end, even if it did lack some of the niceties of the D1 and E1 cylinders and valve gear, they soon showed that they could time the Folkestone 80 minute non-stops with over 300 tons behind them. But within four years they had been knocked from this perch by the magnificent Schools, very special 4-4-0s which are dealt with separately.

Such, then, was the Southern's 4-4-0 fleet. It was the last working stronghold of the traditional design, never undervalued, well cared for and skilfully handled. On duties within their own range they could hold their own with many larger and more modern competitors. It could never be other than a source of joy to look back to the days of the prestige Night Ferry before 1959 (when electric haulage began) and to relive the sight and sound of the up train, 600 tons and more of *fourgons*, dark blue *Wagon-Lits* sleepers and seating coaches, in charge of a Battle of Britain Pacific, with an L1 or D1 as assistant, hammering up Sole Street bank, white feather curling from the safety valves, its throaty bark drowning the thin ragtime rasp of the Bulleid, happily giving its all.

48

Transferred from the Eastern Section in 1959 after electrification, D1 No 31145's grubby paintwork was no credit to Dover (74C) shed. It is seen here arriving at Faversham on a Ramsgate to Victoria train in the summer of 1958. Withdrawal was in October 1961.

Southern Railway: Pre-Grouping 4–4–0s

Class	No built	Dates	Coupled Wheels	S'heated	No to SR 1923	No to BR 1948	Scrapped

London & South Western Railway

William Adams (all with outside cylinders)

Class	No built	Dates	Coupled Wheels	S'heated	No to SR 1923	No to BR 1948	Scrapped
380★	12	1879	5'-7"	-	9	-	1913–25
Steamrollers							
135★	12	1880–1	6'-7"	-	3	-	1913–24
445★	12	1883	7'-1"	-	12	-	1924–5
460★	21	1884	6'-7"	-	21	-	1924–8
X2	20	1890–2	7'-1"	-	20	-	1930–42
Highflyers							
T3	20	1892–3	6'-7"	-	20	-	1930–45
T6	10	1895–6	7'-1"	-	10	-	1933–43
X6	10	1895–6	6'-7"	-	10	-	1933–46

50

Class	No built	Dates	Coupled Wheels	S'heated	No to SR 1923	No to BR 1948	Scrapped
Dugald Drummond							
C8	10	1898	6'–7"	-	10	-	1933–8
T9	66	1899–1901	6'–7"	1922–9	66	66	1951–63
Greyhounds							
K10	40	1901–2	5'–7"	-	40	22	1947–51
Small Hoppers							
L11	40	1903–7	5'–7"	-	40	40	1949–52
Large Hoppers							
S11	10	1903	6'–1"	1920–2	10	10	1951–4
Shorthorns							
L12	20	1904–5	6'–7"	1914–22	20	20	1951–5
Bulldogs							
D15	10	1912	6'–7"	1915–7	10	10	1951–6
London, Brighton & South Coast Railway							
Robert Billinton							
B2X	25R	1907–16	6'–9"	-	25	-	1929–33
B4	33	1899–1902	6'–9"	2 in 1918			
Scotchmen				and 1921	31	7	1934–51
B4X	12R	1922–4	6'–9"	Yes	2	12	1951
South Eastern & Chatham Railway							
William Kirtley (LC&DR)							
M2	8	1884–5	6'–6"	-	1	-	1923
M3	26	1891–1900	6'–6"	-	26	-	1925–8
James Stirling (SER)							
F *	88	1883–98	7'–0"	-	12	-	1924–30
F1	76R	1903–16	7'–0"	-	75	9	1920–49
B	29	1898–9	7'–0"	-	5	-	1930–1
B1	27R	1910–27	7'–0"	-	24	16	1933–51
William Pickersgill (Great North of Scotland Rly, sold to SE&CR)							
G *	5	1900	6'–1"	-	5	-	1924–7
Harry Wainwright							
D	51	1901–7	6'–8"	-	40	28	1944–56
D1	21R	1921–7	6'–8"	Yes	11	20	1944–61
E	26	1905–10	6'–6"	Two in			
				1912	15	15	1951–5
E1	11R	1919–20	6'–6"	Yes	11	11	1949–61
H. Wainwright/Richard Maunsell							
L	22	1914	6'–8"	Yes	22	22	1956–62

* Earmarked for early withdrawal
R Rebuilt

Southern Railway 4–4–0s							
L1	15	1926	6'–8"	Yes	-	15	1959–62
V	40	1930–4	6'–7"	Yes	-	40	1961–2
Schools							

Trains, Trains

In the course of the homeward rush from the seaside on Monday evening last, there were several achievements on the part of the Southern Railway calling for attention. At Brighton a special control tower was installed and brought into use about 4pm, its object being to direct passengers to the various platforms and trains. Between 5pm and 10pm no fewer than 107 trains left Brighton Central, carrying 75,000 passengers. On the average, therefore, a train departed every three minutes – or slightly less – throughout the five hour period, and each train carried on an average just over 700 passengers – 15,000 an hour. The great bulk of this traffic was for London or beyond, and had to be carried over the main line, which has only the one up track as far as Balcombe Tunnel box – 19 miles – and in addition to the trains from Brighton there were those from Worthing and Hove also passing over almost the whole of this distance. More noteworthy still is the fact that from Keymer Junction to Balcombe Tunnel there were also the Hastings, Bexhill, Seaford trains to be accommodated by the single up road in addition to those from Brighton and Worthing. Actually, between Keymer Junction and Haywards Heath the up trains moving over this road were: between 7 and 8pm, 13 trains; between 8 and 9pm, 16; between 9 and 10pm, 18; and between 10 and 11pm, 14 trains, the greatest density being one every 3.3 minutes throughout the hour. Only by the employment of automatic colour-light signalling, and of very heavy electric trains for the most part, could this traffic be moved within so short a period.– *Railway Gazette*, 9 June 1933

Tonbridge shed is host to D1 class 4–4–0 No 31749 and motor-fitted H class 0–4–4T No 31308, both well cleaned, in the twilight of their lives. No 31749 was one of the last of the class to receive a general repair and repaint, in November 1958, and she lasted exactly three more years before withdrawal.

Two ex-SE&CR 4–4–0s, B1 No 1443 and D No 1075, sit out of service at the back of Reading (Southern Region) shed in early BR days, as a Hall in the background slows for a Reading stop. The vertical Stirling steam reverser is prominent on both engines. The B1 was withdrawn in March 1951, almost 53 years old, while the D, built in 1903, lasted until the end of 1956.

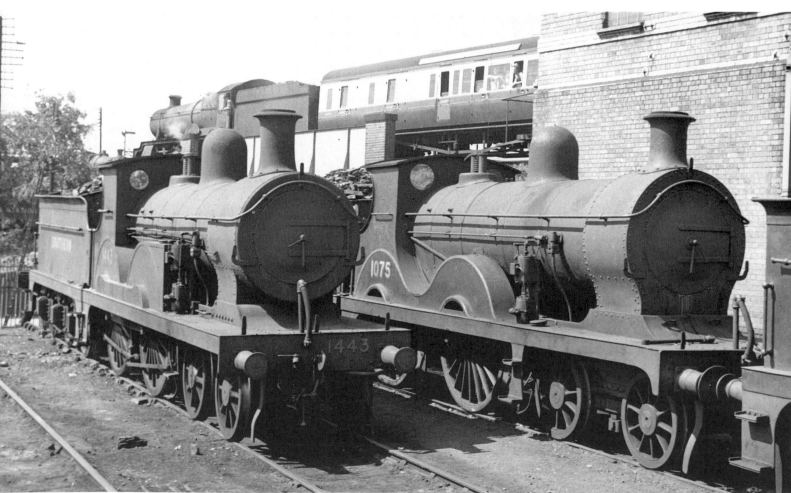

A Day at Hawkhurst

In the rather misty dawn of an early September day in 1946, a short goods train headed by an elderly O1 class 0-6-0 climbs slowly up through the orchards and hop-gardens of the Wealden hills. It left Keylands Yard, Paddock Wood at 5.50am and is making its way up the steeply graded 11½ mile single line to Hawkhurst. After it has called at the three intermediate stations, mainly to unload 'smalls' from the road box wagons, it traverses the short Badger's Oak tunnel, the summit of the line, and rolls into the terminus at 7.18.

Hawkhurst station is high on a hill, a steeply-graded mile from the village. The single platform with its short bay, has a simple wooden, tin-roofed building. One is not surprised Colonel Stephens was the resident engineer of the line. There is a short run round loop and in front of the station are three sidings, one ending in a large brick goods shed, while the far one is equipped for unloading petrol wagons. The two-road engine shed has not been used since 1932. The station is staffed on two shifts by a signalman and a porter who sells tickets among all his other duties, while the stationmaster attends to the accounts.

The engine runs round its train, places the 'roader' (or 'road box', the wagon with 'smalls' for several stations, sometimes known as the station truck) in the goods shed, and the two box wagons of feeding stuffs and the single wagon of coal in the other siding. The shunting completed the loco backs onto the ex-LSWR two-coach pull-and-push set in the bay (note this was Southern terminology, other railways pushed and pulled). By this time the passengers for the first train, the 7.40am are beginning to arrive. There are two or three for Tonbridge and London, but there are also about thirty school-children for Tonbridge, as this is the first day of term. The signalman comes over with the single-line token; unusually for the Southern it is a Tyler's tablet and not a staff. In the aftermath of war there is a staff shortage and promotion is rapid. The tablet is taken by a passed cleaner not yet twenty and the train is driven by a passed fireman not much older.

The 7.40 will pass the 7.35 from Paddock Wood at Goudhurst, Cranbrook is not used to pass trains, and the latter runs into Hawkhurst at 8.10. Headed by an H class 0-4-4T, it consists of a similar ex-LSWR push-and-pull set. With no real connection from London it has no

Hawkhurst Station on 11 March 1961. SECR class H 0–4–4T Fitted with air control push and pull gear has just arrived with the 2.15pm from Paddock Wood. The station is built of corrugated sheet steel with a brick base. Behind the train are the signal box and water tank.

passengers, but brings in some bags of mail, newspapers and a few parcels. It leaves ten minutes later, the H tank propelling, with a handful of passengers going up to London for a day's shopping or business. They will get to Cannon Street at 10.13. Hawkhurst village is an excellent bus centre, with services to Maidstone, Tunbridge Wells and Hastings, so there is virtually no local rail traffic.

The 0-4-4T and set will form all the remaining trains, and they return from Paddock Wood at 9.07am, the journey taking the usual 30 minutes. They leave Hawkhurst with a few more passengers at 09.43. Normally a period of deep peace then settles over the station, but today is the start of the hop-picking season. There will be two hop-pickers' specials.

The first is the 8.15 from London Bridge Low Level and it comes to a halt outside the station a few minutes before its scheduled time of 10.25, having passed the 9.43 at Goudhurst. It is hauled by a D class 4-4-0 with an identification number H5 hung round its chimney and piloting an E1 of similar wheel arrangement, and consists of two trio C sets with their characteristic birdcage guard's lookouts, and four long wheelbased four-wheeled utility vans. The loop is too short to allow a loco to run-

round, so the D class is acting as 'pull-off' engine. It is uncoupled and run into a siding, the train then entering the platform. It has already shed most of its passengers at Goudhurst and Cranbrook, but the station is briefly loud with activity as children are rounded up and pram loads of luggage retrieved from the vans, noisy humanity fading down the approach on their way to the farms. The pull-off locomotive frees the train engine by transferring the train to a siding, the train engine backs on and the two take the empties away tender first.

The pull-and-push comes back at 1pm and leaves again at 1.10. The Southern treat it as a multiple unit, requiring only two crew, so there is no guard. Then the peace of the sunny autumn afternoon is shattered by the arrival of special H12 at 2.20 (the 11.45am from London Bridge). Of similar formation to the morning special, it carries rather more Hawkhurst hop-pickers. The empties are finally despatched about 3.15.

This is just as well as the daily freight train is due at 4pm having made its leisurely way along the branch since leaving Keylands Yard at 12.42. It comes in behind a C class 0-6-0 and brings back the set for to-morrow's 7.40am. It also brings a couple of tank wagons of fuel oil for the hop oasts, three coal wagons, and two bogie brakes. Hawkhurst's main outwards traffic is pot plants for Woolworth's from a local nursery, and the bogie van for this evening is already being loaded.

Shunting operations are completed by the time the H

tank appears again at 4.52. It connected at Paddock Wood with the 3.15 from Charing Cross and conveys the scholars on their way home from Tonbridge. It goes out again at 5.05 and when it has cleared Goudhurst it is followed by the goods. It has two round trips still to make. The first leaves Paddock Wood at 5.53 as a connection with the 4.38 departure from Cannon Street. It reaches Hawkhurst at 6.23 and leaves five minutes later. The last trip leaves Paddock Wood at 7.28, the 6.18 Cannon Street–Ramsgate stops at Tonbridge where the last three coaches are detached to form a stopping train to Margate via Ashford and Canterbury West, which calls at Paddock Wood at 7.25. The Hawkhurst leaves promptly, a dozen passengers having crossed the bridge, and makes a race of it with the main line train until the branch swings away southward. Hawkhurst is reached at 7.58. The pot-plant van is picked up and is towed away behind the propelling H tank, a handful of day trippers and the outward mail in the train. The blast of the exhaust has not been cut off by the tunnel before the late-turn porter has locked up the station. The signalman waits until the tablet has been placed in the instrument at Cranbrook before he too can go off duty. It is the end of another day at this typical yet unique Southern branch line station.

Famous Bottleneck

The layout at Borough Market Junction was resignalled in 1928, controlled by a new 35 lever power frame in the old and scruffy signal box. The flat junctions to Cannon Street and Charing Cross were a bottleneck handling 41 up and 48 down trains between 17.00 and 18.00 in the late 1940s. See plan of how the layout then was. The London Bridge resignalling in 1976 brought a new track layout to concentrate all the Cannon Street trains on to the two southerly ones any further sorting being done between London Bridge and St John's. It is now proposed to provide an additional two tracks towards Charing Cross by bridging over the Market premises.

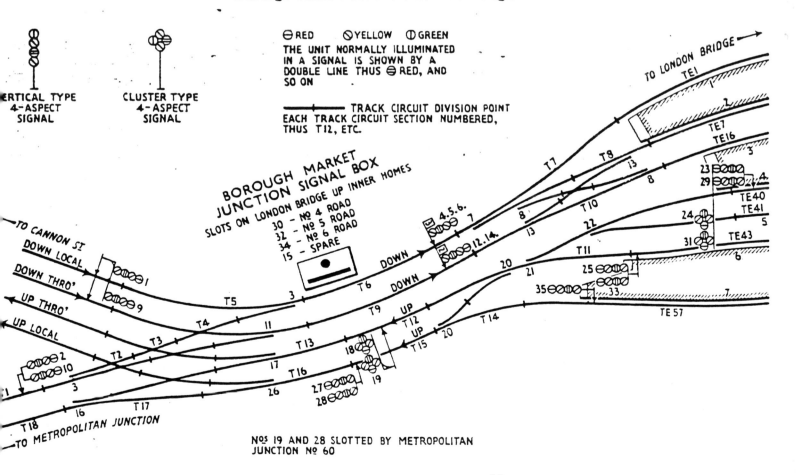

Borough Market Junction, Southern Region

NOS 19 AND 28 SLOTTED BY METROPOLITAN JUNCTION No 60

Silver Thaw

The first winter of the War probably brought the worst weather conditions within living memory, although reports were restricted due to censorship.

A rare phenomenon was the 'silver thaw' of the night of 27/28 January 1940. Throughout the month the weather had been intensely cold but on Saturday evening the 27th a fine rain was falling in South East England hopefully preceding a thaw. But by Sunday morning there was a coating of ice up to half an inch thick. The evening drizzle had frozen and subsequent rain had thickened the coating of ice which broke branches of trees and of course covered the Southern's conductor rails making it virtually impossible to run an electric service.

Steam trains were able to run more or less normally and after getting locomotives organised some electric trains ran hauled by steam. These where possible were Westinghouse fitted and thus able to operate the train brakes with electric current when available, as in tunnels, fortunately supplying lighting! It was not always possible to provide an air braked locomotive and in these cases the steam driver had to rely on his own engine brake and as much help as was possible from the air brake reservoirs on the train – operated by the rostered electric driver from the leading cab. Running speed had of course to be drastically reduced to allow for the extra braking distance required.

One unfortunate passenger who missed the 3.25pm Charing Cross to Hastings train on Sunday 28 January was advised to travel *electric* via East Croydon, Brighton and Polegate which he did, eventually reaching Hastings about 4am after being stranded and rescued by steam. If he had taken refreshment in London and caught the next steam service to Hastings, the 7.25pm he would have been home by 10pm! *See also page 108.*

SOUTHERN RAILWAY

EPSOM RACES

APRIL 20th, 21st and 22nd,

Cheap Tickets
To Epsom
Epsom Downs,
Tattenham Corner,

By ALL Trains.

FROM	RETURN FARES.		FROM	RETURN FARES.	
	1st Class	3rd Class		1st Class	3rd Class
	s. d.	s. d.		s. d.	s. d.
KENSINGTON (Addison Rd.)			STREATHAM COMMON		
WEST BROMPTON	5 / -	3 / -	NORBURY	4 / -	2 / 6
CHELSEA AND FULHAM			THORNTON HEATH		
BATTERSEA	4 / 6	2 / 9	SELHURST		
BATTERSEA PARK			NORWOOD JUNCTION		
CLAPHAM JUNCTION			NEW CROSS GATE	5 / -	3 / -
WANDSWORTH COMMON	4 / -	2 / 6	BROCKLEY		
BALHAM			HONOR OAK PARK	4 / 6	2 / 9
SOUTH BERMONDSEY			FOREST HILL		
QUEEN'S ROAD (Peckham)			SYDENHAM		
PECKHAM RYE			PENGE WEST		
EAST BRIXTON (Via Peckham Rye)			ANERLEY	4 / -	2 / 6
DENMARK HILL	5 / -	3 / -	STREATHAM HILL		
EAST DULWICH			WEST NORWOOD		
NORTH DULWICH			GIPSY HILL		
BRIXTON (via Victoria)			CRYSTAL PALACE (L.L.)		
LOUGHBOROUGH JCT.			BIRKBECK (via Crystal Palace, Low Level)	4 / 6	2 / 9
HERNE HILL					
TULSE HILL	4 / -	2 / 6	BECKENHAM JCT. (via Crystal Palace, Low Level)	4 / 9	3 / -
STREATHAM					

Tickets available for return by any Train on the day of issue.

FREQUENT ELECTRIC TRAINS.

Tickets may be obtained in advance at Stations and Agencies.

Refreshments can be obtained at the Refreshment Rooms at Tattenham Corner and Epsom Downs Station.

NOTICE AS TO CONDITIONS.—These tickets are issued at less than the ordinary fares, and are subject to the notice and conditions shown in the current Time Tables. No luggage allowed except small handbags, luncheon baskets or other small articles intended for the passenger's personal use during the day.

Waterloo Station, S.E. 1. March, 1931.

H. A. WALKER, General Manager.

C.X. 635/$\frac{55}{26831}$

Waterlow & Sons Limited, London, Dunstable & Watford.

3
HAVING A FLUTTER ON THE SOUTHERN

HAD you been one of the crowd that turned up at Nine Elms Station on 21 May 1838 expecting to be taken by special train to the races you would probably have been very annoyed and disappointed at missing the Derby that day. So many people came along that the railway could not cope and the police had to be called.

The opening of the line from London to the vicinity of the present Surbiton station had been brought forward to take advantage of the occasion, people thinking little of the ten mile walk to and from the course at Epsom.

The overwhelming demand for rail travel to a race meeting was not lost on the directors of the fledgling London & Southampton Railway nor on their successors of the Southern. They inherited territory containing no less than sixteen rail-associated courses.

Indeed the very next station from Surbiton down their main line to Weymouth and the West Country, Esher, was to become the focal point for race traffic to Sandown Park. There were stairways to Lower Green Road, opened only on race days, and a special entrance there to the course. To overcome the peak congestion arising at the end of meetings, when winners and losers alike are anxious to leave for home, an island platform was brought into use for the London traffic immediately west of the station and, before the advent of the next station, Hersham, steam trains queued along the up local line from Walton-on-Thames so as to be ready for a quick getaway. There are two up and two down lines at this location and they were not electrified until 1937. So that train crews were not confused under normal day-to-day conditions the signal at the London end of the special platform was of a slotted variety with the arm tucked away inside the post except on race days.

Ultimately, of course, much of this traffic succumbed to the motor car and nearly twenty years into nationalisation the additional trains to Esher for a Saturday race-meeting numbered only two, from Waterloo at lunchtime. One electric train with a headcode 10 served all stations and then ran empty to Woking; the other with headcode 56 called only at Wimbledon and then continued similarly to Chertsey. To provide a path in the dense suburban traffic the 12.25 from Waterloo to Shepperton had to be retimed to run one minute later to Kingston. The two additional trains returned to London from Esher soon after five o'clock.

Hurst Park, now a housing estate, was adjacent to the Thames just west of Hampton Court and it was along the branch through Thames Ditton from the main line at Surbiton that the extra trains were run from London. The terminus was well-provided with sidings for the leisure

No 119 Is Scrapped
She is made of steel, but not a robot, nor by any means lifeless or without character. She is, in fact, the royal engine of the old LSWR, the famous No 119. Now, after 54 years of service, she has been condemned and is being broken up for scrap at Ashford, in Kent. It happens sooner or later to every railway engine, but when it happens to this one it is rightly news. Fifty years of her life were given to the hauling of kings and queens, for this was the engine which the South Western Railway, and the Southern after them, kept inviolate to pull the royal train when it ran over their metals.

For the rest of the time she
continued overleaf

Hurst Park race course was served by Hampton Court station. Three return specials carrying headcode 94 wait for the punters on Whit Monday 6 June 1960. The two trains on the left are 4 SUBs with stencil route numbers and that on the right is a combination of probably two 4 EPBs with roller blind indicators.

continued
stayed in Nine Elms shed, sheathed in tarpaulins and dust-sheets. Occasionally, it is true, a distracted motive power superintendent, at his wits' end to find enough engines to run the trains he must provide, surreptitiously borrowed her to run a race special to Ascot or a conference special to Bournemouth or a Southampton boat train, hoping against hope that the directors would not hear of it. For the use of No 119 for any purpose other than royal journeys was not encouraged.

In the stud book of the railway she belonged to Class T9, which *continued opposite*

traffic for which it catered and these helped with the stabling of the coaches during racing. The shunting neck, however, adjoined a level crossing and the marshalling of stock necessitated frequent openings and closings of the gates with chaotic effects on road traffic.

Nearby Kempton Park remains in business and boasts its own adjacent station, open only for race meetings, situated between Hampton and Sunbury on the branch to Shepperton. Trains come from Waterloo either via the original route through Richmond and Twickenham or by way of the spur towards Kingston, on the loop line, put in at the turn of the century. Electrification took place shortly before the creation of the Southern and in its day, notably on Easter Mondays, trains ran at four-minute intervals before and after the races. This necessitated the provision and special opening of four intermediate block posts from Fulwell to Kempton Park to shorten the normal lengthy sections and exhausted the capacity of the sidings available at Shepperton for berthing the stock.

Again it became the practice to stand the empty trains on the up line, between Shepperton and Sunbury, ready for the home-going but this time the formation was only double-track. Accordingly, electric tablet instruments were installed permanently in the signal boxes there and when it was too late for trains to be run back to Waterloo for more punters the signal engineer would establish single-line working for the local service on the down line. At the height of the race meeting some sixteen trains were stabled on the up track in an almost unbroken procession over a mile-and-a-half long.

To complicate matters further the Southern provided a number of steam-worked specials to Kempton Park for first class passengers. M7 class 0–4–4 tank engines hauled trains of vintage SECR and LBSCR compartment stock. These spent the afternoon at Sunbury and used a non-electrified loop on the outer face of the up platform to pick up their clientele.

Before we leave the Thames valley for the wider south east we must have a look at the Ascot traffic. The working timetables setting out the arrangements for the principal race meeting annually on five days in mid-June are a tribute to the skills of the Southern management. Their experience and expertise were unparalleled in dealing with crowds quickly and efficiently, in the days when staff and other resources were more readily available. Racing took place between about 2pm and 5pm and thus some of the stock which normally lay idle after the morning peak into London could be used for the many additional services. In the evening the racegoers vacated trains at Waterloo which were instantly filled with those returning from work to the home counties.

The principal station at Ascot is a junction on the line from Waterloo through either Richmond or Hounslow, then Staines and Wokingham to Reading where there are connecting tracks to the Great Western network. Until quite recent years it was possible also to run direct from Waterloo to Ascot via Weybridge and a spur at Virginia Water which avoided the station there. The branch from Ascot itself runs to Ash Vale on the Alton line and again until the recent past there was a triangular junction at the point where the branch passes under the Southern main line to the west. This provided another alternative route from Waterloo via Woking and a direct connection towards Farnborough and Basingstoke.

Following electrification shortly before World War II the regular pattern of trains to Ascot was a half hourly service from Waterloo which divided there for Reading and for Aldershot and, after reversal, Guildford. To cope with the frequent race traffic four temporary signal boxes were brought into use between Virginia Water and Ascot and the signal engineer had to have the signals put in working order by the preceding Sunday. Four other existing boxes had to be manned for far longer periods than usual. The steam engine off the morning Woking–Bagshot goods was sent on to Ascot for shunting and emergency purposes and remained until mid-afternoon in company with another engine that spent most of the day there. A station known as Ascot West, serving only the Reading line, was brought into use for racegoers arriving from Waterloo and those on terminating trains the other way from the Western. Some of the passengers returning to London were directed to Ascot Race Platform, just west of the main station, from which a number of departures were made to ease congestion next door. There was the usual blockage, this time of part of the up main line, to accommodate trains waiting their turn to leave for Waterloo.

The normal service to and from Guildford became a self-contained shuttle working. Because longer trains than usual thus continued to Reading, passengers had to beware of short platforms further down the line. To provide accommodation for home-going workers from Sunningdale and Longcross in the thick of the exodus from Ascot, three coaches at the front of one of the services from Reading had to be locked

continued

in common speech among railwaymen and railway lovers was called the Greyhound class. She was designed by that cantankerous old Scotsman Dugald Drummond in 1899, and by general consent she and her sisters were his masterpieces. People seldom agree on aesthetics in engine design, but few would quarrel with the judgment that Drummond's Greyhounds were the most beautiful engines ever built in Britain. They were not very large even when they were built, but the sheer grace of these 4–4–0s was incomparable then and is so still. Her sisters ran most of the main line traffic for a good many years, and then they were relegated to slow trains and branch-line work. Today those that are left of the class – there are about 20 – run many of the trains between Padstow and Exeter, and a number of the slow trains which converge on Bournemouth. But No 119 was reserved for royalty and kept clean and gleaming in vivid green paint. Only the old Great Eastern and South Western kept the one engine for the use of kings and queens. The Great Eastern's was an old Claud Hamilton 4–4–0 which lived in Cambridge so as to be handy for Sandringham. Very occasionally, when not wanted by royalty, she was allowed to run an ordinary train as far as Ely and back, but it had to be a fine day.

The reign of No 119 as the South Western's royal engine was a long one. She kept her eminence until after the war, and then she was at last demoted, sent to live at Dorchester, and kept pottering about between Weymouth and Bournemouth. Naturally she was the special pride of the Dorchester enginemen, who kept her as spick and span as she had ever been, so that on her last journey she shone as brightly in the sun as on her first. – *The Times*, 4 March 1953.

'The Bug'. In 1898–9 Dugald Drummond built a 4–2–4T combined locomotive and saloon numbered 733 for his daily business journeys from his home at Surbiton to Nine Elms and later to Eastleigh, also longer unscheduled trips. After Drummond's death it was not much used until 1932 when No 733, by then No 58S, was repainted in passenger green livery and with an ex-SER six-wheel saloon conveyed important visitors around the new docks at Southampton. After completion of the new docks 58S retired to Eastleigh paint shop, where it is seen here in 1936, until 1940 when it was stripped to the frames and bogies and used for conveying heavy loads around Eastleigh Works. The frames finally disappeared in 1957.

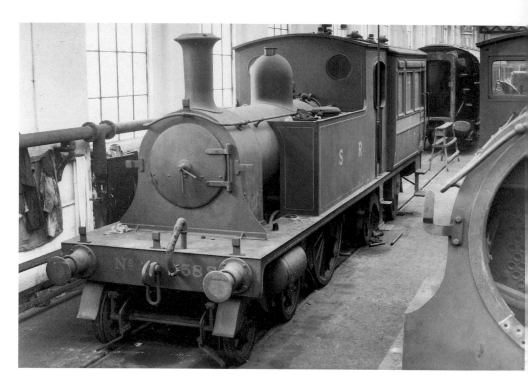

MONDAY, APRIL 29th
FOLKESTONE RACES

FIRST RACE 2.0 P.M.   LAST RACE 4.30 P.M.

EXCURSIONS
TO
WESTENHANGER

FROM †	DEPART				RETURN FARES, Second Class
	a.m.	a.m.	a.m.	a.m.	s. d.
VICTORIA	—	9C 18		10B 35	
CHARING CROSS	9 15	—	11R 6	—	13/6
WATERLOO	9 17	—	11R 9	—	
LONDON BRIDGE	8A 52	—		10A 38	
NEW CROSS	8A 59	—		10A 44	12/6
HITHER GREEN	8E 57	—		10A 50	12/–
GROVE PARK	9A 6	—		10A 53	11/9
BROMLEY SOUTH	9A 2	9C 35		11A 4	11/6
ORPINGTON	9A 18	—		11A 8	10/9
SEVENOAKS	9 50	—		11 50	9/–
			p.m.	p.m.	
Westenhanger (Race Course) arrive	—		12 40	—	
Westenhanger	10 49	11 30	—	12 54	

A—Change at Sevenoaks.   B—Change at Bromley South and Sevenoaks.   C—Change at Maidstone East.   E—Change at Orpington and Sevenoaks.

and brought to a stand beyond the ends of the platforms until they reached their required destination.

Engineer's department staff were stationed at various level crossings, including that over the A30 at Sunningdale, 'to prevent interruption to the trains,' and during the period of return traffic it was stated to be 'of extreme importance that the inspector-in-charge at Ascot should be able to obtain uninterrupted telephonic communication with Waterloo, and station masters on the line are held responsible for seeing that the telephones are not used except in cases of absolute necessity'.

A train conveying first class passengers only at a special fare was generally run from Waterloo to Ascot at 12.40 via Chertsey, returning at 6.33pm via Frimley and Woking. Sometimes excursions would be put on from the West Country, one originating at Exeter Central followed by another with portions from Plymouth Friary and Ilfracombe, a day out lasting more than seventeen hours. These would use the curve from Farnborough to Frimley and run on to Clapham Yard to be serviced. On its return the Exeter empties had to wait in the Sanatorium Siding at Virginia Water for three hours as no other path was available.

Freight train working, too, was affected by the race traffic, particularly as Feltham marshalling yard was situated on the direct route from London to Ascot and the 10.45 Feltham–Exmouth Junction, for instance, had to bide its time in the Sanatorium Siding and be limited to 45 wagons including brake so as not to obstruct its junction. The goods yards at intermediate stations were still in business and the 11.23 Chertsey to Ascot pick-up had to be diverted to Feltham, wagons for Sunningdale having been detached at Virginia Water to be taken forward on a special at 2.10pm.

Excursions from the Western through Reading often came from such places as Swansea and Wolverhampton and on at least one occasion the miners of Nantybwch, travelling on a Thursday, would be preceded by

The race course platform at Westenhanger near Folkestone on 13 August 1956 with the 4.50pm race special to Victoria via Maidstone East loading while passing through on the main line is the 3.45pm Margate–London via Redhill. By a strange coincidence both locomotives are now preserved in the National Collection. No 30777 Sir Lamiel is on the Race Special and No 30925 Cheltenham on the Margate–London Bridge train.

Cross Countries

It is perhaps not often realised that it was the Southern's electrification and great increase in frequency of trains to London that first started the decline in cross-country travel and trains. Those opting for making journeys by London knew that at least on their Southern segment there would be a train when they needed one, avoiding delays in London and indeed in many cases obviating the need even to consult the Southern's timetable. It was of course not always just a question of time and fare but of flexibility.

Among the first casualties were the Southern's own internal cross-country services, such as Deal to Bournemouth (a journey that used to take six and a half hours), Chatham to Brighton and Brighton to Ilfracombe (as well as Brighton to Plymouth which on nationalisation was the only major surviving internal cross-country service).

Liverpool and Manchester to Portsmouth and Bournemouth, Liverpool and Manchester to Whitstable and Ramsgate and also to Brighton and Eastbourne, Birkenhead as well as Cardiff and Bristol to various destinations including Hastings and Sandwich, the Newcastle to Bournemouth, the Pines Express, of course... the pre-war variety was never repeated... and even the tables of 'Coastal Service' showing connections eg via Ashford that were not through trains were dropped from the timetable.

Many of the cross-countries were of course time-honoured institutions, the Sunny South Express having an especially evocative name and history. Though the distances they travelled and how frequently they ran or were duplicated or triplicated at summer weekends naturally varied, and only some of them carried restaurant cars, they shared a number of common char-
continued opposite

their brothers from the Midlands coalfield at Pleasley the previous day. The stock was berthed at Bracknell during the racing. No detail was forgotten: to discourage fraudulent travel the Southern remembered to suspend the validity of platform tickets on platforms used by race trains at Waterloo and their sale at Ascot from 4pm until after the last special had left. Mail and parcels traffic between Frimley, Camberley and Bagshot and Waterloo had to be rerouted by the Cobham line via Guildford and staff there had 'to arrange prompt transfer'.

For her visits to Royal Ascot the Queen usually drives from Windsor. For the Derby, however, Her Majesty normally travels by special train from Victoria to one of the terminals near the course, either Epsom Downs or, more frequently, Tattenham Corner. On one occasion in post-Southern days the Royal Train returned to London from Chessington South.

The two terminal stations on the downs boasted extensive facilities with many lengthy sidings and there was no need to store trains on running lines prior to the conclusion of the races. Turntables were available for steam engines though electrification came to both routes, from Sutton and from Purley, in 1928 and the following comments date from after that time. The principal race meeting is held at the beginning of June and includes peak days for the Derby and the Oaks. The special workings began with the steam-hauled 7.10 from London Bridge to Epsom Downs (arrive 8.02), which had originated at New Cross Gate and consisted of horse boxes for the Metropolitan Police. The men, generally up to 660 from London augmented by 95 from Epsom, travelled in reserved accommodation soon afterwards.

Again there was modification in block working, at Epsom Downs, and the provision of signals at intermediate points between the stations on the branch. The breakdown tool van from Stewart's Lane Shed had to be stabled there most of the week and that from Norwood at Tattenham Corner where two steam engines were in attendance. A steam crane was sent from Guildford to Purley via Deepdene in the early hours of Wednesday and Friday morning.

The many additional trains included one from Cannon Street at lunchtime for businessmen from the City and two from Streatham Hill. On Derby Day eight Pullman cars left Stewarts Lane Yard at 10.45 and passed through Nunhead to Blackheath where, 45 minutes later, they were steamed back through Lewisham to be ready to form the 12.46 super service from Charing Cross to Tattenham Corner (arrive 1.38pm). The train returned from there at 5.47pm and performed the same itinerary in reverse. At certain times the regular Victoria–Epsom service was diverted from Sutton to Epsom Downs. An up and a down Bognor–Victoria express via Dorking made a special stop at Epsom; one of the trains which normally started out from Effingham Junction began its journey back at Guildford and returned there later. The Caterham service became a shuttle from Purley; trains which normally terminated at Coulsdon North were diverted to Smitham and sent on to Tattenham Corner. Emphasis was placed on the need for race trains to carry side destination boards.

Lingfield Park Races

FRIDAY { First Race 2.30 p.m. / Last Race 5.0 p.m.   SATURDAY { First Race 2.0 p.m. / Last Race 4.30 p.m.

FRIDAY & SATURDAY, JUNE 30th & JULY 1st

DAY RETURN TICKETS
to Lingfield

FROM ↓	DEPART									RETURN FARES, Second Class
	Friday only				Saturday only					
	p.m.	p.m.	p.m.	p.m.	a.m.	a.m.	p.m.	p.m.	p.m.	s. d.
VICTORIA	12 5	12 8	12R 39	1 8	11 38	11P 50	12 4	12P 39	—	9 / 2
CHARING CROSS ..	—	a.m. 11A 53	12A 23	12A 53	—	—	11D 45	—	12E 28	} 9 / 6
WATERLOO	—	11A 55	12A 25	12A 55	—	—	11D 47	—	12E 30	
CANNON STREET ..	—	—	—	—	—	—	11D 41	—	12E 31	} 9 / 2
LONDON BRIDGE ..	—	p.m. 12A 0	12A 31	1A 0	—	—	12A 0	—	12 47	
CLAPHAM JUNCTION ..	12 11	12 14	12A 34	1 14	—	11P 55	—	—	12A 41	8 / 2
BALHAM	—	12A 1	—	1A 1	—	—	p.m. 12A 1	—	12A 31	7 / 6
STREATHAM COMMON ..	—	12A 5	—	1A 5	—	—	12A 5	—	12A 35	6 / 10
NORBURY	—	12A 7	—	1A 7	—	—	12A 7	—	12A 37	6 / 6
THORNTON HEATH ..	—	12A 10	—	1A 10	—	—	12A 10	—	12A 40	} 6 / 2
SELHURST	—	12A 13	—	1A 13	—	—	12A 12	—	12A 43	
NEW CROSS GATE ..	—	a.m. 11B 40	12B 10	12B 40	—	—	12A 5	—	12B 37	8 / 2
FOREST HILL	—	11B 47	12B 17	12B 47	—	—	a.m. 11B 47	—	12B 27	7 / 2
NORWOOD JUNCTION ..	—	p.m. 12A 14	12A 43	1A 14	—	—	p.m. 12A 3	—	12A 51	6 / 2
EAST CROYDON	12 25	12 29	12R 58	1 29	—	p.m. 12P 9	12 24	12 57	1 5	5 / 6
OXTED	—	12 59	—	1 59	—	—	12C 59	—	1 34	2 / 4
Lingfield .. .. ..arrive	12 54	1 11	1 25	2 11	p.m. 12 22	p.m. 12 35	12 50	1 25	1 45	

A—Change at East Croydon.   B—Change at Norwood Junction and East Croydon.   C—Arrives Lingfield 1.11 p.m.
D—Change at London Bridge and East Croydon.   E—Change at London Bridge.

FIRST CLASS **DAY** RETURN TICKETS ARE ALSO OBTAINABLE WHERE SUCH ACCOMMODATION IS AVAILABLE

RETURN BY ANY TRAIN SAME DAY
Including LINGFIELD depart:—

FRIDAY
5R18 p.m. to East Croydon and Victoria.
5P29 p.m. to East Croydon, Clapham Junction and Victoria.
5.34 p.m. to Oxted, East Croydon and Victoria.
6.9 p.m. to Oxted, East Croydon and London Bridge.

SATURDAY
4P48 & 4P58 p.m. to East Croydon, Clapham Junction and Victoria.
5.9 p.m. to Oxted, East Croydon, Clapham Junction and Victoria.
5.18 p.m. to East Croydon and Victoria.

P—PULLMAN CARS 1st CLASS WILL RUN IN THESE TRAINS
R—PULLMAN CARS 1st & 2nd CLASS WILL RUN IN THESE TRAINS
(A supplementary charge, 2/6 1st Class, 1/6 2nd Class, is made in each direction)
Luncheon will be obtainable on forward journey and tea on the return
Light refreshments may be obtained in both directions

FROM ↓	DEPART						RETURN FARES, Second Class	RETURN BY ANY TRAIN SAME DAY INCLUDING:—
	Friday only			Saturday only				
	a.m.	p.m.	p.m.	a.m.	p.m.	p.m.	s. d.	Lingfield depart:—
UPPER WARLINGHAM	11 46	12 46	1 46	11 46	12 46	1 20	4 / 0	4.34, 5.34, and 6FO9 p.m.
WOLDINGHAM	11 50	12 51	1 51	11 50	12 51	1 25	3 / 8	
Lingfield .. arrive ..	p.m. 12 11	1 11	2 11	p.m. 12 11	1 11	1 45		FO—Friday only.

Passengers should ascertain before return if (and where) change of carriage is necessary
CHILDREN 3 AND UNDER 14 YEARS, HALF FARE
Tickets may be obtained in advance at Stations or Travel Agencies

continued
acteristics. The chief of these was their slowness. Most of them called at every likely traffic source, and changing locomotives at the hand-over point between the different railways and dividing sections for different destinations (occasionally twice within an hour) took time. Then the timetablers added recovery time, since late running heavy steam-hauled trains on busy electrified routes were not popular.

You could sense the atmosphere on a cross-country train, whatever its coaching stock. The coaches were of course seldom the latest models, and often included Southern green and chocolate-and-cream, maroon or teak according to which of the other big three the particular journey was shared between, though when things went according to the text book there would usually be complete sets of the two companies' stock on alternate days.

Except at summer weekends the trains were seldom crowded, though on Southern metals they often carried substantial numbers of passengers short distances. Many of the long-distance travellers were of course families going to or from holiday; remember the days when dad treated himself to lunch in the restaurant car while the rest of the family tucked into sandwiches?

Not only was the pace generally leisurely but everyone expected it to be. Increasingly those in a hurry, especially morning and evening, went via London, the cross countries being left with leisure travellers, who appreciated not having to cross the capital with heavy luggage.

At one time under State ownership it looked as though all the cross countries would disappear, only the Newcastle–Poole running north to south. That more use the route between Reading and Basingstoke, and that Kensington
continued overleaf

continued

Olympia sees north to south trains once more, reverses recent trends. Lack of porters, greater hassle in crossing London, increased Channel ferry business via Dover, and above all the rise of Gatwick as the holiday airport have all contributed.

So Kensington Olympia (ex-Addison Road) is very still on the map... but not Reading West so far as long-distance services go. How the atmosphere used to change there when taxis started dropping off passengers (and waited for any incoming) and the Newcastle to Bournemouth squealed round the western curve now not used by regular passenger services. But then who would have thought that HSTs would one day serve the New Forest?

The course at Lingfield in Surrey is one of a number provided with a so-called 'covered way' from the station. Posts supporting arched corrugated-iron wind their way across the fields, giving it has to be said meagre protection from the elements. On the now electrified line from London through Oxted to East Grinstead, the station was reached direct too, pre-Beeching, from the coast through Lewes or Haywards Heath and from Tunbridge Wells.

Another Surrey station that has changed out of all recognition since the days of the Southern is Gatwick Racecourse on the direct London–Brighton line. Racing has ceased and it has been completely rebuilt to serve the international airport.

One complete casualty has to be recorded. The Southern withdrew its passenger service between Midhurst and Chichester in Sussex in July 1935 and henceforth race-goers for Goodwood had to travel to Chichester on the main South Coast line (which already served Fontwell Park at Barnham) rather than Singleton. This had been a wayside station in the heart of the South Downs boasting two island platforms to cope with race meeting needs, and approached by a fine tree-lined drive. A more modest wayside station in Sussex, Plumpton, between Haywards Heath and Lewes, does survive, though with a peak-hour service only today, and immediately adjoins the course. It comes to life on race days when expresses call en route between Victoria, Eastbourne and Hastings.

The association of railways and race courses seems set fair to continue and even expand. Folkestone race course in Kent is adjacent to Westenhanger station, where the Southern used separate platforms for race meetings, and is but a stone's throw from the Channel Tunnel. Its location on the direct line from the Continent suggests that future Southern handbills will be aimed at encouraging racegoers to travel from Paris and Brussels as well as the more customary London and provincial stations.

A portion of the southbound Sunny South Express entering Kensington Addison Road in 1932. Still very much a pre-Grouping scene nine years on. The locomotive, an LBSC class K 2–6–0, is still in original condition with boiler mountings and cab to the larger Brighton loading gauge and some of the coaches are ex-LNWR. All the signals are LNWR including, rather unusually for that railway, one on a concrete post. The lines are electrified for the LNWR/LMS service from Willesden to Earls Court and the Metropolitan and GWR trains via Uxbridge Road and Latimer Road.

Preservation

It could be said (but it would be unkind) that the Southern Railway was a preservation organisation in its own right. Even into the second half of the century and well into nationalisation engines and stock which could have been seen by Queen Victoria – had she elevated herself to the status of an enthusiast – were apparent not only on the branch lines of the south but also at the stately London termini. Drummond's Greyhounds in the form of rebuilt T9s abounded in North Devon and Cornwall, his 0–4–4 tanks of classes M7 and Adams O2 in push-pull and Isle of Wight services respectively and his 0-6-0s on pick up freights. In North Cornwall, on the Wenford Bridge branch out of Wadebridge even earlier ex LSWR dinosaurs, Beattie 2-4-0 outside cylinder well tanks, trundled their trains in daily service until 1962. On the old South Eastern lines original D and E and rebuilt D1 and E1 4-4-0s, next to the LNWR George the Fifths possibly the finest inside cylinder types to be built, ran their trains from London to the Kent coast watering holes and ports, H class 0-4-4 tanks emulated their LSWR sisters on push-pulls on, for example, the Westerham branch and again the 0-6-0s worked the pick ups – and the passenger service on what was once the Kent & East Sussex Light Railway. The LBSC did not

fare quite so well as electrification decimated much of its passenger motive power, even so the Marsh Atlantics had a long innings, the last survivor going in 1958.

Of course, the knowledge of pending electrification discouraged wholesale replacement of steam power and perhaps the wonder is that Bulleid could spend what he did. At all events, if you were into classic late-Victorian or Edwardian types, the SR was well worth a visit. These were not leaking and clanking relics but well cared for elderly ladies. Indeed those who have read Richard Hardy's tales of the D1s and E1s at Stewarts Lane depot when he was shedmaster in the 1950s have stories of sterling work with men who may have been tough trade unionists but who also cared about their Victoriana.

So it was the Brighton engines which went to the torch first, but even these were great survivors with Stroudley's beautifully proportioned 0-6-0 tanks so rightly called 'Terriers' heading the geriatric list – working not only as shunters but also on lightly-laid branches such as the Hayling Island line with its wooden trestle link with the

Ex-LBSCR class A1 0–6–0T Terrier No 82 Boxhill *is seen outside the open roundhouse at Guildford probably soon after restoration for the Waterloo Station Centenary celebrations.* Boxhill *is now preserved in the National Collection.*

Three of the Schools class 4–4–0s have been saved. No 926 Repton was originally preserved in Canada on the Cape Breton Steam Railroad, Nova Scotia. It is seen here ready to leave Port Morien in 1974 hauling typical North American coaches and complete with headlamp, cowcatcher and buckeye coupling. Fortunately Repton has returned to England and is currently running on the Great Central Railway based on Loughborough.

mainland at Langstone. The Brighton had an aura of its own and many of its devotees were members of what was then a very august railway enthusiast organisation indeed, the Stephenson Locomotive Society – one which regarded itself as being semi professional having links with the Institution of Locomotive Engineers. Perhaps it was because the LBSC ran the famous Southern Belle (later to become the Brighton Belle) perhaps a treasured memory of Stroudley's magnificent livery of ochre christened 'improved engine green', or dreams of spotless engines or their very grace; no one will ever know, but undoubtedly it evoked considerable loyalty. So in retrospect it is not all that surprising to find that the first engine to be officially preserved under Southern auspices was LBSC, an elderly Stroudley 0-4-2 express, once an unusual flyer (when thinking of its wheel arrangement)

named *Gladstone*, the standard bearer of a unique class.

Back in the 1920s dieselisation was not even on the horizon but suburban electrification most certainly was; this led to the comparatively (for the Southern) early demise of the Gladstones, an event which would have passed unnoticed in the more northern sections of the UK had it not been for members of the SLS led by an eminent engineer, gentleman and son of a world famous magician, J. N. Maskelyne. These stalwart enthusiasts persuaded SR management that *Gladstone* should be saved and even raised the money to pay for it – one hundred and fifty pounds, equal to a year's money for many (and possibly the scrap price of the engine) which was withdrawn from service in December 1926. The actual date of purchase was early the following year but the Southern showed considerable willingness in repainting *Gladstone* in full Stroudley livery at Brighton Works. Goodwill indeed must have abounded for she found a resting place in the then LNER's railway museum at York. Quite how she got there and who carried the cost is not evident. The old lady was handed over to LNER care on 31 May 1927 by the well known photographer Will Whitworth on behalf of the SLS. *Gladstone* was formally presented to the then British Transport Commission on 18 September 1959.

So it all began. Other ex-constituent Southern engines to earn a reprieve (and escape World War II scrap drives) were an ex LSWR Adams class T3 4-4-0 No 563, a graceful outside cylinder locomotive and Stroudley 0-6-0 'Terrier' No 82 *Boxhill*. Both were repainted in their pre-Grouping liveries for the Waterloo station centenary in 1948. No SE&C engine was so requisitioned probably because they were still hard at work, the D class 4-4-0 No 737 lasting in service until November 1956 and restored in 1960.

Then into the postwar era of preservation, and first off the mark was the Bluebell, part of the charmingly entitled 'Bluebell Line' of the LBSC from East Grinstead to Lewes via Horsted Keynes. The section in preservation today is that from Horsted Keynes to Sheffield Park, though the link through to East Grinstead is being pursued step by step, and will become reality given time. The Bluebell Railway is one of today's success stories, a pleasant rural one-time secondary line, close enough to London *and* Sussex resorts, a short enough run for passengers to enjoy themselves without getting bored and above all a really historic atmosphere: it seems to relive the Southern and at times pre-grouping Southern. The Bluebell Railway also has very adequate engineering facilities at Sheffield Park, completing its rebuilds and overhauls to a very high standard.

Its birth came about by an Act of Parliament! Like so many secondary and branch lines, the Bluebell was an unwanted adjunct – a loss maker. The usual closure notices were issued. BR, however, reckoned without the determination of a few stalwarts. They found a clause in the original Act whereby the stations were to be kept open in perpetuity and so forced the national colossus to keep trains running (after an initial closure on 25 May 1955) until a clause could be slipped into a further BR Act on its way through the Parliamentary system. Final closure was thus delayed until 16 March 1958 though the temporary service of trains quite deliberately failed to call at Kingscote and Barcombe stations which were not mentioned in the original Act. Another piece of BR spite.

Although the presence of large main line steam locomotives and their attendant workshops has overwhelmed once peaceful Sheffield Park, T. H. Myres' original and delightful building of 1882 remains virtually intact, while at Horsted Keynes, the authentic atmosphere of a 19th century LBSC country junction with its friendly little buffet remains almost unspoilt, at any rate when short trains with elderly small tank locomotives form the only moveable scenery.

The Mid-Hants is a section of the old LSWR cross country branch from Alton to Winchester now open from Alton to Alresford, a distance of nine and a half miles. Like the Bluebell this is single track but it is over twice the length and tends to use larger locomotives such as reconstituted ex-Barry West Country Pacifics No 34016 *Bodmin* (rebuilt) and No 34105 *Swanage* (in air-smoothed form) as well as by some smaller engines and several Maunsell moguls. The railway has not been without its

problems but again captures a slice of Southern country atmosphere, especially when trains are lightly loaded.

Then the Kent & East Sussex Railway based on Tenterden station in Kent and once part of the Colonel Stephens light railway carrying the same name. In preservation the line follows the old atmosphere well, using small engines and ambling through the countryside. It is excellently run with one of its main success stories the *Wealden Pullman*, an evening wine and dine train of some luxury though this is really foreign to anything Colonel Stephens ever thought of. Money is now being raised for a final push to Northiam with the intention of reaching Bodiam where the lovely moated castle will help to combine history and historic travel.

Perhaps the preservation scheme that has had to work hardest for survival and progress is the Swanage Railway down on the Dorset coast. Swanage is still a popular resort; once indeed several daily expresses for Weymouth detached a rear through coach at Wareham for Swanage, where a down departure in the bay platform would be waiting for its arrival. Swanage station survived to be restored and one of two examples of a preserved standard gauge once thriving seaside terminus with all that implies; the other is at Minehead. The local council eventually gave the scheme its backing, but Swanage still being busy in summer there was inevitably a road problem: would a bypass at Corfe Castle (of which there was a splendid view from the train, and may now one day be again) take over the railway's route? After years of anxiety, happily not. Trains hauled by Southern engines now have far enough to travel out of Swanage to show their paces, and there is the possibility of an ultimate link with BR's freight route (part of the original Swanage branch) to the oil-loading sidings at Furzebrook. But first the decline and demise of the clay traffic (it used to be loaded from narrow-gauge systems of great charm that alas nobody could preserve) and then the increased output from the Dorset oilfield have added further delays and anxiety.

Mention has been made elsewhere of the preservation scheme on the Isle of Wight, bringing back to life something of the unique island railway character of Southern days, using two classes which abounded there: an O2 0-4-4 tank and (like the K&ESR) a Stroudley Terrier but unique island large bunker version. This

Overleaf The Bluebell Railway was founded in 1960 to preserve a typical Southern subsidiary line and has gone from strength to strength. The original four mile line from Sheffield Park to Horsted Keynes is being extended to East Grinstead. Ex-SECR class C 0–6–0 No 592 is seen at Sheffield Park in 1976 with a train for Horsted Keynes. The leading coach is a Bulleid brake third and the signal is LBSC.

glimpse of what was once a small part of a very busy system is indeed a pleasant reminder not only of the past but what can be done by sheer determination and after years of talks the link up with BR at Smallbrook Junction is no longer a dream.

In recent years steam main-line running has become varied and successful, for several locomotives have been either acquired directly from BR for private or national preservation, as well as a number from the renowned Woodham Bros scrapyard at Barry and restored. Of these, Oliver Bulleid's rebuilt Merchant Navy Pacific No 35028 *Clan Line* is front runner, the National Collection's King Arthur No 777 *Sir Lamiel* not far behind; the other engine from the National Collection which has been used on main line steam specials has been No 850 *Lord Nelson*, while No 925 *Cheltenham*, one of three Schools 4-4-0s in preservation, appeared at the Rainhill celebrations in 1980. (The other two are No 928 *Stowe*, on the Bluebell, and No 926 *Repton*, on the Great Central Railway). Of the carefully restored engines out of Barry perhaps the best known is the unrebuilt West Country Pacific No 34092 *City of Wells*, though S15 class 4-6-0 No 841 did some good work a few years back and it is still working on the North Yorkshire Moors Railway.

Most have acquitted themselves well on the main specials, on BR's Marylebone to Stratford Shakespeare Limited and over such scenic routes well beyond their designers dreams as the Settle & Carlisle. There is obviously little scope for express steam working on today's busy and mainly electrified lines, but recently there have been welcome seasons of specials on the Exeter road out of Salisbury, recapturing some of the magic of the days of the *ACE*.

Specially Prepared

The prestige all-Pullman Golden Arrow between Victoria and Dover was reinstated after the war on 15 April 1946, and considerable care was lavished on the engine, allocated to Stewarts Lane shed, to achieve a spectacularly smart turnout – to Royal train standards, in fact. The usual power until 1951–2 was a Bulleid light Pacific, after which a pair of Britannias shared the bulk of the Arrow workings.

Each morning saw the engine worked on until its paintwork gleamed, the motion was scoured bright, copper pipework shone and brasswork was polished. There were extra touches also, such as the burnished smokebox door hinges and front frame edges. Specially machined buffers were fitted. Once cleaned, woe betide any driver who wanted to go back under the coaling plant to top up the tender; that was taboo lest the paintwork was besmirched with coal dust.

Before leaving the shed the special circular Golden Arrow headboard was mounted on its brackets on the smokebox door and the long horizontal arrows – actually made of wood – were secured on special attachments on the side of the casing. The white route discs, freshly painted, were placed on the lamp brackets above each buffer. And finally, as Dick Hardy has recorded: 'that comical character, Syd Newman, the shop officeman, would appear with the Union Jack and the Tricolour on a vee-shaped carrier for the buffer beam – washed flags if the weather was wet, new ones if it was set fair.'

The engine was now ready to leave the shed and meet its Pullmans at Victoria. This routine was maintained until the last steam working of the Golden Arrow on 11 June 1961. Thereafter the power was provided by an electric locomotive (later Class 71). It was commendably clean, it carried a plain rectangular headboard and the two flags, and short horizontal arrows on its flanks behind the cab doors. But it was never quite the same.

Southern Railway class Q 0–6–0 No 541 climbing Freshfield bank on the Bluebell Railway hauling the 10.30 Santa Special from Sheffield Park to Horsted Keynes on Sunday 8 December 1991. The class Q was introduced in 1938 and twenty were built. Never in the limelight, the last member of the class was withdrawn in 1965. No 541 is the only one preserved.

4
AN ENGINEER'S VIEW
FROM THE BRIDGE

HARD it was: 'Southern man, eh? That's not a real railway, just a glorified tramline' – the likely greeting from staff of the other three pre-nationalisation companies, from manager to train crew. 'You don't know what it is to run fast long-distance expresses or to handle millions of tons of coal and steel.'

Granted, the Southern did not run 400 mile expresses. Nor did it figure prominently in speed tables; in the summer of 1939 it could only muster five trains daily (all on the Western Section) averaging 58mph or more start-to-stop, over no greater distance than 84 miles. By contrast the LMS ran 99 such trains, the GWR 52 and the LNER 46. Over its generally shorter distances, its geography dominated by the North and South Downs, and its timetable built round intensive commuter services within outer London, it could hardly be otherwise.

And what is wrong with being a tramline in commuter territory, anyway? The electric tram owed its meteoric rise to frequency of service, frequent stops and convenient interchange between routes. It was easy to forget, in the 1930s, that it was the tram's inexorable rise, particularly south of the Thames, which had goaded the London, Brighton & South Coast and the London & South Western Railways to begin electrifying their suburban areas, and made the South Eastern & Chatham plan similar action. This enabled trains to emulate the tram and beat it, or at least compete on more equal terms, in the mass movement of people.

No, it did not have steel works, and only one modest coalfield. A large slice of its freight traffic was handed over by the other three companies, mainly in the London area. *They* did the easy trunk haul, and the Southern was landed with the remarshalling and distribution. What is more, it all had to be done over the same metals and junctions as an intensive passenger service. The other companies had no monopoly of tricky operating problems.

So how did the Southern develop and how good was it? 1923 of course saw two incompatible electrification systems in use; in some localities the two existed, side by side but immiscible. The Brighton company, first in the field, had looked to the longer term future when electrification would reach South Coast destinations. With such longer distances in mind the overhead contact wire at 6600V single phase AC was chosen, on expert advice. While it was more costly to install than a third rail, it would save in the number of substations and feeders as the system grew.

The South Western had entered the field five years later than the Brighton, and had no long distance ambitions for electric traction. They therefore were well suited by the third rail with top contact energised at

Merchant Navy class 4–6–2 No 35019 French Line CGT *has had the full treatment — even to painting the heads of bolts securing the front platform white! — in readiness for hauling the French President from Dover Marine to Victoria on 7 March 1950. She was little over a month from general repair and was in blue livery with black and white lining.*

Bickley Junction is being prepared for electrification of the Kent Coast line in 1958 as the up Night Ferry picks its way off the Chatham route. Battle of Britain class No 34070 Manston *is being given a helping hand with this heavy train by Maunsell's L1 class No 31754. There are two fourgons and seven Wagons-Lits sleepers plus seating vehicles. The train conveyed sleeping cars between Victoria and Brussels as well as Paris.*

73

Rocking Bridge

As a cadet seconded for the summer to the Western division as 'train runner' I was often called to do very minor station inspections or look into problems which were unlikely to need the attention of anyone of importance.

The stationmaster at the little country station of Crewkerne was an elderly Devonian on the point of retirement and apparently he was worried about the footbridge over the line there, which he seemed to think might fall down. A highly improbable occurrence which looked even less probable when I alighted from an up main line stopping train and saw the footbridge.

It was an old-fashioned, heavy, ponderous structure made of wood and the whole of it, stairways as well, was not only built up high at the sides but roofed over. None of your modern structures with waist high wire-netting sides and a few girders. It seemed even to have a reasonably recently painted exterior.

I greeted the old stationmaster and spent some time commiserating with him on the ailments of old age, finally bringing the subject round to the footbridge. I said it looked really solid to me. 'Ah', said the stationmaster, 'but wait till 'ee zee a train!'

Soon after, the down line cleared for a Waterloo–North Devon Express, which came thundering up the bank at high speed with all steam on and plenty erupting from the chimney. To my total incredulity, as it roared under the footbridge I thought I saw the whole structure actually move.

The train gone, I went to the side of the footbridge between the stairs and the platform fencing where the thickest wooden timber supports were. Unbelieving, I leaned my weight on one of them and distinctly felt it move. I then alternately leaned, pulled back,

continued opposite

660V DC. By the Grouping they had over twice as many route miles in electric operation. In this situation, and with Sir Herbert Walker of the LSWR in the general manager's seat the decision to standardise the third rail for the Southern's future was probably inevitable. On technical grounds it was almost certainly the wrong one. However, knowing how the Southern expanded its electric network on the cheap, it is possible that less would have been achieved with ac overhead wire. With hindsight it is arguable where the overall balance of advantage lay.

Technically Southern electric stock was not in the forefront of innovation – and perhaps passengers could give modest thanks for that. Having reached a watershed in the development of the on-train equipment, notably the simple camshaft controller with resistance grids, whose reliability was fabled, the Southern stuck with it for many years after it was nationalised. Breakdowns could so easily stitch up the service, even off-peak, but they were almost unknown. Perhaps the weakest link was the pickup shoe and the third rail itself, even in good weather.

Neither the Brighton nor the South Western had pampered their commuters, and this tradition continued for a decade. While the North Eastern, the Lancashire & Yorkshire and the London & North Western had built electric stock with end doors and fair comfort, the Southern season ticket holder had to put up with slam-door compartment stock of some age and distinctly sit-up-and-beg dimensions to maximise seating capacity. The frequency of service and the improved and relatively short journey times were evidently thought sufficient to take the passenger's mind off the re-use of old wooden bodies from the steam era as they rattled their way to Waterloo and the City. Only from 1931–2, when the supply of old coaches ran out, was this practice abandoned.

Even when the third rail reached the South Coast, coach layouts trailed well behind the best of what was being done north of the Thames. Pullmans excepted, even on the express services compartment-type gangwayed stock with individual slam doors was the Southern norm, lasting well into BR days. The operating demand for rapid station work counted for more than passenger amenity.

There were good features in Maunsell's express stock, however, both electric and steam-hauled. There were the pullman gangways and buckeye couplers. The corridor windows were taken up to cantrail level, giving an uninterrupted view to those unfortunate enough to stand. The door droplight with leather strap was banished in favour of a balanced droplight.

It was largely left to Bulleid to produce stock postwar with large picture windows and sliding ventilators in compartments, and with end *and* centre vestibules to improve ease of boarding and alighting. Even this stock was marred by detail; was it really necessary to fit compartment doors with a thumb latch, albeit chromium plated, more suitable for a back yard gate or privy door?

The steam locomotive under Maunsell reflected to a considerable extent the upbringing of his assistants, Clayton (chief draughtsman) from Derby (witness the appearance of the L1 class) and Holcroft, his technical assistant with a Swindon background, who was behind some of the modern influences in the 2–6–0s. Maunsell looked for high standards in

design; he also encouraged soundly based ingenuity. Take the three-cylinder Z class 0–8–0 shunting tanks. With the inside cylinder inclined in order to drive the second axle, there was insufficient height to locate the piston valve above it, and not enough space in front of or behind the cylinders to operate it by a conjugated valve gear. So a novel variant of Walschaerts valve gear was used to operate a valve alongside the inside cylinder, driven by *two* eccentrics, one of which moved the bottom of a much-shortened combination lever rather than the crosshead.

It was a regime in which nothing was wasted. Anything redundant but in good condition, for which a possible future use could be envisaged, was put on one side, for years if necessary. When the K class 2–6–4 tanks were withdrawn after Sevenoaks and rebuilt as tender engines in 1927–8, the side tanks, bunkers and bogies appeared four years later on the W class 2–6–4 tanks built for freight transfer work. Likewise the underframes of AC motor coaches displaced in 1929 by the changeover to third rail lay for several years before appearing in a new guise, de-motored, as 27 ton goods brake vans in 1934.

Pre-war locomotive orders tended to come in penny numbers, reflecting the diversion of available capital towards electrification. An order for ten locomotives of a class in any year's programme was quite normal; the North British Locomotive Company order for thirty King

A Urie King Arthur No 30457 Sir Bedivere *hurries through Farnborough with an up Southampton boat train for Waterloo on 23 June 1957. The signals are still the electro-pneumatic semaphores installed by the LSWR in 1905 and 1907, many of which were automatics; note the co-acting arms almost hidden amongst the lattice girders.*

continued
leaned harder, pulled back and leaned until – it really takes some believing – the entire vast footbridge was rocking to and fro. Speechless, I turned horrified to the justified stationmaster and I shall never forget his comment. 'Lord, sir, doan 'ee du that or we'll never get anyone to cross by um!' – P. S

75

Arthurs in 1925 was wholly exceptional, and that for fifty N class 2–6–0s in 1924–5 was only precipitated by the availability of kits of parts made by the Royal Ordnance Factory, Woolwich, and on the market at knock-down prices. What a contrast with the post-war situation; it seemed that demand-led building programmes had given way to an annual estimate of what was needed to keep Brighton works busy on new construction at any price. At a time when the LMS calculated – utterly ludicrously – that they only needed 91 Pacifics and big 4–6–0s to run their entire postwar express service, here was the Southern churning out West Country/Battle of Britain Pacifics to a total of 110 in under five years. Many of them were grossly under-employed on light duties; other Regions could be excused for looking longingly at them – the rebuilt ones, at any rate – to supplement the upper end of their own fleets.

How different it all was from the prewar dependence on ageing 4–4–0s on the main holiday routes. Ex-South Eastern & Chatham D1s and E1s cheerfully tackled heavy expresses to Kent Coast resorts over a difficult road; their work is touched on elsewhere. And even the glut of light Pacifics did not wholly displace 4–4–0s. Their availability was so poor that on the Bournemouth line Drummond D15s were still called upon to work Lymington boat trains as late as the mid-1950s.

Steam locomotive activity might not be on the scale of the other railways, but experimental work was sustained and in some respects led the

The anachronistic layout at Dorchester South, whereby up trains had to pass through and then back into the platform, lasted until 1970, when a new platform was built on the up line curve. Urie King Arthur No 30739 King Leodegrance *had backed in with the 2.20pm Weymouth–Andover Junction on 27 August 1954 and is now ready to depart.*

field. The problem of drifting exhaust steam obscuring the driver's view, which became acute with the Southern-built King Arthurs, was tackled in 1926 when several designs of deflector plates were on trial. By 1928 a standard type was being fitted to the Arthurs and, shortly after, to the Nelsons also. At this time the LMS was just *beginning* parallel experiments with the Royal Scots, which were similarly afflicted, but the decision to fit deflector plates was not taken until prodded by the comments of the Inspecting Officer following the Leighton Buzzard derailment in March 1931.

There was a willingness, too, to look at more fundamental issues affecting the steam locomotive if the proposals held out prospects of tangible benefit. Maunsell fitted a U class 2-6-0 in 1929 to burn pulverised coal, since the Kent field was producing quantities of small coal for which the market was limited. Its short life and spectacular demise are described separately. In 1930 an N Class 2-6-0 was equipped with proprietary heat conservation equipment which condensed and reused exhaust steam by a mixture of cooling and compression. Trials continued for more than four years before abandonment.

With Bulleid's arrival in 1937 innovation found a new protagonist in a number of fields, often springing from his patents jointly with the railway. Some of those incorporated into his steam locomotives are covered elsewhere in this book. But even the humble four-wheeled wagon was involved, with his patented triangulated underframe, which was reckoned to save a modicum of weight. Likewise vans were built with plastic panels instead of wood. They tended to *be* innovations, however, having no lasting advantage over more conventional design.

A.W. Szlumper, who came from the London & South Western to be the Southern's chief civil engineer, must have wondered what he had taken on amongst his extended responsibilities. He was faced with completing a heavy renewal programme of no less than 588 bridges started by the South Eastern & Chatham before World War I, together with upgrading of main line track with heavier rail and stone ballast (shingle had been widely used). Until that was completed the Chatham line to Dover, a prime boat train route, could accept nothing bigger than 4-4-0s with 17½ ton maximum axleload, of which the D1s and E1s were the star turns. Not until the summer of 1927 did completion of the bridgework allow the new King Arthur 4-6-0s to work to Thanet and Dover via Chatham.

The catastrophic Sevenoaks derailment in August 1927 put the spotlight back on to track condition, which left much to be desired and compared very poorly with the LNER main line during the post-Sevenoaks testing of River class engines. As a result a major campaign of renewals, with attention to ballast and drainage, was launched.

As this work was gradually improving the quality of the track, a more insidious influence was at work degrading it. The simplicity and low cost of the nose-suspended electric traction motor was attractive to the rolling stock engineer, but particularly with the inception of express electric services it played considerable havoc with the track. The high unsprung weight of the motors pounded any weakness in the rails, sleepers and ballast, making it difficult to maintain a good top, leading to rough riding,

Much Filmed

Not overlooking the favourite, *London to Brighton in Four Minutes*, undoubtedly seen by more people than any other railway film and full of interest including steam locomotives, perhaps the place of honour for filming on the Southern Railway must go to the first line to be built under the Light Railway Act of 1896. The Basingstoke & Alton Light Railway was opened in 1901. It was sent to the battlefields of France in 1916; reinstated in 1924, with passenger services withdrawn in 1932 and freight in 1936, before final abandonment. First came Arnold Ridley's classic *The Wrecker*, filmed by Gainsborough Films in 1928. In addition to views of SE&C Wainwright D Class, Maunsell SE&C 2-6-0s, LSWR H16 class, SR L class, a Maunsell U class No A803, a D15 class 4-4-0 and a King Arthur class No 773 *Sir Lavaine*, the film featured a spectacular wreck in which an SE&C Stirling 4-4-0 crashed into a Foden Steam lorry loaded with ballast on Spain's Crossing near Herriard. This was staged on the afternoon of 19 August 1928, using 22 cameras. It could only be done once! Much material shot in the making of *The Wrecker* and the crash itself, along with various shots of the Stirling 4-4-0 in action, was built into a 1936 sound film called *Seven Sinners*. It even includes an interesting 'dummy run' with a car racing over the level crossing just in front of the train.

As the Basingstoke & Alton track was being lifted in 1937, a final film used the station of Cliddesden and the line back to the terminus, including Basingstoke Yard. *Oh! Mr Porter* must surely be just about the best known of all railway films. Featuring Will Hay, Moore Marriott and Graham Moffat, the early scenes are all based on
continued overleaf

One of the last batch of Maunsell King Arthurs to be built, No 801 Sir Meliot de Logres *stands at Victoria ready to depart with a Ramsgate train of non-corridor birdcage stock in the mid-1930s, the six-wheeled tender was originally specified for use on the Central Section, where the usual bogie tender would have been too long for the turntables.*

continued
Cliddesden and involve the 'express' train, with a William Adams X6 class 4–4–0 No 657 of LSWR 1895 vintage and LSWR stock and the 'excursion' train, with an Adams LSWR 0395 class 0–6–0 on the front. The 'star' was a Kent & East Sussex locomotive No 2 *Northiam*, remodelled and *continued opposite*

increased bogie wear and potential danger from rail end fractures. The weakest point was the rail joint; the technique of producing and laying long welded rails was two or three decades away. While the LNER and LMS experimented with short two-bolt fishplates and close joint sleepers – and soon abandoned them – the Southern tried a more radical form of rail joint having the rail ends machined with interlocking tongues. But it was not cost-effective and was not extended. While traction motors have been progressively lightened over the years, the basic problem continues to exist on even the most modern electric multiple units.

If the civil engineer's efforts on the permanent way were not always crowned with glorious achievement, much of his building work – stations, signal boxes, engine sheds, and so on – did him great credit. Much praise could be directed towards management also for the sheer scale of the renewal programmes. Pre-war station renewals and new construction used both traditional brick (eg Hastings) and *art deco* styling in concrete (as Wimbledon), culminating in the rather flamboyant cinema-styled stations on the new Chessington branch. Signal boxes, with operating floors reminiscent of a cross between airport control tower and ship's upperworks sat on an extended relay room at ground level. Woking was a classic example of this complete break from traditional style.

Widespread running shed renewal went on over the years, initially with reinforced concrete walls and roof trusses following the style of Feltham, completed by the LSWR in its last year. When the shortcomings of this material in such a highly corrosive atmosphere became painfully apparent – the last of this type, Ashford, was completed in 1931 – a change was made to steel framing with sheet cladding of asbestos cement or corrugated steel, concrete being confined to the pits and (in block form) dwarf walls. The new shed at Hither Green, a key element in a total reorganisation of London area freight working, ushered in this style in 1933.

A curious feature of Southern running sheds was the seeming indecision about the mechanical handling of locomotive coal supplies. The LSWR had been early in the field with large mechanical coaling plants at Feltham and Nine Elms. Ramsgate followed in 1927 and Exmouth Junction a year later. But the Southern was largely run on Welsh and Kent coal, soft and friable and ill-suited to being dropped from towering heights. It was the cause of an almost total reversion to coal stages with small hand-tipped tubs, even at sizeable sheds such as Ashford and Hither Green, though Stewarts Lane bucked the trend.

If concrete had its limitations for engine sheds, produced on a prodigious scale from the company's own concrete works at Exmouth Junction which published a catalogue of components to drum up demand around the system, it was joyously exploited for a host of smaller items. The passenger would particularly note platform fencing, lamp standards, a variety of huts and perhaps gradient posts. While ideal for some uses, one wondered about both the durability and the economics of concrete fence panels, neat as they might appear.

Last but far from being least, if any engineering discipline *made* the

continued

renamed *Gladstone* for the filming. This charming Hawthorn Leslie 2–4–0 of 1899 was built for the Rother Valley Railway, went under its own steam to Basingstoke for the film, and returned to the Kent & East Sussex; alas, it was broken up in 1941.

There are many great railway moments in *Oh! Mr Porter*. The first appearance of *Gladstone*, decorated for the relief of Mafeking, shows the K&ESR engine with cab cut back for filming purposes and a spiked-top chimney added for effect. For certain action scenes, the camera crew worked from a wooden platform built out on the side of the Adams X6; for the fight on the roof, Graham Moffat went from Cliddesden to Basingstoke Yard with one leg tied to the top of the carriage. The final crash into the buffers was shot from a high camera platform in Basingstoke Yard and a small bit of film still survives showing the crew in action and *Gladstone* charging the specially-built sand pit. Thus it was that an obscure little branch line secured for itself a permanent place in the history of the Southern Railway.

Bromley South on 1 August 1936. A down Continental bound for Dover via Maidstone East appears to be starting from a signal check, hauled by class E 4–4–0 No 1514 and class B1 4–4–0 No 1448. The train is a heavy one of 12 or 13 coaches with an SEC brake second leading and one or two Pullmans in the centre of the train.

Steam Taxi

Coming up to London one summer afternoon having spent the morning at Eastleigh works, I was just going to walk up to the station when the foreman called out 'There's 44 going up to Nine Elms after overhaul – she's over there. Why not go up with her? So I joined a Drummond M7 0–4–4 tank, all newly painted and smelling of it, and she became my private taxi to London through the lazy summer woods and fields. There was an element of running-in about the trip so we went quite slowly and easily – between 35 and *continued opposite*

Pre-war Hayling Island train leaving Havant behind Stroudley Terrier (class A1X) No 2644. These little engines, used because of the weight-restricted Langstone viaduct and swing bridge, maintained an intensive service until the line closed in 1963.

Southern what it became, that of the signal engineer could well claim the honours. He it was who provided a total system for the control of trains which met the sometimes conflicting operating requirements of line capacity, safety and unambiguity to drivers. In this the Southern could justifiably claim to have established a considerable lead, spurred on by the needs of route electrification. The colour-light signalling scheme completed in June 1926 covering the Charing Cross, Cannon Street and Holborn Viaduct to London Bridge lines introduced to Britain the four-aspect signal with the new double yellow aspect. The system was designed to handle an intensive service at short headways despite the presence of three major flat junctions. Where physical space for the signal heads was tight the four aspects were arranged in a circular cluster, a configuration copied by the LMS at Manchester Victoria but nowhere else in Britain. At that time separate signal heads or theatre-type route indicators were provided at divergences; the modern illuminated junction indicator or feather, another Southern first, was still to come. When it did, it used three white lights as distinct from the five on the LMS and LNER. Failure of a single bulb could give a doubtful indication. A measure of what was involved in maximising track capacity at Borough Market Junction was the very short overlaps beyond a signal to the fouling point with another movement; in one instance a down Charing Cross train could draw up to a red signal, just twenty yards beyond which an up train for Cannon Street on the local line was crossing its path!

The Southern willingness carefully to think a problem through to an elegant, if sometimes radical, solution permeated the whole organisation. It showed in the major 1926 scheme at Ramsgate to rationalise stations

and other facilities in order to improve operations. It saw the construction of the Wimbledon flyover in 1936 to avoid conflicting movements, and the associated rearrangement and resignalling of the running lines thence into Waterloo. It brought the partnership which set up the Dover–Dunkerque train ferry service and the Night Ferry train, also in 1936. And it was fully in keeping with the Southern ethos that in 1938 it should have put a new diesel-powered double ended car ferry into service on the Lymington– Yarmouth (IoW) route which, thanks to its state-of-the-art Voith-Schneider propellors, could outmanouevre the paddle steamers in the difficult and shallow Lymington approaches.

It was quite a tramline, the Southern!

continued

45mph. At Micheldever we were shunted into the tiny yard to allow two boat rains and the 1.35 Weymouth to pass. Unprepared for the pleasure, I had time to go to the country pub b the station to get something to eat. The sun shone down; the M7 simmered quietly; we had all the time in the world to reach Nine Elms and it was heaven. – P.S.

A New Boy's Impression of the Last Years

This schoolboy's first sight of England was in August 1945. Trains seemed to be everywhere: red ones to the right and green to the left, as the ship slowly felt its way up river to London Docks; more red ones burrowing underfoot in Central London. Red trains were familiar in New Zealand; green was a new experience.

The route to be inspected to a new school, was out of Waterloo. We steamed out behind a locomotive the like of which the schoolboy could not possibly have imagined. It later became clear that the rest of the world had a rather similar first reaction to the 'Merchant Navies'. It rolled away to the West, through the vertical-sided chalk cuttings and along the enormous embankments of the South Western main line; another relieved it at Salisbury. It demanded attention out of the window. We climbed an obvious gradient for the first few miles. In New Zealand locomotives made a great fuss and disturbance about gradients. Not this one. It just whuffled, a rapid muttering exhaust beat, with fairly frequent bursts of slipping. Odd.

That first impression provided a good key. The Southern was *different*. Indoctrination down under had been pro-Great Western, mainly due to that masterly official history by MacDermot. The bias alas did not survive the first journey in a train out of Paddington, in a cramped and uncomfortable, sit-up-and-beg third-class compartment all the way to Cornwall. The GWR, it seemed, was excellent at image-building; not so good at realities. The London & North Eastern had style, and nothing could beat the prestige and solid comfort of its best trains; but all too obviously by 1945 it was physically the most run-down railway of them all. Things creaked, and there seemed to be an awful lot of derailments. The LMS was enormous and anonymous, complicated and obviously not very efficient. Euston was a beehive, but a lot of the confusion seemed to be due to the fact that everything arrived late; and mostly double-headed. Surely it could not make sense to have so many small engines. But even in the run-down post-war years, the Southern gave the impression that it was coping effectively; of course it was a smaller concern, but even busier

and more complex than the rest of the Big Four.

During the last three years before nationalisation, there were extensive travels round Britain, but more was seen of the Southern (and the Somerset & Dorset) than the rest. Slowly it became apparent that the three main constituent companies, which still formed the Central, Eastern, and Western Divisions, had been railways of very different kinds. Their characters still remained, under a top layer of uniformity imposed since 1923. The most obvious feature of this top layer was of course electrification. It is perhaps hard now to remember how far ahead of everybody in this field the Southern was; for there were practically no electric trains anywhere else. Liverpool had a fair suburban system; there were a couple of lines in Manchester and Newcastle; and that was that. The LNER had actually de-electrified one section. But the Southern had beavered away and made a howling success of its electrifications; effectively all its suburban lines were converted, plus Brighton and Portsmouth by 1939, and Kent was on the way. Admittedly the SR electric trains were rather *uninteresting*; but obviously they were what people wanted. The most diehard steam enthusiast had to admit the SR was right about them. And there was still a surprising amount of steam about, even on electrified lines; all the freight was steam-worked (and freight trains still ran everywhere), as well as through trains from other railways. Brighton, with tracks electrified everywhere, had an enormous steam shed full of engines, with lots of work for them. And there were some other uniformities, including a fair sprinkling of rebuilt modern stations, of which the Southern had more than all the other railways put together. It had obviously been trying.

But perhaps it was the unreformed character of the rest of the system that gave the Southern so much of its final flavour. The lines in Kent were the most marked example. The old South Eastern & Chatham still was rather a raffish concern. Ancient 4-4-0s hauling ancient and often rather disreputable trains still jangled their way across the county; some of the coaches were more or less officially called Birdcages, a word rather more descriptive than was probably intended. Everything had obviously been done on the cheap; tracks snaked round bends and

The Southern was probably the best of the big four in dragging itself out of the slough of the war years. Locomotives were repainted malachite green and coaching stock was renovated and spruced up as far as possible. Here Schools class 4–4–0 No 903 Charterhouse *climbs Hildenborough bank on an up Hastings train in 1947. The locomotive is in post-war malachite green and the leading coach although rather dowdy appears to be reasonably clean. The coal supply looks pretty poor, the Southern's equivalent of nutty slack, mainly dust with a few small lumps.*

over hills and even the original Dover main line with a better alignment suffered from poor drainage and consequent rough riding. There were lots of trains, well-filled; but the textbooks said that short-journey passengers were bad news, so obviously geography was against the prosperity of the South Eastern.

This comfortable theory was however exploded at once by the Central Division. The old London Brighton & South Coast had had the same difficulties of short distances, hilly country, and unstable ground to contend with as the South Eastern, and yet it had always been one of the most prosperous railways in Britain, and it still showed. It was *solid*. The overlay of Southern style had been applied much more thickly on the Brighton than

elsewhere, mainly through electrification, and so the Brighton's old character had been buried more deeply – but it still showed through, most clearly on the surprisingly rural branches in Sussex.

But it was the old London & South Western, as the largest constituent company, which contributed most to the Southern style, and not only because the SR rather unwisely chose to adopt the South Western's system of third-rail electrification instead of the Brighton's greatly superior overhead AC. The South Western, with its long main lines to Bournemouth and Exeter and beyond, had more in common with the railways of the rest of the country than with its stablemates, with the one exception that even here passenger revenue exceeded freight revenue, though the balance was closer than on the other two divisions. And it was certainly the South Western which provided the modernising impetus, illustrated by the fact that even before 1914 it had substantial lengths of automatically-signalled main line, including the unique (in Britain) electro-pneumatic semaphore installation between Woking and Basingstoke.

The Southern's modernising policy continued up to the end, though it had been subverted to some extent. By what feat of persuasion, one wondered, had Oliver Bulleid persuaded the Board that they had neglected their fleet of steam locomotives for too long, and that priority had to shift away from electrification for a period to enable it to be brought up to date? Anyway, he succeeded, and so during the late 1940s a tidal wave of Bulleid Pacifics swelled and spread, to the extent that cheap and simple 4-4-0s on two-coach locals in North Cornwall were replaced by the highly complex and costly three-cylinder machines, while lurking behind dust-sheets and clouds of doubt and rumour were the infinitely more complex and costly 'Leaders'. This diversion of policy was of course a mistake; but a mistake of good intention. Not all the mistakes made by railway management after 1948 can be so described.

But what of the flavour of the South Western in these final years? One can only describe an image to give an impression. First, it was an efficient railway; trains ran pretty much to time, impeccably so by the standards of the northern lines, even if on paper they often promised (but markedly failed to deliver) higher overall speeds. The trains were comfortable, especially the final Bulleid stock, even if somehow the Southern never managed to heat a train properly with steam. But it remained a railway with local roots; the company appointed station-masters in country towns and laid on them a duty to discover what the people thought of the railway, and what they wanted it to *do*; a far cry from the remit given to local management by, for example, the LMS or BR.

And then to become a beneficiary, just once, of this local sensitivity. A car breakdown had made it impossible to be delivered to Salisbury in time to catch the last train with a Somerset & Dorset connection at Templecombe back to school. The signalman without hesitation said he would stop the down express: 'but get on quickly, because I will clear the signal as soon as the train stops.' So the six o'clock from Waterloo paused momentarily at Wilton to collect one stranded schoolboy!

Not a way to run a railway nowadays, of course; and not a thing one could do lightly even then. But what an example of good local management taking an exceptional decision for good reason, and what an example of good public relations. The modern centralised 125mph railway may be splendid, but it has lost something. Perhaps the most significant thing about the Southern was that, for all its modernisation, it remained a human-scale enterprise. One comes back to the familiar story of Sir Herbert Walker, noticing a Fareham supervisor about to send away the day's last train up the Meon Valley branch while passengers were still on the footbridge; pulling down the window of his coach on the main-line train and calling to the man *by name* to hold the connection. The story of an incident like that would have gone through the whole staff like wildfire, and done a power of good. It is a tragedy that this sort of management skill did not survive the Southern Railway Company.

The Belle Theme

One of the redeeming features for better-off travellers south of the Thames was the large number of Pullmans employed: in addition to individual coaches for refreshments there were a number of complete trains of Pullman cars and complete trains. Possibly unconsciously a 'Belle' theme was developed, starting with The Southern Belle in November 1908. This ran between Victoria and Brighton and back at first once, but from June 1910 twice daily — in one hour. It was, of course, steam hauled. It ran, with a break of sorts during World War I, until 31 December 1932, when the full Brighton line electric service commenced.

The all-electric Southern Belle was unique so it was the only all-Pullman electric multiple unit. Three five car sets were provided and the train ran with either one set or two coupled together according to traffic requirements. The Southern Belle was originally first class only but from 1 January 1913 third class ordinary carriages were added to the formation. These continued on and off until 14 July 1924 when the train became all Pullman again with third class cars.

The title Southern Belle was a bit vague as the train only served one destination so some eighteen months after electrification it was renamed Brighton Belle. Apart from a break in World War II when Brighton was in a restricted area, the Brighton Belle continued to run with the original three 5 PUL sets until April 1972. Latterly the coaches were painted in reverse 1964 livery, blue upper panels and grey below the waist. It did not suit them.

The second Belle ran between Waterloo and Bournemouth West and return once a day and naturally was christened the Bournemouth Belle. It operated from 1931 to 1967, except for World War II, and apart from some runs in 1966 and 1967 which were diesel hauled (Class 47) was steam hauled throughout.

The two other Belles were post war innovations. The Devon Belle began in 1947, while the Thanet Belle, although a Southern Railway project did not commence until after nationalisation, in May 1948. At the time of its introduction, the Devon Belle, a summer weekend only service, was popular because it offered reserved seats, not yet restored out of Paddington or on the Atlantic Coast Express. The train was a heavy one, 12 cars made up of four for Plymouth and seven plus observation car for Ilfracombe. Though successful at first, patronage soon declined and from 1950 only the Ilfracombe section ran and then on fewer days. Final withdrawal was at the end of the 1954 summer timetable.

The Thanet Belle was introduced, five months into BR, on 31 May 1948 and ran between Victoria and Ramsgate via Chatham, again only in summer. In Festival of Britain year, 1951, three coaches were detached at Faversham and ran to Canterbury East which caused a change to Kentish Belle which name the train retained until September 1958 the last full summer before electrification. The Canterbury portion was not well patronised (sometimes having no passengers) and ceased after one season.

	Date commenced	Date ceased running	
Southern Belle (Victoria–Brighton)	1 November 1908	28 June 1934	Partially suspended during World War I Electric from 1 January 1933
Brighton Belle (Victoria–Brighton)	29 June 1934	30 April 1972	Suspended during World War II
Bournemouth Belle (Waterloo–Bournemouth West)	5 July 1931	9 July 1967	Daily Summer. Sundays only Winter until 1 January 1936 when became daily. Suspended during World War II
Devon Belle (Waterloo–Ilfracombe and Plymouth)	20 June 1947	19 September 1954	Summer only
Thanet Belle (Victoria–Ramsgate)	31 May 1948	24 September 1950	Summer only
Kentish Belle (Victoria–Ramsgate: Canterbury 1951 only)	2 July 1951	14 September 1958	Summer only

Opposite *Electric Pullman, the Brighton Belle during a busy period (thus using two five car sets) entering Brighton on 18 August 1948. The leading unit is No 3051. Note the Pullman armorial bearing on the front, the (as yet) absence of a yellow warning panel, and the roofboards. On the right is the erstwhile Brighton locomotive works of the LBSCR which at the time was still turning out steam engines and where in the 1950s the design work for the rebuilding of Bulleid Pacifics was carried out under the direction of R. G. Jarvis. The Brighton Belle has now gone the way of all good railway things – withdrawn, superseded by expediency.*

```
      "The SOUTHERN BELLE"  First and
                                      Third Class
LONDON (Victoria)    ..    ..   B11.5 a.m.    ..  B3.5 p.m.
BRIGHTON  ..   ..    ..    ..    12.5 p.m.    ..   4.5 p.m.

BRIGHTON  ..   ..    ..    ..   c1.35 p.m.    ..  B5.35 p.m.
LONDON (Victoria)    ..    ..    2.35 p.m.    ..   6.35 p.m.
               FARES—WEEKDAYS
First Class —Single  ..  10/8   PULLMAN  Supplement  2/-
             Return  ..  21/4        ,,         ,,    4/-
Third Class—Single   ..   6/5        ,,         ,.    1/-
             Return  ..  12/10       ,,         ,,    2/-
             SUNDAYS—First Class only
       LONDON (Victoria)    ..    ..   B11.5 a.m.
       BRIGHTON  ..   ..    ..    ..    12.5 p.m.

       BRIGHTON  ..   ..    ..    ..   B5.0 p.m.
       LONDON (Victoria)    ..    ..    6.0 p.m.

       "PULLMAN LIMITED"  SUNDAYS
LONDON (Victoria)    ..    ..   D9.45 a.m.   ..  B†4.35 p.m.
BRIGHTON  ..   ..    ..    ..   D10.55 a.m.  ..   5.35 p.m.

BRIGHTON  ..   ..    ..    ..   B†11.35 a.m. ..  DB6.35 p.m.
LONDON (Victoria)    ..    ..   B12.38 p.m.  ..  DB7.45 p.m.
SUNDAYS:— Cheap Day return tickets issued from Victoria as under:
First Class, 18/- inclusive of Pullman Supplement, 11.5 a.m., 12.5 and 1.5 p.m
Third   ,,   10/6      ,,        ,,      9.45, 11.10 a.m. and 12.5 and 1.5 p.m.
    Children under 14—Half fare.  Single Fares as on weekdays (see above)
         † First and Third Class.        D Third Class only.
Passengers travelling by "The Southern Belle" must obtain their Pullman tickets
                      at the Booking Office.
• These fares are subject to revision.    B Buffet Cars, Tea and Light Refreshments.
```

The down Southern Belle, Victoria to Brighton, near Coulsdon between 1926 and 1929 hauled by class L 4–6–4T No B328 in early Southern Railway livery. The first few Pullman cars are elliptical roof 12-wheel vehicles, probably some of those built in 1908 for this service. The overhead AC electrification was extended to Coulsdon in 1926 and converted to third rail in 1929. The two tracks on the far side are the SE&CR Tattenham Corner branch.

The down Bournemouth Belle in the New Forest near Ashurst Walks on 4 April 1953. The locomotive is No 35010 Blue Star *recently ex shops in BR green livery. The train consists of 10 Pullmans probably built circa 1928.*

The "Thanet" Pullman Ltd.

Every Sunday during the Year.

Any Seat can be Reserved in Advance by Purchasing a Ticket for the Journey
Private Coupés to hold Four Passengers can also be Reserved.

Teas and Light Refreshments supplied and Special Meals to order.

* CHEAP DAY RETURN FARES, including Pullman Car Supplement—

Margate .. .. .. } 20/- (Children under 14, half fare)
Broadstairs, Ramsgate .. }

DOWN				UP			
	a.m.	a.m.			p.m.	p.m.	p.m
VICTORIA	dep. 9. 4	10. 8		**RAMSGATE**	dep. 5. 5	6.40	7.35
		p.m.					
Margate	arr. 11. 5	12.12		Broadstairs	,, 5.14	6.45	7.43
Broadstairs	,, 11.14	12.22		Margate	,, 5.25	6.53	7.52
RAMSGATE	,, 11.23	12.32		**VICTORIA**	arr. 7.10	9. 1	10.21

* These fares are subject to revision.

The Devon Belle near Barnstaple behind West Country Pacific No 34017 Ilfracombe on 27 August 1949 still in Southern Railway green with no lettering or emblem on the tender. The BR number was applied in May 1948. This is the Ilfracombe portion of the train (7 coaches) which had split at Exeter Central, the other portion running to Plymouth (4 coaches).

The Thanet Belle, although planned by the Southern Railway, was introduced by BR in May 1948. The down train consisting of 10 Pullmans is seen here passing Ravensbourne on 29 August 1948 hauled by Battle of Britain class 4–6–2 No 34075 in SR colours and as yet un-named. It later became 264 Squadron.

This later picture shows class N15 No 30768 Sir Balin (North British June 1925 to October 1961) in charge of the down Kentish Belle near Reculver between Herne Bay and Birchington around 1953. The Stewarts Lane based engine still carries the old LSWR/SR power classification A under the number but appears to have the BR one above it.

Class T14 4–6–0 No 462 on a down local to Southampton Terminus near Hook on 5 June 1938. The leading three coaches are ex-LSWR non corridors with Maunsell corridors bringing up the rear.

Class N15X 4–6–0 No 2333 Remembrance at Bournemouth Central in 1939 with a relief to Waterloo, reporting number 119. The locomotive has been modified with opened cylinder ports, shorter blast pipe and altered brick arch. The livery is dark green with new style lettering and numbers.

5
AN OBSERVER
REMEMBERS

FROM childhood memories centred around trains, followed by the number collecting phase, a systematic record of observations began to be made in 1938, chiefly those seen on the nearby main line out of Waterloo, though it must be confessed that the comings and goings of electric trains were rarely noted.

During the summer of 1939, with war clouds looming, a special effort was made to watch the Saturday holiday traffic to Bournemouth and the West of England, also to Portsmouth, where twelve-car electrics shuttled four times an hour to and from Waterloo. On Saturday 19 August observation extended from 6.54am to 10.37pm, though there were various gaps caused by what BR now term 'Physical Needs Breaks', but some of these were covered by a school friend.

The full summer Saturday service was running on 19 August, plus a few relief trains and some specials bringing organised camping parties (Boy Scouts and so on) back to London. There were also nine ocean liner boat trains from Waterloo. Altogether 201 steam trains were seen, hauled by 114 different locomotives.

Most of the boat trains left during the morning, with Cunard specials at 8.22, 8.59 and 9.24, conveying passengers for the *Queen Mary* on the express service to New York. These were followed by Canadian Pacific Line trains to Southampton New Docks at 9.30 and 10.00 and two P&O departures at 11.03 and 11.41. There were also a short all-Pullman train to the Docks at 10.06, headed by T9 4–4–0 337, which returned during the evening. These extra trains caused some congestion at Waterloo. There were already 25 scheduled steam departures between 8.30am and noon and even though the boat trains ran to conditional 'Q' timings, trains during the morning were leaving up to ten minutes late.

The five-and-a-half day week was general in 1939, so there was a movement of commuters up to Waterloo before 9.00am and a return flow after mid-day. Humble office workers mostly travelled in suburban electrics, though some of their seniors (the term 'executive' had not been invented) lived further out on the Portsmouth, Alton and Basingstoke routes and paths had to be found on the through lines for their homeward trains. The Basingstoke semi-fasts tended to get the scrapings of the motive power barrel on busy Saturdays; Feltham put L11 4–4–0 158 on the 1.24pm from Waterloo, while 'Small Hopper' K10 4–4–0 139 appeared on the 7.40pm up from Basingstoke. Many of the additional Saturday trains were berthed during the week in sidings at Woking, Walton, Esher and Surbiton and M7 0–4–4Ts 25 and 248, 2–6–0 1619 and 4–4–0s 343, 396, 409, 414 and 730 headed empty stock workings into Waterloo during the morning.

1940 Loco Notes

The Stephenson Locomotive Society's *Journal* Southern notes for the April issue of 1940 make one rather envious of the passengers suffering wartime and cold weather disruption.

All the Lord Nelson engines are now allocated to Nine Elms, Nos 850–1, 853–5/7/9, 861/3, which normally worked the Folkestone and Dover boat expresses, having been transferred there from Stewarts Lane. In exchange, Stewarts Lane received King Arthurs Nos 772–4/6/8–80, which had been at Nine Elms all their lives, plus 784–5 from Eastleigh, which until lately were always at Bournemouth. Urie N15 4–6–0s Nos 741/2 have moved to Eastleigh. King Arthurs continue to be employed partially on heavy Eastern Section goods trains.

A special formed of 12 LNE coaches was recently noted passing Tonbridge from the up main to the Redhill route hauled by Redhill U 2–6–0 No 1800. It was probably bound for the GC *via* Reading and Banbury.

The evacuees' friends' excursion, from Kent suburban stations to Hastings, on March 3 was hauled by L1 4–4–0, No 1782 (B Arms spl duty 15). All four Wainwright D class 4–4–0s at St Leonards were on the dead road this week: Nos 1075 (for shops), 1734/8/44. Class L No 1768 is in works and No 1781 from B Arms on loan in lieu.

Eastbourne duty 737, running 108 miles (to Tunbridge Wells Tonbridge, Redhill and back) is

continued overleaf

continued
frequently worked by B1 Stirling 4–4–0 1449; on other occasions by Billinton E4 0–6–2T of about the same age, or by the rebuilt Brighton D3X 0–4–4T 2397. Atlantic No 2425 (new paint, unlined) and rebuilt Wainwright 4–4–0 E1 1179 were on Brighton stopping trains from London *via* country routes last week. A reported journey from the Sussex borders to Victoria was interesting. The veteran Stroudley D1 0–4–2T 2244 to Oxted: on behind Wainwright H 0–4–4T 1266, working through on the 9.50am from Tunbridge Wells *via* East Grinstead and Oxted, on S Lane Cen duty 501; this trip alone being 48 miles.

Lord Nelson No 859 (6ft 3ins DW) has now been fitted with the self trimming tender and painted in the new style. Other engines repainted with new lettering include No 495 (4–8–0T), No 3520 (4–4–2T), No 955 (0–8–0T), No 327 (0–6–0), No 1637 (2–6–0 U class). O2 No 231 has been repaired again after being withdrawn and No 0334 (0–6–0ST) has been returned from K&ESR and sent to Eastleigh. During the great frost in January and February the Reading service reverted to steam for some days and a strange collection of locos were noted, including Nos 158, 441 and 705 (4–4–0), 517 (4–6–2T), 545 (Q class 0–6–0), No 532 (Q class) was also observed on an Alton electric set.

On the Bournemouth line, 29 scheduled trains and one relief in each direction were noted and eight of Bournemouth's ten Schools 4–4–0s were seen. A ninth may have started out for Waterloo, but the 1.35pm from Weymouth appeared 32 minutes late behind Basingstoke's pilot engine, L12 4–4–0 428, and its return working on the 7.30pm was taken by N15 4–6–0 741. L11 4–4–0 155 replaced a Basingstoke L12 or U class Mogul on the 11.38am to Lymington Pier and made the return trip with ten corridors, including the restaurant car provided on almost all of these Saturday extras. This small Drummond 4–4–0 did well to reach Surbiton at 6.41 instead of 6.18 on its return journey, but unfortunately stopped on dead centre and took five minutes to restart.

The 8.30 and 11.17 to Weymouth and the 10.30am Bournemouth Belle were Lord Nelson hauled (Nine Elms' other two Nelsons were on the 10.24 to Ilfracombe and the 11.00 to Plymouth), but the up Belle with 858 had been delayed badly and was 37 minutes late passing Surbiton. Drummond's T14 'Paddlebox' 4–6–0s were much in evidence with six on Bournemouth or Swanage trains, one on the 1.04pm to the West of England and two on boat trains – only 446 was absent. Fifteen H15 4–6–0s were seen, including eight of the original 1914 series; one of these worked the 10.41 to Padstow, two others took later Atlantic Coast Express portions leaving at 11.47 and 12.00. Of the N15x 4–6–0 Remembrance rebuilds only 2329 was missing; the others were employed on a variety of duties to Bournemouth, Salisbury and Southampton Docks.

Nineteen down and 21 up West of England trains were seen, including reliefs from Seaton and Plymouth. Normally, engines were changed at Salisbury, but on summer Saturdays some Exmouth Junction locos worked into Waterloo. King Arthur 789 came up on the 6.57am slow from Salisbury and returned to the west on the 12.09pm to Exeter and Seaton, while 786 on duty 509 was on the 11.05am from Exeter Central instead of the 10.30 ACE from Ilfracombe, having exchanged with 774, but still returned on the 6.00pm from Waterloo as booked. Of the 26 Arthurs noted, 16 were on West of England trains and many others would be at work west of Salisbury.

The heaviest outward traffic to the west was the ACE group of eight trains leaving Waterloo between 10.24 and 12.09, while the corresponding flow of up trains arrived from 2.58pm onwards. The later members of this sequence crossed the morning's down trains in the Exeter area, where they had also to find a path through the GWR's traffic at St David's station. The twelve minutes' lateness of the 10.30am from Ilfracombe steadily increased for services later in the afternoon, with added delays due to the 1.48pm from Exmouth (H15 487 on twelve) running 44 minutes late and the succeeding 2.20pm from Sidmouth with 'Paddlebox' 459 being 61 minutes down.

Besides the ocean liner expresses already mentioned, Southampton Docks handled considerable Cross-Channel traffic on this day. N15 738 brought the Le Havre Continental Express into Waterloo punctually at 9.02am, followed by 755 and 753 on two divisions of the overnight service from St Malo. 521 and 2331 worked the two corresponding down trains for the return sailing, while at intervals during the evening six trains came

A rare wartime photograph of an up local from Bournemouth to Southampton leaving Brockenhurst on 30 June 1940. The locomotive is class T9 4–4–0 No 707 with three ex-LSWR non corridors.

up with passengers off the day services from the Channel Islands, mostly hauled by engines which had worked down on the morning's boat trains. During the afternoon T9 707 had passed with the 'flying boat special' from Southampton Docks to Victoria, but the usual 8.00pm departure from Victoria did not appear.

Several milk, parcels and local freight trains ran; the goods yard at Surbiton was shunted by K10 349 during the morning and by 0395 class 0–6–0 3442 in the evening. A rare appearance of an Adams 'Jubilee' 0–4–2 was made by 599, which collected an engineer's train from Wimbledon for some overnight work. A race meeting at Hurst Park brought extra electric trains to Hampton Court and a steam special for first class passengers hauled by M7 672, also a horsebox working with S11 4–4–0 400. An all-day LMS excursion to Portsmouth had L12 432 in both directions, while the up campers' specials produced 730 and 400 again. The evening also saw a return procession of six workmens' trains from Bramshot Halt, which had left Waterloo some twelve hours earlier. Conscription had recently been introduced and strenuous efforts were being made to complete the large army camp at Cove, beyond Farnborough. The trains were formed of a motley collection of LSWR non-corridors, SECR first class race train sets and even some Brighton 'balloon' stock; successive trains on 19 August were hauled by 442, 427, 1796, 420, 688 and 154.

Two weeks later German tanks were rolling into Poland and the evacuation of Britain's cities was under way. On the SR the plan was to run the

Under a Cloud!

The steam locomotive functioned best when fired with medium size lump coal containing a minimum of fines. Welsh steam coal and some Kent coals were soft and friable, needing careful handling to avoid undue amounts of slack and dust.

Maunsell knew that in 1927 the German State Railways had built a 2–8–0 freight engine adapted to burn pulverised coal of relatively low quality, using equipment supplied by the firm of AEG. It was claimed to burn coal without smoke, with a total absence of sparks and at higher efficiency
continued overleaf

91

continued

than on a grate. No doubt a Southern representative visited Germany to see this locomotive in action.

There was small coal available in the Kent coalfield at a favourable price. It was therefore decided to modify a U class 2-6-0 No A629 to burn this in pulverised form, using similar German equipment; this involved major alterations to the boiler and tender, in which an enclosed bunker was fitted. Coal in this form, in the presence of air, *can* be highly unstable in some circumstances. The work was completed at the end of 1929 and the engine allocated to Eastbourne shed, where a small crushing plant and closed storage hopper for the pulverised coal was erected.

The German experience was certainly not repeated on the Southern. The engine produced clouds of black smoke and deposited considerable amounts of unburnt and part-burnt coal over Sussex; in dry weather it seemed to need an escort of fire engines to extinguish crop fires. The engine spent a lot of time in store pending modifications to overcome this tendency – in vain. Matters came to a head one fine day in the summer of 1932. The hopper was seen to be showing signs of internal distress, and its contents were hastily discharged into wagons as much as possible. The lid was opened and the hopper blown through to remove any remaining dust. It promptly burst into flames and there was a loud explosion. A dense black cloud of smoke and coal dust floated over Eastbourne, covering burghers and holiday makers alike in coal dust and smuts. Claims poured in to the Southern's solicitors.

That was enough for Maunsell. By October the engine had been converted back to standard.

normal Monday to Friday service, so that commuters could still get to work and back, but to use most of the outward services from London during the middle of the day for the transport of evacuees. Thus all the even hour Bournemouth expresses, alternate Portsmouth fasts and two thirds of the trains to Basingstoke and down the New Guildford line were requisitioned. Only on the Aldershot and Salisbury lines were services maintained to cater for army reservists rejoining their units. Many of the evacuees joined the SR trains at Clapham Junction or Wimbledon (often via the Underground) to avoid causing congestion at Waterloo under the threat of air attack. Special trains were run for groups travelling to the West Country – 456, 486, 2332, 491, 443, 739, 779, 462 and 741 all followed each other westward with these on 1 September, the first day of the evacuation. Official cameramen were on hand to record the departure of these trains from Wimbledon and their arrival at such stations as Exeter Central, Crediton and Bideford, film which is now among the archives of the Imperial War Museum.

A year later, on 28 September 1940, the Southern Railway was coping with the worst of the 'blitz'. Waterloo was open once again for main line traffic after eleven days' closure following the bomb at Juxon Street, Lambeth, but the crater under the Windsor lines there was still not filled. Temporary girders spanning these holes in the viaduct and hastily filled bomb craters elsewhere were causing many speed restrictions and most down trains were running 15 to 20 minutes late. At Surbiton all trains were diverted on to the local lines as an unexploded bomb was thought to be lying between the through lines, on which two trains of coal wagons were standing to provide a protective screening for traffic passing slowly on the local lines.

Some of the Basingstoke semi-fasts had been cancelled but the 3.54pm from Waterloo ran, hauled by 'Paddlebox' 458, which was destroyed on Nine Elms shed two nights later. Up trains were running well behind time, probably delayed by air raid warnings elsewhere before reaching the Surbiton bottleneck. 925 on the 11.02am from Bournemouth passed 77 minutes late, followed by three divisions of the 8.20am from Plymouth behind 2330, 736 and 864 respectively, the last being 91 minutes in arrears. Down freight and parcels traffic was heavy and some trains were held at Surbiton to let passenger trains precede them. The usual 7.25pm Nine Elms to Southampton Docks goods passed at 5.20 (with S15 500) and the 9.30pm to Exmouth Junction at 7.20 (behind 843), in an effort to clear traffic from Nine Elms yard before the start of the nightly bombing. Two ballast trains went up behind L12 429 and T9 705, probably with material to fill the hole under the Windsor lines at Juxon Street. They were closely followed at 6.55pm by T14 445 on the stock for the 2.40am newspaper train to Bournemouth, which was shunted into the up sidings in readiness for its departure from Surbiton the following morning, loaded with papers brought from Fleet Street by road.

By the summer of 1942, wartime life had settled to a routine. Some of the restrictions on travel to the South Coast had been lifted and there was holiday traffic again to Bournemouth on a modest scale. The West of England line was very busy with the movements of servicemen, families visiting evacuees and those fortunate people able to take a break from wartime duties. On 22 August 1942 a long leave provided the opportunity to spend twelve hours (less the usual breaks) watching SR traffic; this was much quieter than on the corresponding Saturday in 1939, but 80 steam trains worked by 59 different locos were noted.

Most Bournemouth line trains ran in two portions, with restaurant cars provided on the regular services. The Schools were in charge of the Bournemouth-based workings, but the Lord Nelsons (all of which were now shedded at Nine Elms) provided added power on 14-coach trains, such as the 8.30, 9.30 and 11.30 from Waterloo. On the West of England line, the new Merchant Navy Pacifics had one venture into passenger traffic; 21C8 arrived at Waterloo on a semi-fast from Yeovil and returned to Salisbury on the 2.50pm Ilfracombe train. The wartime version of the ACE ran in four parts, hauled respectively by 785, 861, 854 and 770. Punctuality was fair – 784 with 13 coaches on the 8.15am from Ilfracombe was 32 minutes late, followed by 863 on the 8.20 from Plymouth 39 minutes in arrears. Of the evening arrivals, the 13-coach 12.20pm from Ilfracombe with 857 was 42 minutes behind time.

T9 118 passed at 10.28am with the 'flying boat special' from Victoria to Poole (the wartime terminal of the service), while another T9, 115, was

An immediate post-war view of Waterloo (note the glass missing in the roof) with King Arthur class 4–6–0 No 755 The Red Knight *backing down on to its train on 27 September 1946. The multiple jet blast pipe and large diameter chimney was fitted in March 1940.*

The post-war Bournemouth Belle 4.35pm ex Waterloo hauled by Merchant Navy class 4–6–2 No 21C16 Elders Fyffes *near Maybury between West Byfleet and Woking on 29 June 1947.*

on both of the troop trains seen. Some of the Western Section's motive power imports were in action; B4X 4–4–0 2073 worked the 9.54am to Basingstoke, D1 4–4–0 1739 piloted King Arthur 781 on the 10.54, while J class 4–6–2T 2326 and SECR D class 4–4–0 1734 were on local parcel and freight duties; nothing of Basingstoke's Brighton Atlantics was seen.

Twelve months later, on Saturday 21 August 1943, service and civilian traffic had grown to the stage where the Schools were no longer able to cope with the loads on the Bournemouth line, despite the withdrawal of restaurant cars, and they had been demoted to the Basingstoke semi-fasts. Their place had been taken by the Nelsons, and this day saw the 8.30, 9.30 and 11.30am from Waterloo each made up to fifteen coaches, headed respectively by 862, 859 and 857. Each of these trains was preceded by a relief, unusually formed of twelve ex-SECR non-corridor coaches. The answer to a parliamentary question at this period declared that trains conveying troops and prisoners of war had priority for corridor stock – or maybe the authorities were just trying to bring home the point 'Is your journey really necessary?'

On the West of England line the SR found an opportunity to demonstrate the contribution their controversial new Merchant Navy Pacifics could make to the war effort. Much publicity was given to the combination in mid-week of the two divisions of the wartime ACE into one 16-coach Pacific hauled train. However, it was soon found that you did not need a Pacific to work a 16-coach train and on 21 August, while the 10.50am to Ilfracombe had 21C7, the 10.59 to Plymouth, also with sixteen on, had 865. There were two other relief trains to the 10.50; 755 on twelve coaches and 771 on fourteen. The latter was followed by E1 4-4-0 1497 on the 'flying boat special'; this being one of the occasions when no T9 was available at Stewarts Lane off an incoming service. Shortness of leave prevented any observation of up trains during the afternoon, but a month earlier on 24 July, there had been some substantial delays.

The return of peace brought only a gradual restoration of normal train services and the acute coal shortage of 1947 severely restricted the passenger train mileage which could be run. The SR showed great enterprise in the last summer of its existence by introducing the new Devon Belle, making use of Pullman cars stored during the war, but under the Ministry of Transport's rules extra mileage had to be offset elsewhere, thus there were three hour gaps in the service to Farnborough. However, the summer timetable included a few of the customary Saturday additional trains.

Once again it was possible to observe traffic on the third Saturday in August, and the 23 August 1947 found a number of unadvertised relief trains also running (did the Ministry of Transport know of their existence?), including the 11.38am to Lymington Pier with Mogul 1634. The ACE ran in six parts – an Ilfracombe relief behind 21C158, the 10.20 to Padstow with 755, the 10.35 to Ilfracombe with 21C160, the 10.50 itself behind 21C12, followed later by sections for Exmouth and Seaton worked by 21C161 and 792 respectively. The new Devon Belle with fourteen Pullmans was in charge of 21C16, while the restored Bournemouth Belle had 21C20. Despite the influx of Pacifics, large and small, Urie N15s 747 and 753 could still be found on the 11.15am from Padstow and 12.40pm from Ilfracombe respectively – both, however, running well behind time. Ocean Liner and Channel Islands traffic had begun to flow again through Southampton Docks – 782 and 856 were on two Cunard specials from Waterloo during the morning, the latter returning with 737 on evening Channel Islands trains.

It fell to British Railways (Southern Region) to experience the full resumption of Saturday holiday traffic on the pre-war scale, so fascinating to the lineside observer, for a few brief years in the 1950s before the motor car and Mediterranean sun enticed holidaymakers away from the train.

Maximum Effort

During the 1948 Locomotive Interchanges I fired to Jack Swain of Nine Elms. On 11 June we were working south from Manchester (London Road) to Marylebone with West Country No 34006 *Bude* and had called at Leicester in the normal way. As Jack restarted the train (12 on including dynamometer car, 376 tons) Mr Sharpe, chief of the squad in the car, called out over the Loudaphone 'Give us a pull, Jack'. He did so and as the engine accelerated in no uncertain manner the cutoff was adjusted to about 33 per cent and the regulator set to maintain 230lb per sq in in the steam chest.

I was somewhat unprepared for such exuberance but quickly started the injector and commenced continuous firing. Fortunately the coal was of the right size for firing so I did not have to pause to crack it up. It was the fastest bout of shovelling that I have ever done and the episode resulted in the highest sustained drawbar HP recorded by an engine during the Exchanges, namely 2010. After Lutterworth our pilot driver called to Jack: For —'s sake, shut off, mate, or we'll be in Rugby a week before time. We have to knock hell out of our B1s to do this section in 24 minutes!' *Bude* did it in 22 minutes and had coasted for some considerable distance approaching Rugby! A Bulleid Pacific will certainly go up a bank. – A.E. Hooker.

Footnote: The official report on the trials, says of this occasion that No 34006 achieved with 260lb per sq in in the boiler, 240lb per sq in in the steam chest, cutoff 27 per cent, speed 67.8mph, recorded drawbar horsepower 1667, equivalent drawbar horsepower 2010, at 107.6 miles from Manchester, ie Whetstone station.

War Memories

The summer of 1939 was hot, dry and menacing. Continental traffic flourished. The Southern introduced a London–Paris season ticket available for 12, 18 or 24 journeys and the package tour business was booming as never before.

Then 3 September, Mr Chamberlain announced that we were at war and, immediately, the sirens sounded all over the London area. No bombs fell – just one unidentified aircraft over the Medway Towns.

Trains were being equipped with dim blue compartment lights as fast as supplies permitted. Notices invited passengers to lie on the floor in the event of an air raid. Whilst this had possibilities for two or three, it was clearly impossible for the full compartment loads still being carried in the business periods.

Train stop marks were indicated on platforms by a figure 8 or letter S in a box with a lighted headlamp behind.

French troops were also evacuated from Dunkirk and some elected to return home. One is seen here at Margate circa May 1940 in conversation with three SR staff. The station name has not yet been removed for security and the staff are wearing their oval railway service badges.

Hoods were fitted over colour light signals, but 'Navigating by Bradshaw' was the RAF term for following the rails which remained easy.

After one bombless week during which peak travel remained normal the Railway Executive decided to relieve the monotony by having a wartime timetable. There was a half-hourly business service on suburban lines except between Holborn and Orpington and over the Nunhead-Lewisham line where there were no trains at all. Main line services were slashed to three or four a day. The result was instant completely unnecessary misery. Hundreds were left behind and, so overloaded were the SR peak period trains that the coach bodies sank on the springs and several stepboards were taken off by platform edges.

This 'Crazy Week' timetable was withdrawn after a few days and the normal timetable reinstated until some sensible alterations could be made. It was the evening services which needed pruning because few people were venturing out in the blackout unless necessary.

Another self-inflicted blow was the decision of the recently created Ministry of Food to decentralise Billingsgate fish market. The result was a classic example of organised chaos. Fish for Kent was concentrated at Maidstone for local distribution. Since all the arrange-

ments were geared to trains from Hull and Grimsby to London, Kings Cross, with trips to the SR London termini, the working had to be completely changed with the result that the fish trains reached their destination some hours late. After sale, quantities of not quite so fresh began their final journeys – most of it back to the London suburban area. This innovation was also short lived. Many things got back to normal. As trains became more crowded with troops, posters began to appear to enquire 'Is Your Journey Really Necessary?' but the discomfort of weekend travel was probably the greater deterrent. Troops went on weekend leave, parents visited their evacuated offspring and there was busy ordinary weekend traffic stimulated by the restoration of cheap tickets in October – despite the questioning posters!

During the first few months of the war, the Germans frequently sent over the odd reconnaissance aircraft whereupon the sirens sounded, all work stopped as everyone was directed to go to shelter. Although trains were permitted to run at 15mph during an 'alert' this was not possible for long as the signalmen left their boxes and took shelter. By late summer of 1940 it was realised that the loss of production was playing enormous dividends to the enemy, and a system of 'spotters' was inaugurated, whereby people were posted to give warning of imminent danger. There were, of course, no 'spotters' at signal boxes so now the signalmen just carried on.

Then, on 26 May, 1940, the jovial divisional superintendent Percy Nunn made one of his rare Sunday visits to the office and called an emergency meeting. For once, he was not beaming. 'The Railway Executive want to know whether we can run a train every ten minutes from Dover to Ramsgate for twenty four hours, or possibly longer. It is a top priority military job and the other railways will provide trains to work in a pool with ours. They want to know how long we can cope. It is all very secret.'

There was no need to explain. It was obvious that we were getting out of France – if we could. There was the sudden, sickening thought that Britain was to be invaded because this, too, seemed obvious. The war suddenly seemed frightening and personal. Mr D.S. Sheppy, the district loco running superintendent told his staff that he had just come from Bricklayers Arms and Stewarts Lane. There was no need to appeal to them to work long hours; many had sons over there. He was further assured that, when all the drivers had fallen down, they would put the shed foremen at B Arms on the footplate and sweat some of the fat off them. When told this, Stewarts Lane said they would not need to do the same as they would just be getting into their stride and would cover the B Arms work as well. Rivalry between these two depots had always been quite fierce. Both performed marvels.

Staff were called in to the office and station masters and signalmen were called out to immediate duty. All main line signal boxes were manned continuously. Mechanical and signal fitters were called out.

The SR headquarters, evacuated to Deepdene, dealt with the Naval authorities and the Railway Executive. They were told that most of the trains would go via Redhill to Aldershot, Salisbury and the West of England. This was not going to help the operating as it meant a reversal at Redhill.

It was not until Thursday that the armada of little ships reached Dunkirk. Consisting of everything capable of crossing the Channel from sturdy lifeboats, brightly burnished cabin cruisers, motor launches, barges and tugs, these little ships were capable of getting close inshore and offered much smaller and more agile targets to the Luftwaffe dive bombers.

Thursday's total of 54,000 evacuees rose to 68,000 on Friday and held at 64,000 on Saturday.

Fred Hemphrey, a senior special traffic clerk, had been sent to Dover Marine to work with Admiral Bertram Ramsey's staff and the Army officers who gave destinations for the various trains. These were frequently altered as the trains were in transit. The job of accommodating such vast and unpredictable numbers must have been aggravated for the Army by the fact that some 50,000 Allied (mainly French and Belgian) troops were mixed with the British. It was not unusual for trains to set out with such destinations as 'Report to RTO at Woking.' Or it might be Salisbury. Or Crewe. Or anywhere.

The down line between Folkestone and Dover was turned into a permissive working 'cab rank' on which empty trains were queued up nose to tail. Volunteer retired drivers and men not passed for main line work looked after the engines and pulled the trains forward while the exhausted crews snatched a few hours or few minutes sleep. Ambulance trains were kept apart and held at Shorncliffe but there were few of them.

It all worked from hand to mouth. Within an hour, two or three destroyers or our own cross-Channel ships might arrive, the cab rank empty and staff would be on to the other railway controls for priority to be given to empty trains for Dover. The ships were, of course, packed. The old SR Isle of Wight paddle steamer *Whippingham* licensed for 800 passengers, brought over 2,700 on one trip.

The problem of route knowledge was uniquely solved. If the guard did not know the road he found out who the driver was to be and arranged that, in any emergency, the fireman would come back and tell him where they were and where he had to go for any assistance. Similarly, guards rode on the engines where neither the driver nor the fireman knew the way. Actually, this was rare as the locomotive depots were able to use all their passed firemen and cleaners to augment their resources so that the shortage of guards was worse than that of loco crews.

South Eastern guards found themselves far down on the Western section and Salisbury men found out what Dover looked like. An ambulance train guard due to be relieved at Willesden Junction, on being told by the station inspector that there would be some delay while they found a guard to take the train forward, though the LMS engine was on and the signal off, simply waved his green flag and said he would get off at Rugby.

Many were on duty for 24 hours or longer and then came back after a few hours for a similar stint. Everything

Mother and son, impeccably dressed, watch the departure of the Golden Arrow behind Merchant Navy Pacific No 35027 Port Line *from Victoria in March 1954.*

Merchant Navy Pacific No 35024 East Asiatic Company, *in BR early dark blue livery for top line express locomotives, leaves Waterloo with a special train in June 1949. Great care has been taken with the engine's turnout, white lining, polished rods, etc. as the train includes a Pullman carrying HRH Princess Elizabeth on a visit to Weymouth.*

Victoria station, London in 1939. D class 4–4–0 No 1726 stands in the Chatham side with a train for Maidstone East via Chatham. The train is Maunsell side corridor stock. Most SR coaches found themselves in semi-permanent sets, hence the number 450 at the end adjacent to the engine's tender. No 1726 carries a shed duty number 339 and still bears its SR numberplate on the cab side as well as tender numerals. The original SECR Ashford works plate is just below the smokebox.

Waterloo station, London on 29 April 1965 with rebuilt Battle of Britain class Pacific No 34050 Royal Observer Corps on a local to Southampton terminus using BR Mk I coaches as set No 573. There is a small Smith's bookstall on the adjacent platform and a rather ancient petrol tractor for dragging trolleys about.

requested was done quickly and without complaint. The evacuation became fairly common knowledge in Kent well before any official announcement. At Tonbridge, the station master's wife organised refreshments. Tables appeared on the platforms and money and supplies rolled in. At Penge East where most of the trains got stopped by signal because of the length of Penge Tunnel a local dairy sent thousands of cartons of milk. Down at the country stations the local Women's Institute members set up stalls of food and drink, waiting for a train to stop.

The LNER and LMS Controls who would normally be shouting their heads off if they had a hundred or so wagons for the South Eastern waiting in their London marshalling yards called to say that they did not want to worry us but thought we ought to know that they were holding a couple of thousand and were blocking back all the way to the Midlands. There never were such days – and never again will be.

Ambulance trains were always a priority. When there was an especial demand the only one 'about' was at Potters Bar waiting for an engine from Hornsey LNER. 'He'll be moving in about an hour.' When told that would be too late the LNER asked for a few minutes and then reported it was already on its way to Factory Junction, the furthest point to which the LNER could work – tender first. 'We've got orders to let the Southern have anything they ask for. So we took the engine off the Night Scot. That's why he is tender first. I reckon the people in our train are better able to wait an hour than your lot at Dover.'

Whenever there was an air raid alert at Dover and activity was reported by Dover Control, which was quite frequently during the night, everyone feared for the whole 'Dynamo' operation, code word for the Dunkirk evacuation, if the Luftwaffe could manage to drop a couple of bombs on the railway line where it ran between Shakespeare Cliff and the sea and bring about a landslide. But, providentially, it did not happen.

The murderous German bombing had turned the waters round Dunkirk into a naval graveyard of over 200 ships including a dozen of the Southern's cross-Channel fleet. On Saturday, the Naval authorities were compelled to issue orders to confine the evacuation to the hours of darkness. Even so, another 52,000 men were brought off before Dynamo finally wound down on Tuesday 4 June. Many seriously wounded were taken to Shorncliffe Military Hospital. After the evacuation the SR had the unhappy and unique job of arranging several trains of coffins bringing home to families those who did not survive their injuries. But that was after the 'train every ten minutes for twenty four hours' had grown to 734 trains, lifting over 300,000 men.

After Dunkirk, an 'invasion train' equipped with bedding, basic rations and wireless telegraph gear was provided at Orpington. The Control staff were told that if need be they would be taken by it to a secret destination, leaving families to fend for themselves. The closer that we were brought to the near-certainty of invasion, the more outwardly nonchalant the staff became. The aerial Battle of Britain raged through the hot summer and reached its crescendo in late August. People in Kent and the London suburbs became the recipients of much assorted and explosive ironmongery dropped from a great height. A Spitfire fell on the quiet country station at Pluckley and killed the staff. Another fell on Forest Hill and badly damaged the station. Pieces of aircraft fell across the railway and destroyed the telephone lines.

Then on Saturday afternoon 7 September, the Luftwaffe got past the exhausted and battered RAF to deliver the first devastating daylight raid on London's dockland.

Next day in Control, all was confusion. There was heavy damage in London and all over the suburban area. The night shift had been trying to plan services without much success. Never before had they been called on to deal with anything like it. By the early evening, the sirens were wailing again. This was, of course, the beginning of the 'blitz' which went on more or less continuously for eight months, waxing and waning according to the phases of the moon. Par for the repair of a bomb hole on plain track was four hours. The people of London and the south east learned a new way of life and Orpington Control had to learn a new way of working. It soon got down to daily programmes, simply based. The passenger controller on the night shift produced an outline train service based on the position at midnight or thereabouts. This covered the start-up and the morning business period. It had to be thought out, written up, typed and duplicated for sending out by despatch riders leaving at 04.00 for the London termini and the principal stations.

Usually, the governing factor was the number of trains (if any) that could be run above New Cross. This would be limited by present or past unrepaired damage to signalling circuitry, bridges or arches. These pathways were then allocated amongst the routes still open. The evening service was produced by the early shift, based on the position at 11.00 and the forecasts of the engineers. It was completed, typed and duplicated for a 13.30 departure by the despatch riders. It was much easier to prepare than the other because there were usually no daylight raids big enough to upset calculations and the evening services had the benefit of a full day's work by the engineers. The evening rush always started well before dark so that people could be out of central London before the nightly raid began.

The worst period on the night shift was from around 06.00 when, after a long, hard night they were faced with a flood of incoming telephone calls from the early turn supervisors, fresh from a night in bed, pointing out why this or that would not work. The steam trains had to be balanced and berthing grounds specified so that engine power and crews could be provided. There never seemed to be much trouble with the train crews of the electric trains, probably because the service was so much reduced.

Apart from the holes blown in the track or, worse, in the arches between New Cross and London there was a lot of trouble with incendiaries setting alight the fat, pitch covered traction current cables or their slimmer but equally vital brothers carrying the signalling circuits.

Although widespread in effect, damage to the traction cables was usually fairly quickly repaired but the signals were much more difficult and took longer.

The geographical complexities of the SE&C with its multiplicity of routes gave many alternatives but made the work of preparing the night emergency train service very difficult because so many possibilities had to be weighed.

When there was only one line open between New Cross and London Bridge with restricted or no signalling the line capacity was twelve trains an hour. If most routes were open, this meant many diversions over the Lewisham–Nunhead route to Holborn Viaduct. Assuming that the only other blockage was on the North Kent line – say at Abbey Wood – the outline timetable might have looked like this:

During the war express engines took on more menial tasks from time to time 'in the national interest'. Here King Arthur 4–6–0 No 797 Sir Blamor de Ganis *climbs the bank from Tonbridge to Sevenoaks with a train of empty coal wagons, now all also pooled as a wartime economy.*

Overleaf Slumbering Giant *by Philip D. Hawkins G.R.A., oils on canvas, 30in × 20in, to be published in a collection of this popular railway artist's work in 1993. Nine Elms locomotive shed was a magical place. Bulleids Pacifics gathered together at one shed was an awe-inspiring sight. Here in the early 1960s a rebuilt Merchant Navy No 35004* Cunard White Star *is being made ready to back down to Waterloo to work the Atlantic Coast Express. Also seen are West Country No 34092* City of Wells *and Battle of Britain No 34086* 219 *Squadron.*

Philip D. Hawkins

From	Dep	To
Cannon Street	03	Hayes via Lewisham
Charing Cross	05	Sevenoaks via Orpington
Cannon Street	13	Dartford via Parks Bridge and Loop
Charing Cross	15	Gillingham via Bexleyheath
Cannon Street	23	Hayes via Lewisham
Charing Cross	25	Gravesend Central via Bexleyheath
Cannon Street	33	Dartford via Parks Bridge and Loop
Charing Cross	35	Sevenoaks via Orpington
Cannon Street	43	Hayes via Lewisham
Charing Cross	45	Gillingham via Bexleyheath
Cannon Street	53	Dartford via Parks Bridge and Loop
Charing Cross	55	Gravesend Central via Bexleyheath
Blackfriars	03 23 43	Addiscombe via Nunhead and Lewisham
Holborn Viaduct	15 35 55	Plumstead via Nunhead and Lewisham

The differing running times of five minutes from Charing Cross and two minutes from Cannon Street would make an even five minutes departure from London Bridge. There would have been shuttle services to cover the Bromley North and Sanderstead lines and another from Dartford to Abbey Wood with a bus connection to Plumstead. Another bus service would cover the Greenwich line.

The Post Office operators were splendid in getting the regular 03.00 call to Abbey 1234 – the London Transport bus controller. One might hear the Orpington exchange operator talking to Guildford, Woking, Chatham or anywhere to which he had a line working – 'can you help me to London? Railway priority'. The bus controller was calm in face of our fantastic demands which might total several hundred buses an hour between the London termini and the various suburban stations at which trains were terminated.

The preparation of the morning train service was not, of course, helped by the efforts of the adverse parties overhead. It was not uncommon to get almost through the service and have to start all over again because the principal route into London had just been blown up somewhere or was thought to have been. Signalmen would telephone to say that there had been a 'nasty crump' between them and the next place and should they stop traffic? Control worked on the simple theory that any bomb which fell near enough to damage the railway would also blow down the lineside telephone wires. So, if there was communication, the signalman was usually told to allow a train to proceed under extreme caution. If it was dark, passengers would be turned out first. After all, there was considerable risk in allowing a passenger train to stand for perhaps an hour or longer while somebody stumbled along to search the line with bombs dropping all around.

The author of this piece was however once caught out one night, when bombing was severe. St John's signalman sought advice about despatching an empty troop train to Stewarts Lane following a 'tidy bang up the bank towards Nunhead.' As the telephones and signal equipment were all working, it seemed sensible to let the train go with the usual caution. Soon afterwards, St John's was back.

'You know that train you told me to send up to Nunhead? The 'you told me' bit was clear indication that something was wrong. 'The driver is back here. His engine is down a bomb hole. Big as a house, he says. Near Brockley Lane.' This was probably the only semaphore signalling area with underground cabling. How was one to know?

Since it was not possible to balance the electric units in the emergency train services, which never ran as programmed anyway, the passenger controller and his other assistant on night duty first concentrated on getting trains off the road and the crews home. Inevitably, some berthing was lost by enemy action. So the few electrified sidings at wayside stations not normally used for berthing were used first to give the crews the chance to get home while there was still a fair train service running.

As the night bombing intensified, more and more anti-aircraft guns of all kinds were deployed in the suburban area. In the first days it was generally recognised that, whether or not they did much in the way of bringing down enemy aircraft, they made a splendid noise and were good for morale. Not quite so happy from a railway standpoint was the idea of firing off shells containing coils of wire which were intended to tangle in the blades of enemy aircraft. This happened in September 1940 and, although one never heard of any enemy aircraft being entangled, the tangle they caused on the ground was phenomenal. The falling wires festooned themselves round telephone wires, bringing them down, fell across railway lines and caused short circuits and fell into streets which were promptly closed by Police and Air Raid Wardens.

In the early days of the blitz, a staff 'hostel' of passenger coaches was berthed in Elmstead Woods tunnel. Although fairly safe, it was not very comfortable. Users stretched out on the compartment seats and tried to ignore the incessant noise and smoke from trains passing on the adjacent lines and the pervading sulphurous smell. Blankets and candles were provided and that was all. In the mornings the washrooms at Orpington were cluttered with people changing their shirts and boiling up water to wash and shave.

Landmines fluttered down by parachute. In size and shape they resembled a torpedo. Their virtue to the enemy was that they exploded on impact with the ground, so making only a shallow crater and achieving maximum blast and damage. The disadvantage from his point of view was their tendency of the parachute lines to catch in trees, chimney pots and similar obstructions to descent. One of the most remarkable of these entanglements occurred in the early hours of 12 December 1940. A scraping noise was heard by the signalmen at London Bridge Box. Cautiously opening the door, the signalman came face to face with a landmine, hooked to the corner of the roof and swaying gently to and fro. The signalman stopped to send 'Obstruction, Danger' in all directions before tip-toeing to a safer spot.

The night of 16–17 April 1941 was one of the worst. At Charing Cross an unexploded landmine was welded to the conductor rail where the timbers of the adjacent river bridge were alight. The Holborn lines were blocked by a direct hit on a bridge over Southwark Street. The Elephant & Castle station and signal box were destroyed, a block of flats was brought down across the Metropolitan Widened Lines at Snow Hill and damage elsewhere was serious. A direct hit demolished Blackfriars signal box just as the signalmen were leaving to take shelter. They were both killed. This was one of the very few days when trains were unable to reach any London terminal. The original train service circular for the evening period is reproduced. The signalling in the Blackfriars–Elephant & Castle area was completely wiped out and was temporarily replaced with a simplified system, capable of displaying only red and yellow aspects. This may have had some influence on the LMS driver who, during another air raid, ran through a pair of points at Blackfriars and carried on along the up local line in the wrong direction to Walworth Road – some 3 miles – fortunately without colliding with anything.

Cannon Street station was a ruin. The booking hall and offices were badly burned and soaking wet. In No 7 platform was a train of metal underframes each with a steel angle sticking up from each corner, which is what a burned out van train looks like at close quarters. The platforms were covered with glass and debris from the roof above. Just outside the signal box stood an engine which had received a direct hit. It was still in one piece and still standing on the rails which had been driven into the ground, fracturing the fishplates. The boiler and superstructure were flattened and the whole thing looked exactly as though a giant foot had stepped on it. The driver and fireman heard the bomb coming, dived under their engine – and lived.

SOUTHERN RAILWAY.

London East Divisional Superintendent's Office,
Orpington, Kent.

17th April, 1941.

THURSDAY, APRIL 17th – TRAIN SERVICE.

According to the position at 1.0 p.m. the following train service arrangements will apply this evening.

Service	Route	UP	DOWN
Gillingham & Blackheath	Bexleyheath	18. 48	10. 40
Dartford & Blackheath	Bexleyheath	15. 30	25. 55
Dartford & Lee.	Loop	0. 15. 30. 45.	0. 15. 30. 45
Sevenoaks & Herne Hill.	Orpington	4. 24 44	15. 35. 55
Sevenoaks & Herne Hill	Swanley	1. 21.41	9. 29. 49
Orpington & Grove Park		2. 22.42	0. 20. 40
Dartford & Erith.		20 50.	5. 35
Addiscombe & New Beckenham		0. 30	25. 55
Sanderstead & New Beckenham		15. 45	10. 40
Shortlands & Bellingham	Catford Loop	Shuttle Service	
Abbey Wood & Maze Hill		Shuttle Service	
Maidstone E. & Bromley Sth.		Normal Service Bromley South	Terminating
Farningham Rd. & Sole St.		Shuttle	Steam Service.

105

The newly introduced Night Ferry from a frontispiece in the Railway Magazine *for* July 1937. *It is a 528 ton train headed by class L1 4–4–0 No 1758 and class D1 4–4–0 No 1145. The train includes sleeping cars and vans of the Wagons-Lits company specially built for the Dover–Dunkirk train ferry service, Pullman cars as 1st class diners and SR Maunsell stock. From a painting by J.D. Goffey based on a photograph by L.T. Catchpole.*

The Southern's only narrow gauge line, the 1ft 11¾in Lynton & Barnstaple Railway closed in September 1935. Manning Wardle built 2–6–2 tank No 761 Taw (supplied for the opening of the line) leaves Barnstaple with a mixed train for Lynton probably around 1932–3.

The train is running alongside the creek where the barges were unloaded. From a painting by J.E. Hoyland.

One of the Urie King Arthur class 4–6–0s No 747 Elaine *about to leave Exeter Central station with an up West of England express in August 1936. The train is drawn well forward on the platform extension provided when the station was rebuilt in 1933. Note Exeter gaol in the background.*

The 'Royal T9', No 30119 *was specially reserved for working Royal trains – a unique position for a pre-Grouping engine. When not in such service it worked from Dorchester shed where it is seen here about 1948 still in malachite green but with its new BR numbering and lettering.*

The Great Frost 1940

The exceptionally severe 1939–40 winter, with snow in Kent measured in feet rather than inches, was kept secret under wartime security. But the third-rail system was badly affected. Unexpectedly 21 of us were marched into the company commander's office to say were were to be sent to Malta, writes K.W. Wightman, rather than France as we had expected, that island then at peace, and we were even issued with peacetime uniforms prior to 10 days leave. I resided in Beckenham, and though local services were disrupted the EMU trains coped. Despite the severe weather I decided to see what was happening elsewhere, and went to Clapham Junction, to see unprecedented steam piloting of local and main-line electrics. I noted the following workings, some of which were EMU trains:

30 Jan 1940

Loco	Class	Working	Shed
416	L12	Brighton EMU semi-fast	BAT
2344	K	Up Bognor	FRA
845	S15	Up Portsmouth	FEL
1837	N	Reading Fast	EXJ
547	Q	Up EMU semi-fast	GFD
676	M7	Up EMU semi-fast ex-Alton	GFD
2333	N15X	Up Bournemouth Express	9E
156	L11	9E–Feltham goods	FEL
451	N15	Up West of England Express	SAL
2349	K	Up Brighton semi-fast EMU	3B
347	K10	ECS duty	9E
439	L11	Feltham goods	FEL

Seen at Waterloo

620	A12	Down local EMU (LSWR type)	Note 1
503	S15	Light to 9E	FEL
167	L11	Light ex 9E	9E
700	700	EMU pilot	FEL
1805	U	Semi-fast Basingstoke	9E
1616	U	Light to 9E	GFD
753	N15	Arr ex-Bournemouth	ELH
115	T9	Up Portsmouth EMU	9E
513	S15	Arr on semi-fast	FEL

At Clapham Junction

518	H16	Goods Feltham–9E	FEL
399	S11	Up Bournemouth semi-fast	BM
32	M7	Down local (steam stock)	9E
1157	E	Up Bognor EMU	BA
1616	U	Down semi-fast EMU	GFD
2333	N15X	Down Bournemouth Express	9E
451	N15	Down West of England Express	SAL
430	L12	Up Portsmouth EMU	BAT
1266	H	Up Oxted line	BAT
1160	E1	Down Oxted line	BAT
1195	F1	Up light. Note 2	EBN

Note 1: This amazing spectacle even more unexpected as this 0-4-2 was last seen withdrawn on Eastleigh dump, 19 March 1939, but reinstated for World War II.

Note 2: Driven by motorman, according to cap badge.

The observations were continued on 31 January 1940.

Beckenham

1019	E1	Down van train	BAT
863	LN	Down Ramsgate Express	BAT
1377	O1	Beckenham Junction shunt	HIT

Norwood Junction

1763	L	noted on shed	AFD
2407	E6X	noted on shed	NOR

Clapham Junction

212	O2	ECS duty	9E
213	O2	ECS duty	9E
38	M7	ECS duty	9E
347	K10	ECS duty	9E
692	700	Down local EMU (LSWR)	
1611	U	Up semi-fast EMU	GFD
860	LN	Down 9.30 Bournemouth Express	9E
2070	B4X	Up Oxted line	BTN
141	K10	Down local EMU (LSWR)	GFD
402	S11	Up semi-fast	FEL
1909	U1	Up Brighton EMU Express	BAT
2553	C2X	WLER shunt	NX
130	M7	ECS duty	9E
249	M7	ECS duty	9E
1618	U	Down Portsmouth XP EMU	
1900	U1	Up Oxted line	BAT
447	T14	Basingstoke semi-fast	SAL

Waterloo

141	K10	Down local EMU	GFD
1630	U	Down Alton EMU	RED
1896	U1	Arr semi-fast	GFD
1899	U1	EMU pilot	
1414	N	Arr semi-fast	9E

Clapham Junction

1872	N	Goods to Feltham	BA
1497	E1	Down Brighton semi-fast EMU	DOV
1624	U	Up semi-fast	SAL
319	M7	Up semi-fast	
422	L12	Up Oxted line	BAT
865	LN	Down Atlantic Coast Express	9E
2073	B4X	Up Oxted line	BTN
166	L11	Down Reading fast	
1896	U1	Down Portsmouth Express EMU	GFD
430	L12	Up Brighton Express EMU	BAT
1917	W	BAT-NOR transfer goods	NOR
1632	U	Dep Basingstoke semi-fast	
327	700	Goods to Battersea	
2027	I3	Up Tunbridge Wells semi-fast	TWW

The conditions were arduous, extremely cold, ice everywhere, but it was worth it to see such sights!

6
A PROFILE ON TANKS

SOMETHING of the rich diversity of locomotives inherited and made great use of by the Southern is conveyed in these biographies of four tank locomotives.

2329

By 1913 the LB&SC was well equipped with modern passenger locomotives for all but the heaviest express services and tended to rely on its eleven Atlantics and two J-Tanks, *Abergavenny* and *Bessborough*, for these important trains.

In his desire to furnish the company with additional express locomotives L.B. Billinton ordered five large tank engines of the 4–6–4 Baltic wheel arrangement. The first two of these, No 327 *Charles C. Macrae* and No 328 (unnamed), were turned out from Brighton works during 1914 but following some initial problems with stability and several minor derailments the construction of the remaining locos was temporarily postponed.

Class M7 0–4–4T, by now BR No 30108 working the Swanage branch. It is seen on 17 June 1957 after leaving Corfe Castle on the 4.23pm Swanage–Wareham. Unusually the locomotive is not carrying a headcode disc. There should be one at the centre of the buffer beam. There is a fine mixture of stock, two Maunsells, a corridor brake composite and a second open, and three LSWR non-corridors.

Very much Great Days of the Southern. West Country Pacific No 34008 Padstow leaves Southampton Central with a down express from Waterloo bound for Bournemouth West. The tender carries the first BR emblem dating the picture as around the mid 1950s as the engine is clean but scarcely ex-works. The signal cabin and name Southampton Central are typically Southern as are the upper quadrant signals. The shed code is 70A Nine Elms.

The Southern Belle, later the Brighton Belle was the Central (ex-LBSCR) Sections major express. Running what was in effect a fast, supremely comfortable non-stop commuter service it carried many famous passengers as regular travellers. It was on this train that the actor Sir Laurence Olivier made that famous fuss when kippers were temporarily withdrawn from the breakfast service. The last Belle ran on 30 April 1972 and the Pullman coach units were dispersed far and wide, many to end up as sections of private restaurants using a railway theme.

The up Brighton Belle in Pullman livery with the small yellow warning panel at Brighton station in June 1968. The train was in unit sets; here 5BEL, 3051 leads 3052. Note the name on the roof boards and the stencil route indicator.

110

Ex-LBSCR Terrier 0–6–0 tank (as Brighton works departmental engine) No DS377 on a Locomotive Club of Great Britain special, The Rother Valley Limited coming off the erstwhile Kent & East Sussex Railway at Robertsbridge on 19 October 1958. The K & ESR, independent until nationalisation, came into the Southern Region of BR. It was closed to traffic on 12 June 1961. In latter days trains did not run beyond Tenterden, the terminus for this special. Due to the short loops here another Terrier (No 32678) was attached to the furthest end of the train. Although No DS377 (old No 2635) was kept as a pet in Stroudley's 'improved engine green' at Brighton it was not preserved, being broken up in 1963.

One of the more authentic pieces of tourist line preservation, the Bluebell Railway, presently running from Horsted Keynes to Sheffield Park, had a special Cavalcade Day on 27 June 1982. Schools class No 928 Stowe double heads U class Mogul No 1618 (the second engine to be rescued from Barry scrap yard) on the 11.27 from Sheffield Park in Three Arches cutting.

Ex-LSWR class M7 0–4–4T No 30108 at Rogate & Harting on 26 January 1952 hauling the 12.35pm from Petersfield to Midhurst. The signal box is still extant but apparently only controls the points unlocked by a key on the train staff.

In the meantime both locos were towed to Brighton Works where No 327 was stripped down to the frames and fitted with a large well tank, while the original side tanks were modified so that the water depth was restricted to 15 inches. *Charles C. Macrae* left the erecting shop for the second time in August 1915 and over the ensuing weeks was thoroughly tested before being released to normal traffic.

Because of the outbreak of war and the prolonged teething troubles of Nos 327 and 328, the remaining three engines of the initial order were cancelled in January 1916. However on the resumption of peace a further five Baltic Tanks were ordered to the modified design and thus No 329 *Stephenson* emerged from Brighton works in October 1921. In company with other members of the class it quickly settled in on the top-link express duties while working from Brighton shed and soon earnt a good reputation for fast running.

When almost one year old, on 30 September 1922, No 329 received an unexpected surprise when it ran off the turntable at Brighton. The loco demolished an 8ft high brick wall and came to rest in the adjacent roadway, injuring a pedestrian. At the subsequent inquiry the driver was admonished for manoeuvering a superheated engine within the shed yard without having the cylinder drain cocks open.

112

At Grouping the class represented the only tank engines of the Baltic wheel arrangement to be taken into SR stock and *Stephenson* was duly painted in the Maunsell green livery during September 1925, receiving at the same time a set of standard Southern cast nameplates in place of the previously painted version.

Up until 1930 all the Baltic tanks had been overhauled at Brighton works but in April that year No 329 was sent to Eastleigh for repair instead. The economics of this decision must be questioned as before leaving Brighton the loco had to have its cab roof, safety-valve casing, dome cover and chimney removed because they were outside the Western Section loading gauge.

As completion of the electrification of the Brighton line approached all seven Baltic tanks were transferred to Eastbourne in 1933 where they were put to good use on express duties for the next two years. However, with the spectre of electrification following them to Eastbourne, a decision as to their future had to be made fairly rapidly, some commentators predicting their early demise. Fortunately the boilers and frames were still in excellent condition so withdrawal was avoided by Maunsell deciding to rebuild them all as 4–6–0 tender engines for services on the Western Section.

No 2329 *Stephenson* was the first to enter Eastleigh works for rebuilding and it emerged as N95X 4–6–0 on 6 December 1934. Sent to Nine Elms it initially saw regular outings on their Bournemouth express turns, but although on paper the rebuilds were considered to be the equal of a King Arthur 4–6–0, in practice it was a different matter and as a result No 2329 *Stephenson* and her sisters were soon relegated to main line semi-fasts and excursion traffic.

Early in World War II it was becoming increasingly difficult to keep the

Last Steam to Brighton
December 31, 11.45pm. The last steam train of all the hundreds of thousands which have made their way to Brighton stands at No 16. *Stephenson* backs down and couples on.

Eleven-fifty. Passengers busily take their seats. Few know, fewer care, that they are passengers in a train that will go down to history. Some stroll up and take a glance at *Stephenson* and hurriedly go back to their compartments. The clock snicks over from 1932 to 1933. 'Tis well indeed our old friend
continued overleaf

LBSC class L 4–6–4T as SR No B329 Stephenson *is seen here in its first Southern Railway livery of olive green applied in September 1925. Unusually, the two members of the class which retained their names in SR days while still tank engines carried their number and the word 'Southern' on the bunker.*

continued

steam has lasted into the New Year.

12.03am. I climb up and tie a large black bow on *Stephenson's* smoke-box, a last tribute from the RCTS.

12.05am. At last the guard's lamp turns green and swings on high, driver Rogers takes a look at the Sykes banner signal in its neat glass case. All clear, All clear, for the last steam train to Brighton! He gives the short regulation blast on the whistle, and edges over the regulator. The driving wheels of the mighty tank engine slip just half a turn and bite. A long, long blast on the whistle, not for regulation this time, but for farewell, farewell.

Stephenson seems to know, as he gathers his train behind him with smooth steady acceleration, that it is his last chance to show that he too knows the meaning of the word; that electricity has not the sole monopoly of this quality. Driver and fireman wave their caps; the little group left on the platform wave back, Pullman car attendants and guard wave back again, and three resounding cheers crash and echo and re-echo under the steamy roof. The last triumphant pall of steam swirls down and tries in vain to hide the bright red eye which is the tail lamp of the 12.5 to Brighton.

The lights of platform 16 switch out in little jerks, and the high glass roof settles down for her short night's repose; perhaps to dream of other famous engines, engines brown and engines yellow, that she has sped on their way to the south, before the days of Southern green. And the small band of us who have known, and loved the steam engines of the Brighton line since boyhood days, sadly, sadly, and slowly, slowly, make our way along the darkened platform, for the last steam train to Brighton has gone. – *Railway Observer*.

class fully occupied and when the Great Western Railway requested additional motive power in 1941, the SR not surprisingly were quick to despatch Nos 2327 and 2332 to their neighbour. *Stephenson* saw duty at Newton Abbot and Exeter sheds until the arrival of new Swindon built LMS class 8F 2–8–0s made its presence on the GWR unnecessary and it duly returned to Nine Elms in July 1943.

After the war, large scale construction of Bulleid Pacifics saw the former tanks move en masse again, this time to Basingstoke as replacements for the U class 2–6–0s on the Waterloo, Reading and Portsmouth services. Following Nationalisation *Stephenson* received its BR No 32329 in December 1948 but did not lose its malachite green livery until April 1950 when BR lined black was applied.

The class was kept fairly busy at Basingstoke but with the arrival of the BR standard Classes between 1953 and 1955 this really was the end for the former Baltic tanks and the first, No 32328 *Hackworth*, was condemned in January 1955. Before receiving its final call *Stephenson* was used twice on railtour duty. The first of these, on 23 June 1956, saw it return to the Brighton main line (its first visit in rebuilt form) with a special from London Bridge, while its last day in service, 8 July 1956, was spent hauling the RCTS 'Wessex Wyvern' railtour from Andover to Waterloo during which it achieved a recorded speed of 80mph.

A fitting end indeed to a career which spanned 35 years and over 1,119,000 miles. The final *coup de grace* took place at Brighton works later that month.

108

When Dugald Drummond took over from William Adams as locomotive superintendent of the LSWR in 1895 he initially allowed completion of various orders placed for engines of Adams' design, albeit with minor detail differences in external finish and the like. In 1897 the first locomotives of Drummond's own design were introduced, these being a series of 0–4–4 passenger tank engines not unlike those of his predecessor in some ways but quite different in others.

The first 55 of these Class M7 engines were turned out from Nine Elms between March 1897 and October 1900 and to start with they found work on semi-fast main line passenger services on the Waterloo–Portsmouth, Bournemouth–Weymouth and Exeter–Plymouth routes. Such prestigious duties for a relatively humble tank engine design soon came to an end however when No 252 was derailed at speed near Tavistock on 6 March 1898. Although the state of the track was partly to blame the wisdom of using tank engines without leading bogies on fast passenger work was seriously questioned and thereafter the class was confined principally to suburban and similar work.

No 108 was the first of a batch of five M7s built to order No C12 at Nine Elms in 1904 and it quickly settled down to a busy but unspectacular existence during its period under LSWR ownership. After the Grouping in 1923 the SR gave all their newly acquired motive power a prefix to distinguish between identically numbered locomotives from each of the pre-Grouping companies and also to signify which works had

SR class N15X 4–6–0 No 2329 Stephenson in post-war malachite green livery applied in November 1947. The photograph was taken at Nine Elms probably in 1948 as No 863 is also in SR livery.

The nameplate of N15X class No 32329 Stephenson in June 1956 with its subsidiary identification 'Remembrance class' below. The engine is in rather grubby BR lined black livery.

Squeezing Out the Mileage
Steam locomotives on the Southern were cared for by their allocated depots, and when a number of King Arthurs were transferred to Heaton on the LNER in 1942 it
continued overleaf

continued

was complained that their condition rapidly deteriorated because of the 'common user methods in vogue on the East Coast main line'. But electrics were different. Even before the war the out-and-back to the same depot pattern had been abandoned for them as ever greater mileages were squeezed from them. By 1939 half the mileage run on the Southern was by electrics though the number of units was far below that of steam locomotives.

This is a roster for one set in early 1939, much more akin to today's railway practice than that of pre-nationalisation days. It covers nearly all the Eastern section:

continued opposite

Southern Railway class K1 2–6–4T No A890 River Frome *at Bricklayers Arms in July 1927. It is seen here in original condition with Holcroft derived valve gear.*

responsibility for maintenance and repairs. In the case of former LSWR engines this was Eastleigh and accordingly No 108 became No E108 and ran thus adorned until the renumbering of SECR and LBSCR stock in July 1931 allowed removal of the prefix.

By this time No 108 was operating from Feltham shed and therefore remained a common sight in the London area right up until its move down to Bournemouth in 1934. While based here it made its first acquaintance with the Swanage branch, frequently double-heading with the T9 4–4–0s on summer specials to this popular South coast resort.

A further move to Guildford followed in the late 1930s and this particular M7 was destined to remain here right up until Coronation year in 1953, acquiring its new BR number, 30108, in 1949. The Guildford M7s had quite a mixed diet of work to keep them occupied and No 30108 seems to have been a frequent performer on the local duties to Reading South and Horsham. Occasional forays were also made over the five mile branch to Bordon which left the Woking to Alton line at Bentley, in addition to working the final week of passenger services on the equally short branch line between Brookwood and Bisley Camp in July 1952.

In February 1953 No 30108 was transferred to former LBSCR territory at Horsham. The shed here was rather unusual in design, consisting of a half-roundhouse with the turntable out in the open, not dissimilar to the arrangement at Guildford albeit on a smaller scale. The handful of M7s based at Horsham were principally used on the Guildford and East

Grinstead lines although they were just as commonly seen on the Pulborough–Midhurst–Petersfield push-pull services before withdrawal of these unremunerative trains in February 1955. There were also times when No 30108 worked down to Brighton via Shoreham and on more than one occasion it was 'borrowed' to help out with station pilot duties at Brighton, a task which sometimes involved hauling 10 coach trains of empty stock out of the station. A far cry form its normal 2 coach load!

In June 1956 No 30108 made its final move back to Bournemouth and was quickly put to work on the service across to Brockenhurst via Ringwood, a route with which it was to remain associated until closure of the line in May 1964, an event leading to the locomotive's own demise. In the interim, however, No 30108 had a spell as regular engine on the Swanage branch during the summer of 1963, while in March of that year it hauled the Railway Enthusiasts' Club 'Rambling Rose' railtour of Southern lines.

This tour included in its itinerary a trip down the Bulford Camp branch near Salisbury as well as over the remnants of the Basingstoke to Alton line. During this excursion a number of small rose transfers were applied to the cabside of No 30108 and thus for the remainder of its career this engine was affectionately known to railwaymen as 'Rosie'.

The withdrawal or dieselisation of local services led to No 30108's redundancy in May 1964 and during the summer of that year it was towed all the way to Ward's at Briton Ferry in Glamorgan to be reduced to scrap metal during October.

890

To all intents and purposes Maunsell's Class K1 2–6–4T was a tank version of his earlier N1 2–6–0 design but with 6ft coupled wheels, the tender replaced by side tanks and the provision of a trailing bogie and coal bunker.

Destined to be the sole representative of its class No A890 *River Frome* left Ashford works on 1 December 1925. Following a successful period of running-in on the Ashford to Tonbridge services it was sent to Bricklayers Arms for main line work and was regularly rostered for the heavy 6.00pm Charing Cross–Dover Priory. Resplendent in SR green with red background to the nameplates this massive yet well proportioned machine must have made an impressive sight at the head of its train.

It soon transpired however that the riding qualities of *River Frome*, together with that of the earlier Class K River tanks, were frequently a source of complaint by engine crews. Work had just commenced on modifications to overcome this problem when A890 derailed itself at 60mph near Wrotham on the Otford–Ashford line, on 31 March 1927. This was soon followed by another derailment near Bearsted on 20 August and unfortunately culminated just four days later with the accident involving A800 *River Cray* at Sevenoaks when thirteen passengers lost their lives.

At once all 21 examples of the K and K1 classes were withdrawn pending the findings of the official inquiry. To gain information on the instability or otherwise of these 2–6–4Ts, arrangements were made for two locomotives (A803 *River Itchen* and A890 *River Frome*) to be sent for

continued

5.00am	Herne Hill sidings to Blackfriars.
5.28am	Blackfriars to Dartford.
6.18am	Dartford to Cannon Street
7.05am	Cannon Street to Gravesend.
8.05am	Gravesend to Charing Cross.
9.10am	Charing Cross to Sevenoaks.
10.08am	Sevenoaks to Cannon Street.
11.02am	Cannon Street to Orpington.
11.45am	Orpington to Holborn Viaduct.
12.31pm	Holborn Viaduct to Sevenoaks.
1.46pm	Sevenoaks to Holborn Viaduct.
2.55pm	Holborn Viaduct to Herne Hill.
3.12pm	Herne Hill to Holborn Viaduct.
3.31pm	Holborn Viaduct to Sevenoaks.
5.03pm	Sevenoaks to Cannon Street.
5.53pm	Cannon Street to Bromley North.
6.28pm	Bromley North to Charing Cross.
6.59pm	Charing Cross to Bromley North.
7.35pm	Bromley North to Cannon Street.
8.06pm	Cannon Street to Dartford.
8.57pm	Dartford to Charing Cross.
9.48pm	Charing Cross to Bromley North.
10.18pm	Bromley North to Charing Cross.
10.48pm	Charing Cross to Bromley North.
11.20pm	Bromley North to Charing Cross.
11.53pm	Charing Cross to Dartford.
12.40 mdt	Dartford to Slades Green.

Disappeared Into The Night

It must have happened often but without the same consequences.

The signalman at Swanage tucked the locomotive of the day's last rain into the depot, shut off the lights and locked up without giving 'train out of section' to his opposite number at Corfe Castle with whom, at the best of times, relationships were strained.

Instead of telephoning a few minutes after the train should have reached journey's end, when Swanage signal box would still have been open, the Corfe man waited (of course earning overtime) until his call was ignored – and then called Control.

Control's first reaction was that had anything been wrong someone would have heard about it by now, but on reflection felt that a referral to its higher authority could not be simply ignored. So the police were called out.

They first went to the station which, of course, they found in darkness and then woke the station master who went with them to the signalman who by this time was, of course, also fast asleep.

Only when the signalman was dragged back to his box was the Corfe man's overtime terminated. Next day the whole branch and most people in Swanage and Corfe Castle were expressing their views on the incident.

Numerous were the occasions when signalmen failed to turn up to open their boxes in time, and there were even stories of half awake bobbies forgetting to announce their arrival and going about housekeeping chores while the day's first train waited at the next box.

But generally the Southern worked with great precision and failure to send 'train entering section' (so that the box ahead could prepare the way) was seen as a serious offence – so rarely committed that many signalmen never experienced a single instance in their whole career.

running trials on the LNER main line between Huntingdon and St Neots. These trials were supervised by Nigel Gresley and both engines ran smoothly at up to 80mph on this well maintained section of track. Yet when comparative trials were run on the Western Section main line between Woking and Walton the locomotives rolled and bucked alarmingly at speeds of only 55 to 60mph.

The overall findings concluded that the River tanks were unsuitable for the relatively inferior track and because it did not make sense to have 21 locomotives out of traffic until a lengthy programme of permanent way renewals could be completed, it was decided to rebuild them all as tender engines.

So A890 *River Frome* entered Ashford works on 10 April 1928 and over the next two months was stripped of the tank engine's details and converted into the nameless prototype of the U1 class 2–6–0s. Its career in this new form began at Bricklayers Arms, mainly on the Hastings expresses, although during February and March 1929 it also ran in trials between Bournemouth and Weymouth and over the Portsmouth direct line.

Not over popular with the enginemen at Bricklayers Arms A890 was transferred to Battersea in April 1929 for the Kent Coast services. Renumbered 1890 at the beginning of 1932 this locomotive also had a brief spell at Eastbourne and Nine Elms before travelling down to Exmouth Junction in the Autumn of 1937 to provide additional power on the Plymouth road. No 1890's wanderings continued with a reallocation to Guildford in October 1939 and then Redhill in August 1942 for goods and passenger service over the Reading to Redhill line.

Throughout World War II the U1s were often seen on freight working and because of their excellent route availability were in demand during 1944 for use on the numerous troop and equipment specials in connection with the D-Day landings, No 1890 reaching Poole with just such a train in May that year.

By mid 1947 this locomotive had been transferred to Brighton for working the principal services to and from Victoria via Uckfield as well as on duties to Bournemouth, Salisbury and Tonbridge. However by early 1951 the availability of alternative motive power (including the Bulleid light Pacifics) meant the U1s were no longer required at Brighton and therefore the now renumbered 31890 was sent to Nine Elms, along with U class 31620/1 for trials on that depot's lighter main line duties. Two regular workings were the 9.40am Waterloo to Lymington and the 10.38am Waterloo to Swanage via Ringwood.

In the summer of 1953 No 31890 returned to Bricklayers Arms and once again was frequently seen at the head of fast trains to the Kent Coast although electrification of this route in June 1959 saw it move back to Brighton where this time its main source of employment was initially on the inter-regional workings to Willesden.

The period from October 1961 to December 1962 was spent at Three Bridges but 31890's last days were eked out at Brighton until June 1963 when it became the last of the class to be condemned. Its last melancholy duty was to haul E4 No 32468 and Schools No 30923 to Eastleigh where all three were reduced to scrap before the end of the year.

Class U1 2–6–0, BR No 31890, hauls a featherweight train, the 10.12am Sundays Hailsham to Eastbourne, on 25 March 1951; it is leaving the up platform at Hailsham. By now No 31890 has three sets of valve gear and smoke deflectors and is in BR lined black livery.

Ex-SECR class H 0–4–4T No 31184 leaves Brasted with a Westerham to Dunton Green pull-push train on 19 September 1952. The stock is the carriage portion of two ex-SECR steam railmotors.

Southampton or New York?

Until 1947 the American traveller arriving by liner at Southampton was under no illusions; he had arrived in England, and there to take him on to London was a green-painted boat train, though at its head an engine with a name such as *Sir Mador de la Porte* might have puzzled him. And in the background, fussing about with wagons, might well be one of the squat 33½ ton ex-LS&SWR B4 class 0–4–0 shunters (our American would have called it a switcher) dating from 1891–2, which worked the dock estate. Even then, if it happened to be *Honfleur*, *Havre* or *Caen* he might have begun to wonder on which side of the Channel he had landed.

But in that year, off went the little B4s to their Valhalla and in their place came fourteen easily identified 0–6–0 yard goats from the good old US of A. They might have Southern on their tank sides but their ancestry was clear from their bar frames, sand domes, stovepipe chimneys and domes carrying two safety valves and a whistle. They were wartime Pennsylvania products of the H.K. Porter Co of Pittsburgh and Vulcan Iron Works of Wilkes-Barre, built for the US Army in 1942 and shipped to Britain for war service in Europe.

The Southern snapped them up cheaply as surplus to replace the tired B4s. Their bunkers were raised to increase coal capacity – one US ton was insufficient to keep them going all day – and in later years they were fitted with radio equipment so that they could be directed about the docks according to need. They were based at the small three-road shed in the dock estate, and carried numbered 'target' discs on the top lamp bracket indicating their duty.

Their reign ended in 1962 and they were replaced by new machines in the form of the Ruston & Hornsby Class 07
continued opposite

1184

Because of rapid increase in suburban traffic, in this century's first years the South Eastern & Chatham Railway found itself hard pressed to maintain these financially lucrative services with the small Stirling and Kirtley tanks then available, so a new medium sized 0–4–4 passenger tank was designed by Harry Wainwright. The first of the Class H tanks left Ashford works in November 1904 and together with its sister locomotives settled in on the often demanding suburban and secondary passenger services on the South Eastern Section.

When Maunsell took charge at Ashford works in 1913 the story of this class took an unexpected twist. He noticed that although material for 66 Hs had been ordered and charged for, only 64 engines were actually on the books of the traffic department. The subsequent search established that all the parts of the missing two were in stock with the exception of the boilers. Fortunately at this time 15 spare pattern H boilers were on order from Kerr Stuart & Co; accordingly two of these were appropriated to complete the outstanding members of the class and Nos 16 and 184 duly entered traffic in July and April 1915 respectively, some five years after the last of the original H class had been built.

No 184 began its career based at Faversham shed in Kent and like No 16 was distinguishable from the earlier members of the class by having most of its brasswork omitted or covered with the modified Maunsell green livery. However in common with most other SECR engines at this time its number was painted on the tank sides in very large yellow figures, apparently in an attempt to provide readily decipherable numerals in connection with the new style of train control being carried out by the operating department.

No 184 remained in Kent right up to the formation of the Southern Railway although by 1931 (now renumbered 1184) it was operating from Ramsgate shed where amongst other duties it occasionally appeared on Margate to Ashford local services. For a period in the early months of World War II, together with sister loco No 1295, it acted as a temporary air-raid shelter at Ramsgate.

Even more unusual was the drafting of No 1184, along with Nos 1177 and 1259, to the LMS in Scotland at the beginning of 1943. Working from Forfar these three Hs were used on the local passenger workings to Arbroath and according to contemporary reports were kept in very clean condition in contrast to other locomotives in the area. This loan ended in August 1944 with No 1184 returning to SR duty at Stewarts Lane, Battersea.

There were several other members of the class allocated here and although they could be found on a wide assortment of work perhaps the most memorable among enthusiasts in the London area was on the empty coaching stock workings into and out of Victoria. Particularly notable were those engines which brought in the stock of heavy boat trains. In addition to providing steam heating during the winter months, these Hs were also required to bank the outgoing services from Victoria to help give a run at the 1 in 64 up to Grosvenor Bridge.

After years on this arduous work it was a relief to No 31184 (its new number in BR ownership) to be drafted to Tonbridge in April 1951 for local duties in Kent and Sussex. The diagrams were quite varied and No 31184 was kept fully occupied, more so when it was fitted with the necessary equipment for motor train working in June 1952. On occasions it was recorded on the Hawkhurst and Westerham branches as well as stopping trains on the Oxted to Tunbridge Wells West route. Oxted was only 26 miles from London and the presence of a relatively ancient looking locomotive on push-pull trains helped to create a distinctly rural atmosphere.

In its last few years in service No 31184 seems to have been a popular choice for the Paddock Wood to Maidstone West services. This particular H received its call to Ashford works for scrapping in March 1958.

continued
0-6-0 diesel-electric shunters. Firemen were no longer needed. Four of these US tanks live on in preservation to maintain the American influence in Britain. It is ironic that since parting company from BR two of them should have been named *Maunsell* and *Wainwright* after chief mechanical engineers of the Southern and one of its constituents. What would they have thought of these Yankee goats?

Southampton Docks
Class C14 0-4-0T No 30588 shunts in Southampton Docks on 24 July 1951. Built by the LSWR at Eastleigh in 1906 as a 2-2-0T for motor train work, and numbered 741, this small engine was rebuilt as an 0-4-0 shunting tank in 1922, and lasted until 1957. One wonders how much use was made of the vacuum brake equipment in this role. Note the splasher over the rear wheel which distinguished the rebuilds from 2-2-0T from those built as 0-4-0T.

USA 0-6-0T No 70, a product of the Vulcan Iron Works, Wilkes-Barre, Pennsylvania in 1943, marshals a boat train at Southampton New Docks on 7 April 1950. The engine, built as WD No 1960, was surplus after the war and bought with 13 colleagues plus one purchased solely for spares in 1946, being given various modifications before going into service in 1947. It was one of the last to be withdrawn in 1967 following the introduction of the class 07 0-4-0 diesel electric shunters in 1962, and is now to be found on the Kent & East Sussex Railway.

Round the Clock at Clapham Junction

For many travellers by Southern main line services in the 1930s Clapham Junction was little more than a name. A writer in *The Railway Magazine* of March 1940 commented that 'practically no main line trains call', and in the public timetables of the period it was not shown in the Western Section main line pages. The reference 'Main Line' in the index guided one to the Central Section table. Where Clapham Junction appeared in the Western Section suburban tables it was described in a note as 'Mid-Battersea, 1¼ miles from Clapham'.

Looking only at main line services gives a false impression of Clapham Junction, quickly corrected by the fact that in 1938 nearly 2,550 trains of all classes were dealt with or were passed through at the station every day. It was a place of round-the-clock activity, with work in the 52 rolling stock sidings of Clapham Yard going on through the night and platform staff on duty in the small hours to attend to one or two 'Kingston Roundabouts' and others. The working book for July to September 1930 showed a midnight departure for Southampton described as an emigrant special, tickets to be collected before departure. It crept away via Point Pleasant Junction and East Putney to join the main line at Wimbledon.

Milk traffic flourished in the small hours. Clapham is credited with the invention of an unloading ramp with steel runners which enabled churns to slide upright from van to platform without being trundled. The 1.15am from Wimbledon to Clapham performed an interesting 'milk round', travelling via Kingston, Twickenham and Richmond. Between 12.25am and 1.42 Clapham accommodated an LNER fish train, destination Portsmouth, while the 1.30 newspaper and parcels from Waterloo to Exeter ran through on the main line at 1.38. Fast freight trains to and from Nine Elms were also in evidence, the last of the down overnight services passing at 3.01am en route for Southampton, followed at 3.08 by the 3.0 ex-Waterloo newspaper and parcels to Plymouth, and at 3.25 by the 3.15 Waterloo–Exeter milk churns as empties began flowing back to the West Country. Clapham despatched empty churns to Yeovil at 11.35am, the train travelling via Chertsey and the Byfleet curve. The first down passenger to pass was the 4.50am Waterloo to Gosport via Medstead which ran through at 4.59.

There were numerous freight workings through Clapham between the northern companies and the Southern, with 13 LNER and 19 LMS trains to and from Longhedge Junction. Activities on the West London Extension line began with milk empties to Kensington at

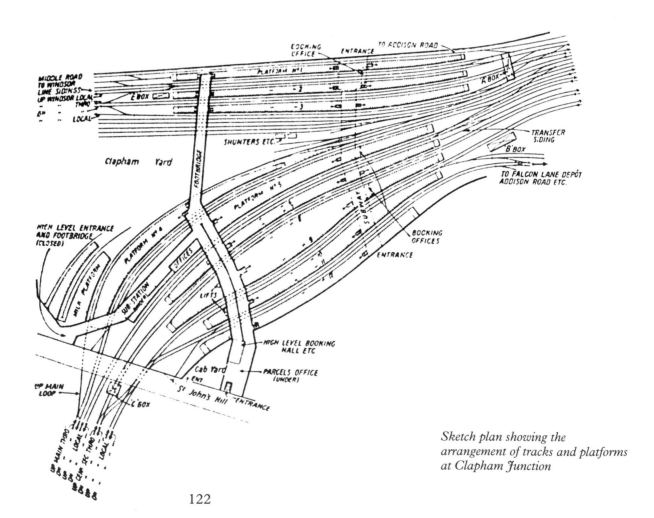

Sketch plan showing the arrangement of tracks and platforms at Clapham Junction

Clapham Junction looking from the Brighton side towards London. The LSWR lines are on the left and the Atlantic Coast Express is running on the down main line. The signal box is Clapham Junction A which partially collapsed with disastrous results onto the LSWR Windsor lines on 10 May 1965. There are at least 12 parallel running roads here, 8 LSWR to Waterloo and 4 LBSCR to Victoria plus connections to the West London Line.

4.20 and 5.33am, followed by the start of the passenger service at 6.5. From then to 7.43pm there were 22 departures. An ex-LNWR 'coal tank' from Willesden took a parcels train to East Croydon, while an ex-Midland engine, came to shunt the LMS's Clapham Junction freight yard and called at Falcon Lane.

The timetable provided 14 paths for boat trains from Waterloo between 6.33 and 11.47am, some of which had to be slotted in between portions of the Atlantic Coast Express. It was the age of Period Excursions and a special for holders of these tickets left at 12.28 on Fridays for Padstow and Plymouth.

Observers at Clapham Junction were rewarded by the spectacle of a sequence of freight trains passing on their way from Nine Elms to the West Country at 8.44, 9.41, 10.20 and 10.57pm. Post Office sorting carriages were conveyed in the 10.34pm passenger and mails service to Dorchester, returning with the service due Waterloo at 3.49am.

On the Brighton side of the station a number of down main line trains called in the evening rush hour and later, including Brighton 'fasts' with Pullman Cars at 7.11 and 10.12pm. Services from the coast calling at Clapham were more numerous, the trains arriving at intervals between 10.50am (from Hastings and Eastbourne) and 10.16pm (from Portsmouth). Four from Brighton and one from Portsmouth included Pullmans. In 1930 these were all steam trains. The Brighton's overhead electrification had been converted to third rail by September 1929 but there were nearly three years to go before the first electrics ran to the coast.

7
MAUNSELL AND BULLEID: A COMPARISON

IN its 25 years existence the Southern Railway had just two chief mechanical engineers. Richard Maunsell, who occupied the post until 1937, had laid a foundation of technical excellence on the South Eastern & Chatham and was happy to build on it by slow development. Let no one suppose, however, that he was a stick-in-the-mud; far from it. But he was jealous of his fine engineering reputation, and would do nothing to jeopardise it. His successor, Oliver Bulleid, an unbridled extrovert, was the very antithesis of what had gone before. Slow development of ideas was anathema. If OVB felt that something new was right it was absolutely useless to argue an alternative case. He was the fountainhead, and his design staff were there to translate his raw ideas into hard steel without question.

But let us not oversimplify their characteristics and draw dubious conclusions, for they functioned under very different circumstances. The Southern of the twenties and thirties was preoccupied with electrification, firstly of the London suburban area and then of longer tentacles reaching out to the south coast – Brighton, Hastings, Bognor and Portsmouth. Much of it might necessarily be done on the cheap, but still left little money to invest in new locomotives and rolling stock. Maunsell had perforce to keep elderly locomotives running rather than build new. Indeed, in 1937 when the depression of the early thirties was easing, *no* new locomotives were built for the Southern (In that year the GWR took into stock 150 new locomotives, the LNER 69 and the LMS no less than 266).

By 1940, in contrast, electrification was at a standstill under wartime stringency; no new scheme was implemented by the Southern after July 1939. But with traffic burgeoning and higher revenues forthcoming, not only was capital for new locomotives more readily available but operating needs demanded them. The Southern rightly saw, too, that when hostilities ended there would need to be major service improvements to meet rising public expectations. Only in the shortest of terms would restoration of immediate prewar standards satisfy the travelling public. Bulleid had no alternative (even if he had been so inclined) but to provide locomotives of greater power and rolling stock of new form to meet that demand.

Both Maunsell and Bulleid, in their very different ways, strove mightily for the Southern Railway and both on balance benefited it in the conditions of their period.

Maunsell's experience in Ireland before joining the South Eastern & Chatham in 1913 had been almost entirely on the works production side and he had little experience of the design. So when he took over at Ashford from an ailing Wainwright he recognised the need to assemble a

A down West of England eleven-coach express is ready to leave Templecombe, so the fireman takes a last opportunity to pull coal forward on the tender. The engine is No 35029 Ellerman Lines *based at Nine Elms and the date 1 August 1958. A year later she was being rebuilt in Eastleigh works and is now preserved sectioned at the NRM, to show how it worked.*

Pro Buff?

One often gets the feeling that had the Southern continued its independent existence it would have viewed railway enthusiasts far more kindly than the other railways. Ian Allan and his first *ABC*, published while he worked for the Southern, would have helped, but there were other straws in the wind.

Ten weeks before nationalisation, for example, the Southern celebrated the centenary of Ashford works with an illustrated history of the works and an exhibition of models and photographs. On show outside was a Stirling B1 4–4–0 built in 1898, rebuilt in 1927 and now waiting scrapping. One more further use for a piece of Victorian ironmongery as 'a representative of Ashford production'.

No 850 Lord Nelson, *the first of the class, is in charge of an up Continental Express, including at least one Pullman car, approaching Petts Wood in 1938. The smoke deflectors, fitted circa 1930, seem to be doing the job for which they were designed.*

The cab of a Nelson. The photograph was probably taken with the engine stationary; the regulator is shut and boiler pressure appears to be well down, though steam heat is being applied to the train. The driver is standing in front of the reversing wheel, his seat tipped up beside him. Note the large oilboxes for axlebox lubrication.

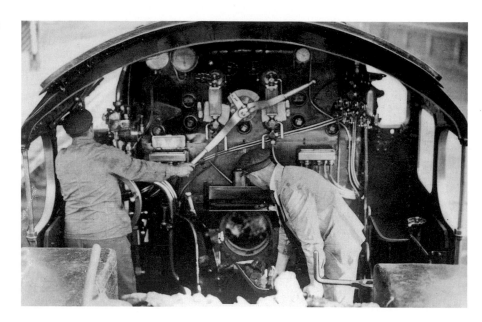

Island Rush

Both before and after World War 2, up to nearly 40,000 passengers arrived at Ryde Pier Head on the busiest summer Saturdays. A few walked, many went by tram, but the majority joined waiting trains. The comings and goings were on a grand scale; it was like peak commuting by sea. Well over a thousand passengers arriving by some boats, such as the *Southsea* and *Whippingham*, two large paddle steamers, the Southern introduced in 1930 and sometimes used for trips round the Isle of Wight or to view ocean liners in Southampton.

The smartness of connections and general organisation on summer Saturdays was outstanding, passenger movement made easier by the common use of passenger luggage in advance. Special PLA trains on Fridays were long a feature of the island's system. But there were of course occasional incidents. Bad weather could delay ships. One old lady refused to detain on arrival at Ryde Pier Head saying that the stationmaster at Shanklin had assured her that she had joined the Waterloo train.

team of competent specialist assistants. That comprised Pearson (Assistant CME and works manager) from Swindon, Clayton (chief locomotive draughtsman) from Derby, Lynes (leading carriage and wagon draughtsman) and Holcroft (works reorganisation assistant, later technical assistant, locomotives) both from Swindon. Ten years later that team translated smoothly into a Southern Railway organisation and remained intact until 1937.

Maunsell took care to work through, and encourage, this team. He would outline the requirements and his thoughts on how they might be met. The assistants had a fairly free hand to initiate the examination of new ideas and, if thought worth while, offer them to the chief, though nothing way out would be tolerated.

Maunsell's future policy in the locomotive field was straightforward; indeed, in large measure it might have been specified by Riddles on British Railways nearly thirty years later. It may be summarised: 1. Engines that were masters of the job, with wide route availability; 2. A minimum number of classes with maximum component standardisation; 3. Belpaire boilers of ample size; 4. Long lap piston valves operated by long travel valve gear; 5. Maximum simplicity and accessibility; 6. Comfortable, convenient cabs; 7. Efficient lubrication; 8. High capacity smokeboxes and ashpans for sustained steaming.

Applying these principles to his inheritance presented few problems. He could continue building his new SE&C 2–6–0 and 2–6–4T designs, dabbling with three-cylinder versions, for all three sections, though the catastrophic derailment of 2–6–4T No 800 *River Cray* at Sevenoaks in August 1927 blighted the use of large passenger tank engines for many years (even though the main culprit proved to be indifferent permanent way rather than the locomotive). The Brighton engines had no place in his plans, but the larger ones needed adaptation to the Southern's composite loading gauge. Urie's 4–6–0s from Eastleigh could be adapted for future construction, subject to improvements to cylinders, valve gear and draughting, together with modifications to bring them within the composite gauge. Only new traffic requirements would bring a need for new designs.

Of these it is sufficient to refer to the two most important. To haul 500 ton trains at average speeds of 55mph – the Eastern Section boat trains and the West of England expresses – the Lord Nelson 4–6–0 was produced in 1926. It was an all-new design built within tight weight limits. As it turned out, it was a very near miss, though Bulleid's later modifications proved beneficial. Maunsell himself was not wholly satisfied with the Nelsons, trying out a number of variants without clear advantage. Design work was also advanced on a modern four-cylinder compound conversion, for which authority was obtained in 1932, but this

London-bound from Hastings in the immediate post-war years, L1 class No 1754, a Dover engine is working hard with a train of narrow flat-sided stock as she tackles the 1 in 122 of Hildenborough bank. She is in wartime black with 'sunshine' lettering.

'Scotch Arthur' No 30784 Sir Nerovens *is on a humble duty, the 10.10 Weymouth–Eastleigh all stations train on 2 January 1951 approaching Southampton. Bulleid had fitted a new large-diameter fabricated chimney and multiple-jet blastpipe, and removed the Maunsell snifting valves on the smokebox. The first vehicle is NER in origin, possibly a conversion from a brake third.*

The pioneer Z class 3-cylinder 0–8–0 tank No 30950 is hard at work on the Eastleigh–Fawley freight as she accelerates away from Southampton on 27 January 1951.

Previous page *Redhill shed plays host to U class 2–6–0 No 31623 (allocated to Guildford) on 18 September 1960. Only a few Southern sheds had mechanical coaling plants; the remainder continued with elevated coal stages where 10cwt wheeled tubs were filled by hand from wagons and the contents tipped into the tender.*

Some Scheme

'Fresh negotiations are, we understand, taking place regarding the abandonment of the present Charing Cross terminus, and its replacement by a remodelled and enlarged Waterloo. The substitution of a through station in place of a terminus is being considered. There are many advantages to be gained by such a proposal – a reduction in area, saving in cost, and greater convenience to the public.'

So *The Locomotive* wrote in January 1929. But this largest of all possible Southern reorganisations was not to be, though *The Locomotive* persisted in supporting it. In September 1930 it compared the proposal with a station merger in Philadelphia, and concluded:

'Although the substitution of the two termini, Waterloo and Charing Cross, with one handsome, *through* station, has been stated to be impracticable by some of the expert advisers to the Government, County Council and railway company, we have not seen the reason why, and many still think a commodious and convenient *through* station, serving all the main line services of the Southern Railway, would be the best and most economical solution of the problem.'

Opposite *The Nine Elms coaling plant, built in 1922–3 to replace an elevated coal stage is masked by the smoke of Battle of Britain class 4–6–2 No 34071 601 Squadron in September 1958.*

was never proceeded with. A year later a Nelson Pacific with wide firebox was schemed out but foundered on civil engineering objections.

Maunsell's other *magnum opus* was the three-cylinder Schools 4–4–0, produced against a requirement to haul 400 ton trains at 55mph average while being capable of working the severely restricted gauge Tonbridge–Hastings line. The locomotive proved a winner which could tackle the heavy Bournemouth expresses on level terms with the 13-ton heavier Arthurs.

On the coaching side non-corridor pre-Grouping stock was altogether too prevalent on the long distance expresses of the twenties. Maunsell's corridor coaches were sound if not adventurous, steel panelled and with early adoption of Buckeye couplers and Pullman gangways, but retaining individual compartment doors with droplights. They might lack armrests and reading lights in the third class, but their seats with separate cushions were supremely comfortable. Until the early 1930s electric stock, of compartment type, was provided by pre-Grouping wooden bodies on new steel underframes. Bodies were lengthened (including the characteristic rounded cabs) to make up a standard length; in some cases two bodies from non-bogie stock were mounted on one underframe. Nothing usable was wasted. But all the express electric sets were built new to foster electrification's modern image, and it saw the first partial breakaway from compartment to saloon coaches, with end doors.

Maunsell's retirement in 1937, at a ripe 69, coincided with a major break-up of his long-standing support team, which particularly on the locomotive side eliminated any chance of continuity. In as CME came Oliver Bulleid from the LNER. At 55 years of age he had been Gresley's personal assistant and 'assistant to' for 25 years and was steeped in Doncaster philosophy, though with a strong independent streak which Gresley had needed to rein in. Meanwhile the Southern had tended to lean towards Swindon and Derby practice. Bulleid now had a much freer hand to follow his inclinations and took an active part in design. His technical assistants, Holcroft for locomotives and Lynes for carriages and wagons, were no longer active initiators in the design process; they were largely bypassed by Bulleid working directly with the chief draughtsmen and even with the men on the board.

Bulleid has been the subject of both adulation and fierce criticism for his locomotive designs. At least in the locomotive field, he was set a truly formidable task. The pre-war specification of 500 tons at 55mph average speed had been stepped up to weights of 550–600 tons at average speeds increased to 60mph on the shorter runs (eg Dover) and up to 70mph to the west. All this had to be done without axleloads exceeding 21 tons. No longer was this realistically within the capability of a narrow firebox, making a 4–6–2 the natural choice. Thus was the Merchant Navy conceived, followed four years later by the lighter West Country.

These Pacifics unquestionably set new performance standards. The operators could hang almost any train behind them and they would handle it with panache. To enginemen, being master of the job was far more important than their healthy appetite for coal. Their steaming was impeccable, their riding excellent and for the most part the cab was well-

Canadian Style
The 48½ sq ft of grate on a Merchant Navy Pacific severely taxed the fireman if the engine was being driven hard, while coal quality was gradually declining in the post-war years. So, Bulleid purchased a reconditioned Berkley mechanical stoker from Canada and fitted it to No 21C5 (later 35005) *Canadian Pacific* in
continued opposite

Dover shed was built in 1928 but did not have a mechanical coaling plant. Bulleid class Q1 0–6–0 No 33016, in filthy condition, gets its supply from the coal stage, while on the adjacent ash pit, in completely different style and fairly clean, Maunsell N class 2–6–0 No 31819 has its fire cleaned.

arranged and comfortable. There were various plus features to gladden the crews' hearts. Unfortunately they demanded high levels of maintenance and gave low availability in return. Bulleid's analysis – or gut feeling – of conventional locomotive problems was flawed and savoured of wishful thinking. Inside big end performance need not have been the weakness it was made out to be in justification for that dreadful oil bath and chain drive. From that decision sprang the unsatisfactory valve gear, the outside admission piston valves and other doubtful features. Throughout the design weight-saving was paramount. The use of thin flat plates for a non-circular smokebox shell, subject to exhaust pressure pulses, suggests a lack of engineering judgement. There was altogether too much thin welded sheet metal to stand up to the vibration of a moving locomotive. Their many weaknesses led to a programme of over 200 modifications; these were stop-gap measures, however, for only rebuilding in more conventional form (but still using most of the original locomotive) could provide good availability and acceptable operating costs. The penalty was a weight increase of just over 5 tons.

Bulleid never seemed satisfied unless his products were talked about and argued over – whether with praise or critically seemed to matter little. His class Q1 0–6–0 freight engine of 1942 was a step forward but visually

The second Co-Co electric locomotive of the Bulleid/Raworth partnership, No 20002 (originally No CC2 when built in 1945) about to leave one of the dog-leg platforms at Victoria with the 9.35am Newhaven boat train on 23 May 1949. These locomotives had four pickup shoes each side with a booster-generator set to provide continuous traction when passing through third rail gaps. The light pantograph for use in certain shunting yards provided with overhead wires can also be seen.

hideous; to many this was not only totally unnecessary but in some respects actively detrimental. Surely simple circular boiler clothing on crinolines, and a matching smokebox, would have been as light, cheaper and more robust than that imitation of a badly-built haystack.

His contribution to coaching stock design – and the requisite construction facilities – was considerable. Out went steel panels on a timber framework; in its place came all-steel construction with the characteristic body side curve and very slender section to provide maximum internal space. Individual compartment doors on corridor stock gave way to end and centre vestibule doors to allow quicker loading. Large numbers of suburban electric sets were built by similar construction techniques (largely using underframes built for their wooden-bodied predecessors), still with slam doors. The mixture of compartment and saloon vehicles was utilitarian rather than comfortable, but was a reasonable answer to London's commuter conditions of the time.

Bulleid will long be remembered less for this general coaching stock than for his two departures from convention, the 'tavern cars' for express services and the double-deck stock for the North Kent line. The outcry about the tavern cars, and their rapid modification, suggest another case of Bulleid plunging in without adequately consulting other interested departments. The double-deck electric sets were a highly ingenious exercise in getting 508 seats in the same train length as a conventional set's 386. But on intensive services, to try to coax 22 passengers through a single door into a complex space on two levels, not all of which was visible from the platform, without exceeding the frequent 15–30 second station stops on which the service depended, was something which this concept could never solve.

continued
March 1948, the first such application in Britain.

On trials it was well liked by enginemen but showed that there was a threshold of coal quality below which it could not be successfully burnt. It also suffered because, being a one-off example, it could not be supplied with coal of graded size from a normal coaling plant, a problem which also afflicted the three Saltley-based BR Standard 2–10–0s fitted in the mid-1950s. The trial with No 35005 ended in 1951.

Island Specials

Anyone visiting the Isle of Wight in Southern days (and well into nationalisation) was amazed at the variety of the island's railways: busy main lines, quiet branch ones, alternative routes, freight trains… and once even specials.

The evening freights to and from the substantial Medina Wharf near Newport were cancelled on the Friday night of the illuminations and fireworks of Cowes Regatta, for example, when 5,000 passengers were carried from various starting points.

Once there were even race specials, perhaps 2,000 passengers from Ryde and 1,000 from Newport going to the Ashey race-course. It more or less ended its career when the grandstand burned down in 1930.

Ugly duckling! Q1 class 0–6–0 No 33007 is working a ballast train in the early 1950s on the Western Section. While the chassis was very conventional (apart from the absence of side platforms) the flat-bottomed smokebox and boiler casing gave the impression that they had been designed to fit something different!

It was Bulleid's last fling, however, which showed him as the innovator for innovation's sake. There was a stated traffic requirement for a passenger tank engine to replace the elderly L&SWR class M7 0–4–4 tanks and the superannuated 4–4–0s working local services west of Exeter. It was the work for which, in BR days, Class 2 and 3 2–6–2 tanks and Class 4 2–6–4 tanks were built and were ideal. But such straightforward locomotives were alien to Bulleid's thinking. He offered a vague but complex double bogie engine which was surprisingly accepted by the Southern top management. Having received authority for five, he piled unconventional Pelion on unproven Ossa to incorporate the greatest number of untried concepts ever assembled in one locomotive. He had created a monster; it was engineering gone mad. Not only that, but by late 1950 costs of £179,000 had been incurred in getting one engine completed for testing and four more in various stages of erection – this at a time when BR standard 2–6–4 tanks were being built for £15,000 apiece! The decision to scrap without ever entering service was inevitable.

How, then, will posterity look back on these two men? Each in his own way was dedicated to keeping the Southern in the front rank of locomotive development and in creditable coaching stock. Maunsell sought this end through teamwork, sound conventional engineering and a willingness to experiment with new developments on a small scale basis until proved one way or the other. He ran a tight ship at a time when it *had* to be tight, and was highly regarded within his own department and by other colleagues. In contrast Bulleid was the brilliant individualist, difficult to work with amicably despite his charm, persuasive with non-engineers, a boiling cauldron of ideas often applied to shaky engineering appreciations, eager to make the next great step forward even while teetering on the last. He reigned at a time when the national psyche was full of hope for achievement, though his own was marred by mistakes – for which he was unapologetic. All in all, a fascinating pair of diametrical opposites.

Holiday At Bexhill

In the 1930s Bexhill was a very superior resort, home to the retired gentry; it suffered rather than relished the summer holiday season, looking down its nose at Hastings but tolerating Eastbourne. The old LB&SCR coast line was a 1935 candidate for electrification but until then the steam services through Bexhill Central were fascinating for those who had an interest in elderly engines but less intriguing to small boys who wanted to see the new sparkling modern 'Schools' which they had read about in the *Meccano Magazine* or, for a rare treat, in *The Railway Magazine*. Most trains seemed to be hauled by antiquarian 4–4–0s – foreigners in the form of ex SE&CR F class from St Leonards shed and diminutive 0–4–2 tanks with a huge single coach working push-pull. Central was truly central in practice as well as in name and only a few steps from the grandeur of the almost adjacent Granville Hotel or Drusilla's Tea Rooms.

There were two highlights of the day. The early riser caught a 4–6–2 tank on the van train from Polegate to Hastings. In the afternoon around 4.30pm another 4–6–2 tank was often found on the final leg of the Sunny South Express from the LMS and the Birkenhead through service from the GWR. By then these Marsh engines led a highly leisured existence due to their displacement from main line express duty with the Brighton line electrification. Then there was Galley Hill gas works at the far east end of the town which was supplied with coal usually

Bexhill West was a late venture by the SECR opened in 1902. Everything was on a grand scale, four platforms, two signal boxes and a large goods yard. Traffic never came up to expectations and only one island platform was used regularly. H class 0–4–4T No 31162 is seen on the 12.19 to Crowhurst on 17 May 1958. The whole lot closed on 15 June 1964.

brought in by a class C2X 0–6–0 which was an object of awe as it was fitted with two domes. The other possibility was a Billinton E4 class 0–6–2 tank from Eastbourne shed, often No 2561. So if one wanted railway excitement

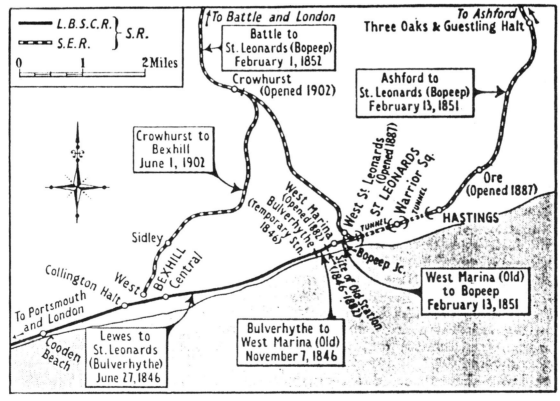

Chronological map of the railways in the Hastings area, showing pre-grouping ownership

Bexhill West No 1 signal box on 23 March 1959 with H class No 31161 shunting stock, the usual two coaches. This signal box had a 123 lever frame of which 80 levers were in use at first but this was much reduced in later years.

The elaborate exterior of Bexhill West station on Tuesday 28 July 1953. There is a wonderful collection of parked vintage cars including a number of pre-war vehicles.

(there was not much of this anywhere at any time in Bexhill) it meant spending holiday pocket money on an afternoon outing to Eastbourne or Hastings; as this was short it was usually Hastings as this enabled a good look at the Schools and a glimpse of St Leonards shed between the tunnels as the train stopped in the station. By 1933 the shed had E904 *Lancing* and E907/908/909 went there new. By 1935 there were twelve Schools there, 900–911. Hastings seemed 'modern' (it was completely rebuilt in 1931) and comparatively full of bustle with the fasts coming down from London and sights of newer looking engines for, until electrification of the LBSC line, the Schools only worked the fast trains, the others being left to the L class 4–4–0s. On weekdays, if one returned in the early evenings there were other interesting sights for boys from the Midlands – returning city gents in pin stripes and bowlers – all very respectable. And there were Pullmans too; commuters could travel in extra comfort for a modest supplement – in those days the 3rd class monthly return from London to Bexhill was 11/3d (55½p).

Later holidays found electrification in place with the remarkable 2NOL sets (a real mark of Southern economy) briskly trading along the lengths of the south coast from Worthing in the west to Ore in the east. Somehow this gave everything a much more lively feeling (especially if one were riding over the leading bogies of a 2NOL) than before. It seemed strange to see the daily LMS and GW through trains still steam hauled and still behind their huge tanks. Freight, such as it was, of course, was still steam. Later one learnt that this 'new' electric stock was

far from the case; only the underframe and electric traction equipment was new, the coach bodies were all re-used pre-Grouping equipment easily distinguished by their door commode handles and also by the numerical designation of the sets (for example the 1400 series was of SE&C origin and the 1700s LBSC with LSW examples from 1200).

The other option was to go to Bexhill West – right on the edge of town whereas Central was just as its name implied – and then via the double tracked but lightly used four miles long branch of the erstwhile SE&C from Crowhurst on the Charing Cross to Hastings line. This was not opened until 1902 whereas the South Eastern had reached Hastings some 50 years earlier in 1852. Overall it was nine miles shorter distance to Bexhill this way but there was always the problem of a change of trains and a longer walk (for most) at the end. Here was another juxtaposition – ex SE&C 4–4–0s helped out the Marsh engines on the coast line but Brighton class D3 0–4–4 tanks worked out of Bexhill West. St Leonards shed had an allocation of six of these, No 2374 being the usual Bexhill West branch engine. The station, a single large island platform always seemed cold and draughty and the whole very much the poor relation, although it managed a reasonably ample station entrance building complete with the customary clock tower.

Crowhurst was a typical small country station with a bay platform for the Bexhill trains. Its big advantage was that everything stopped there and one could have a good look at the 'Germans' as the drivers called the large splasher Ls, and (with some awe) the Schools. Though one only admits to this in later years, it was possible to get on a Hastings bound train and make the journey there and back without a ticket! All it needed was the ability to read the timetable.

One last memory of that railway scene was the proliferation of tunnels. From west to east one encountered Bo-peep tunnel (between Bo-peep junction and St Leonards Warrior Square), Hastings tunnel (between Warrior Square and Hastings), Mount Pleasant tunnel (between Hastings and Ore) and Ore tunnel (east of Ore). The restrictive bore of Bo-peep tunnel meant that the LB&SCR and its successor, the SR, were precluded from using their Baltic tanks on the Hastings expresses via the coast route, much to their vexation; and the general hemmed in nature of central Hastings must have been one of the prime reasons for the electrification of 1935 reaching the comparatively unknown outpost of Ore. It certainly allowed good carriage servicing facilities there.

On Foreign Lines

Largely because it was first and foremost a passenger railway, the Southern took a considerable number of trains from the adjoining LMS and GWR — and of course the heavy summer holiday traffic over the Somerset & Dorset Joint line. There was also that peculiar routing whereby all Southern trains for North Devon and Cornwall had to run (in the opposite direction to GW services) through Exeter St David's station to Cowley Bridge Junction.

The following photographs catch glimpses of Southern engines in foreign territory, including the triumphant Bulleid Pacifics running in the Locomotive Exchanges of 1948.

Somerset & Dorset Joint where the Southern's influence was strengthened by introduction of West Country class 4–6–2s in the early 1950s. A real joint train heading for Bournemouth on 23 August 1952 hauled by S & D 2–8–0 BR No 53808 (still retaining its large boiler) and SR West Country class 4–6–2 No 34095 Brentor *at Masbury Summit.*

Oxford on 13 August 1956 with two SR locomotives on parade. On the left is King Arthur class 4–6–0 No 30789 Sir Guy *with a York to Bournemouth train via Reading West curve (therefore not needing to reverse), thence over Southern metals. On the right is No 30783 Sir Gillemere with the return service Bournemouth to York.*

Reading General as it was in February 1956 with U class 2–6–0 No 31799 (rebuilt from 2–6–4T No A799 River Test) *on an up express freight. The Southern locomotive had probably worked the train from Moreton Cutting near Didcot to the South Eastern section via the wartime connection at Reading.*

Exeter St David's taken from the water tank in June 1962, with N class 2–6–0 No 31845 leaving on a ballast train from Meldon Quarry to Exmouth Junction. The train would be banked up the 1 in 36 probably at this date by a class Z 0–8–0T.

In foreign territory. The locomotive exchanges of 1948 brought SR locomotives to many unusual locations. Merchant Navy class No 35019 French Line CGT passing Beeston Junction Leeds with the 7.40am Leeds Central to Kings Cross. This was a preliminary run on 18 May 1948, a week previous to the actual trial with dynamometer car.

8
BUSTLE AND VARIETY: THE LONDON TERMINI

MURDERERS, royalty, diplomats, film stars, adulterers, sailors, generals, prime ministers, and humble, conforming bowler-hatted commuters in their thousands – all were accepted and disgorged by the SR's seven London termini. These ever-busy stations could offer a great variety of activity, with commuting and holiday journeys always the underlying base. Their already considerable traffic was steadily augmented between 1926 and 1939 with the relentless spread of electrification. By 1938–39 this development had moved the boundaries of the Southern's commuter area to the Sussex Coast and the London end of Hampshire, creating intermediate traffic nodes fed by buses and commuters' cars at places like Haywards Heath and Haslemere. Electrification also increased the profitable daily off-peak traffic into London by over 55 per cent between 1925 and 1938, from 82,300 to 128,000. Yet despite this advance, steam remained present at all seven stations right up to the disappearance of the SR at the end of 1947. Interest was always maintained.

There was less impact on the inherited architecture, which the Southern hardly touched, although the Luftwaffe did what it could to alter things. Electrification did however prompt the Southern to make some important track, signalling and platform changes. And, as we shall see, there was a plan to completely re-site one terminus, which came to nought.

Flagship Waterloo

The L&SWR London terminus held undeniable pride of place throughout the quarter century of the Southern's life. Here the SR took over a station that had just undergone almost total rebuilding on the most up to date lines. It had everything going for it: expresses to the West Country; boat trains for America and France; a healthy variety of special events business (Ascot, *the* Boat Race, International Rugby, a share in the Derby); and a diurnal flood of commuters dwelling in some of London's choicest residential districts. And, overlooking its great curving concourse across the heads of all 21 platforms, were the company's headquarters offices, with the managers ever-present to keep an eye on it all.

Electric trains had been a feature of Waterloo's South Side since 1915–16 but the Southern added many more, until by 1939 the whole of the former L&SWR suburban district was theirs alone, together with the strategically important main lines to Portsmouth and Aldershot and the Windsor and Reading routes. The nature of the area served ensured that Waterloo had a busy war and many a serviceman and his girl experienced

Coal-Oil-Coal

In August 1946 the Minister of Transport announced a plan to convert 1217 locomotives on the four British railways to oil firing to relieve supply problems of coal suitable for locomotive use. The Southern's share was to be 110 engines based at Fratton, Eastleigh and Exmouth Junction, the thinking being that coal would be eliminated from whole districts irrespective of the types of locomotive working there. Large fuelling installations were built at these three depots, with small outbased facilities intended at a number of others.

In fact only 32 locomotives were converted before the scheme collapsed in the autumn of 1947 due to shortage of foreign currency to import the oil. The fuelling installations were quickly abandoned, and soon again coal reigned supreme. The locomotives were:

N15 King Arthur	5
WC West Country	1
D15	1
N	1
U	2
T9	13
L11	8
'Terrier' tank	1

The fuelling installations at the three depots were abandoned. The remainder were never completed.

Waterloo station looking over the main line departure platforms towards the 'Windsor' side in the mid 1950s. A Southampton Docks boat train is leaving behind Lord Nelson 4-6-0 No 30859 Lord Hood. *To its left is a Portsmouth Direct electric and behind the luggage van is an H16 class 4-6-2T, no doubt on an empty carriage train to Clapham Junction. The shot tower on the South Bank had not been demolished when this picture was taken and can be seen behind the Royal Festival Hall. The Windsor side is, of course, to be the London International terminus for trains via the Channel Tunnel.*

sad partings and joyous greetings under its blacked-out roof, perhaps whiling away the time as they waited for a train, in the cinema that had been opened at the south end of the concourse in 1934. German bombs, some 50 in all, wrought havoc both within the station and its immediate approaches in 1940 and 1941, stopping all trains for a time. But the efficiency and dignity of the place were soon enough restored. 1940 also saw modernisation of the tube trains that carried Waterloo's commuters on to the City but little or nothing was done to brighten the lavatorial subterranean premises of this curious Southern sideline.

Victoria's Split Personality

For interest and prestige, Victoria was Waterloo's only serious rival. It remained two separate stations – the 'Brighton' and the 'Chatham', throughout the Grouping period, despite the holes that the SR made in the intervening wall in 1924 and a continuous renumbering of its platforms from 1 to 17. Each side had its own distinctive characteristics. On the west, the former LB&SC premises, beyond the prosaic presence of the South London line and other suburban electrics, there existed a certain, if sometimes slightly sleazy, glamour. Up to 10.30 or later, wealthy businessmen and entrepreneurs commuted in from comfortable Sussex homes; during the afternoons and late evenings, the coastal Pullman trains were patronised by the theatrical profession and its hangers-on, by excited couples bound for an extra-marital romp in a Brighton hotel, and by racegoers and other pleasure seekers, including, in the season, patrons in evening dress for the opera at Glyndebourne. By 1938 the coastal expresses to Hastings, Eastbourne, Brighton, Worthing and Littlehampton were all electric multiple-units, but the traditional Pullman service was faithfully maintained and the all-Pullman non-stop Brighton Belle, a unique multiple unit operation started in 1934 (actually in 1933 as the Southern Belle) and restored after a wartime break in 1947, was always worth a glance.

The former SE&CR station also had its suburban and long distance residential business (in this case, throughout the Southern era, the latter remained steam-hauled). But there was glamour here too, of a rather more dignified and traditional kind, for until the late 1930s, this was the accepted way of travel to and from the European mainland and beyond. Victoria's Folkestone and Dover boat trains carried princes and diplomats, King's Messengers, spies, wealthy holidaymakers and prosperous

Victoria Brighton side on Sunday 5 October 1952. Ex-LBSC class H2 4–4–2 No 32424 Beachy Head *is at the head of an RCTS all-Pullman special train to Brighton, run in connection with celebration of the centenary of Brighton works.*

Test Run

A test run was made with one of the Merchant Navy class on November 9. The load of 16 coaches with a tare of 527 tons was one of the heaviest trains that have ever worked out of Waterloo. A stop was made at Woking and leaving there, the engine steadily accelerated on the almost continuous upgrade to 72mph beyond Fleet. Another stop was made at Basingstoke.

The real test was west of Salisbury where No 21C2 gave a fine example of her effortless pulling power. Sherborne was passed at 70mph and up the bank of 1 in 80 beyond Crewkerne the minimum speed was 25½mph. A stop was made at Axminster. Leaving here, there is about 1¼ miles of down grade where the engine accelerated to 51mph, and then followed the long pull of 1 in 80 to Honiton tunnel. Here the speed fell again to a minimum of 25½mph, with a slight acceleration to 57mph at the summit.

On the following down grade the speed touched 79mph before stopping at Sidmouth Junction. The 12.2 miles from there to Exeter Central were covered in 15 min 8 sec. A little brake trouble in the early part of the run together with a strong side wind helped to handicap the engine but the noiseless running and the splendid acceleration after both leaving Woking and Salisbury amply proved the capabilities of the Bulleid's new type. – *The Locomotive*, 1941.

Opposite, below *Cannon Street in 1958 when the remains of the bomb damaged roof were being removed. Two rush hour steam trains bound for Ramsgate via Chislehurst and Chatham headed by Schools class 4–4–0s Nos 30920* Rugby *and 30923* Bradfield. *In between is a brand new Hastings line diesel electric set. The narrow width of these trains for tunnel clearances is clearly visible.*

international businessmen; only the impecunious used the old LB&SCR route via Newhaven/Dieppe and only a handful of pioneers ventured out to Croydon Airport to fly to Europe. Two famous named trains punctuated the Eastern side's daily round: from 1929 the all-Pullman Golden Arrow, running in connection with the Calais–Paris Flèche d'Or Wagons-Lits Pullman; and from 1936, the Night Ferry, with its purpose-built Wagons-Lits, carrying their sleeping passengers direct into Paris (Nord) via the Dover–Dunkerque train ferry. In 1939, not to be outdone, the Brighton side, or rather a special platform beyond, beneath the new Imperial Airways Terminal building, saw the inauguration of the flying boat trains to and from the Empire Air Base at Southampton. During the war, there were 'Air Specials' from here to Poole Harbour (for flights to Baltimore, USA) and also for Hurn Airport. Bombing at Victoria was less successful than at Waterloo, although damage to the approaches did cause brief closure. In a dramatic few minutes in September 1940 a Dornier bomber, vacated by its crew, crashed against the Eastern Section station, while in 1944 a 'flying bomb' missile further damaged the departure side and Eastern Section offices.

Charing Cross: West End Convenience Under Threat

In January 1920, three years before the birth of the Southern, Charing Cross, in many ways London's most conveniently-sited terminus, had lost its Continental traffic to Victoria. Its Channel boat trains to Folkestone and Dover had been of prime importance right up to 1914 (and during the war for military specials). This aspect of its traffic had a last moment of glory with the arrival of a special train carrying President Woodrow Wilson of the USA in December 1918, King George V and his ministers attending to greet him.

During the Southern era, from 1926 onwards, this terminus became filled with electric suburban trains, their efficient ubiquity punctuated by a strong leavening of steam-hauled services – some with Pullman cars – to Hastings and the Kent Coast. A 1928–29 proposal to close this station in favour of a road bridge across the river, re-locating where the Royal Festival Hall now stands, was reluctantly accepted by the SR board and shareholders after the government had declared the scheme as 'in the national interest'. But Parliament perversely then took objection to a railway terminus in such a prominent bridgehead site, rejecting the Bill. In 1931 after alternative plans had been drawn up, the government had second thoughts, withdrawing its promise of a 75 per cent subsidy for the road bridge and new station, this and the contemporary financial crisis effectively killing the proposal.

By the 1920s, the older part of the controversial river bridge was showing signs of strain and loco movements had to be restricted. Electrification of most of the Charing Cross services saved the SR heavy capital expenditure on rebuilding it, but the running roads were rearranged in 1925 with Up Through, Down Through and a Middle Road on the 1887 structure, leaving only the Up Local and Down Local lines, used solely by electric multiple-units, on the older northern section.

War damage at Charing Cross was mainly confined to the hotel but

Above *Charing Cross, probably the busiest six platform station in the world, is caught in a quieter moment in April 1957. Schools class 4–4–0 No 30929* Malvern *is leaving with a Sunday train for Dover made up of a 4-coach set of Maunsell corridor coaches with 3 BR Mark I corridors bringing up the rear. The roof is the replacement of 1906 built after the collapse of the original arched one. The SR arms and initials still stand proudly over the end girder replacing those of the SECR after grouping.*

there was a hairy morning in 1941, observed by the writer from his office close to the station. A land mine, its parachute caught in the bridge girders, was all but exploded by a fire under No 4 platform, the flames not extinguished until they were but·12ft away from the canister, by then already fused to a conductor rail by the heat.

Cannon Street for the City

Similar in position and appearance to Charing Cross and unlike its West End partner, retaining its original arch-roofed train shed, Cannon Street was almost entirely used by those whose bread and butter was earned by being 'something in the City'. For the first electrifications of the former SER suburban services in 1926, the track layout, platforms and signalling were completely remodelled to allow as many parallel and non-conflicting movements as possible. Facilities for steam locos working the Kent Coast services were retained on the western side. Simplification was another aim; although there were still 77 sets of points, this was 24 less than in the former layout. The dignified train shed was left sheltering eight platforms, their buffers in line at the south end of the small concourse.

Cannon Street's dull daily round was brightened on summer Saturdays between 1936 and 1939 when trains were diverted to relieve the congestion at Victoria. War years saw virtual restriction to rush hour traffic, with just a solitary fast train to the Kent Coast at 17.45. This lasted until the first year of BR. The great walls and high arched roof made a prominent target for bombers and the roof was burnt out on a memorable night in May 1941 as brave railwaymen moved trains out on to the bridge amongst a shower of fiery timbers and molten glass.

The Company's well-appointed Hotels include the following:
LONDON
CANNON STREET HOTEL – Adjoining Cannon Street Station, in the heart of the City. Entrance from Station Platform. Inclusive Terms. Restaurant open to non-residents. Telegrams: Convenient, Canon, London. Phone: City 6463.
CHARING CROSS HOTEL – Adjoining Charing Cross Station. Entrance from Station Platform. Moderate Tariff. Inclusive Terms if desired. Most convenient for Families and Gentlemen who are visiting London. Restaurant on
continued on next page

Ex-LBSC class L 4–6–4T No B333 Remembrance *waits in London Bridge station at the head of the down City Limited, the 5.0pm London Bridge to Brighton, circa 1929. The structure on the right is a water softening plant and storage tank.*

Dowdy and Muddled: London Bridge

During the Southern years, the 14 terminal platforms at London Bridge and their decaying Victorian buildings offered little attraction to the casual passenger and much confusion to those unfamiliar with the complicated topography of the place. Commuters made up most of the traffic, some coming in daily from the Sussex coast, their lot much improved by the electrification of these services in 1933–38. The former SER and LBSCR stations although abutting together, remained physically separate until 1928, when a hole was made in the intervening wall and a connecting footbridge was also provided. The approach tracks to the 'Brighton Side', as it remained known, were also rearranged at this time, and the 21 platforms were continuously numbered from north to south (omitting a No 5). Such colour as London Bridge could muster in these years, apart from its commuter Pullman trains, was confined to the seasonal hop-pickers' specials (carrying household possessions as well as their owners for their free country 'holiday'), and the nightly departure of the 23.50 Dover TPO with its late fee letter box. German bombs here caused much devastation to the station offices, the consequent ruins and improvised replacement remaining well into BR days.

The 'Chatham's' City Stations

This closely-spaced trio, St Paul's (renamed Blackfriars by the SR in 1937), Ludgate Hill, and Holborn Viaduct, on the City extension of the old LC&DR, were not much individually and hardly more impressive if taken together. Several British cities outside London could offer termini that far outclassed them in size and dignity. Such changes as the SR made to this unique inheritance were almost entirely related to shoe-horning electric trains into the narrow confines available. Indeed Ludgate Hill had to go altogether because even its rebuilt island platform of 1912 proved too short to take 8-car multiple units. When the Wimbledon services, which had started from here, were electrified in March 1929, the station was closed. Other local electric services from Holborn Viaduct and St Paul's/Blackfriars were introduced in 1925, 1934 and 1935 and the peak hour Gillingham workings to and from Holborn Viaduct were converted in 1939. Considerable ingenuity was exercised in lengthening the inadequate platforms at Holborn and Blackfriars to accommodate the newcomers.

The hotel across the frontage of Holborn Viaduct, which had been converted to offices in World War I was almost totally destroyed by bombs in October 1940 and May 1941. The destruction of the south bank signal box at Blackfriars and of a nearby bridge by another bomb caused further problems, closing Holborn Viaduct completely for three weeks in May 1941. The terminal roads at Blackfriars remained out of use from this time until restored for peak hour services in August 1946 (they were used to berth empty stock at other times). Blackfriars platforms were then renumbered 1–5 from east to west.

During the SR years, both Holborn Viaduct and Blackfriars retained much of their Victorian steam age aura, despite the pervasive electric multiple units. Both stations repaid careful exploration, as they could

continued
the Ground Floor (with entrance from Station) open to non-residents. Private Rooms for Luncheons, Dinners, Meetings, Receptions &c. Telegrams: Banqueting, Westrand, London. Phone: Gerrard 8025.

CRAVEN HOTEL – Near Charing Cross Station. Phone: Gerrard 2491.

SOUTHAMPTON
SOUTH WESTERN HOTEL – Adjoining Docks Station and facing Harbour. Entrance from Station Platform. Moderate Tariffs. Luggage moved from Station and Docks free of charge. Telegrams: Welcome, Southampton. Phone: 5031 Southampton.

DEAL
SOUTH EASTERN HOTEL – Open throughout the Winter. Situated in commanding position on Marine Parade, facing South. Celebrated for Home Comforts and unequalled for Catering, Service, and Wines. Luncheons, Teas, and Dinners Served in Verandahs facing the Sea. Convenient for Championship Golf Courses at Deal and Sandwich; also for Walmer and Kingsdown. Two Hours from town by Southern Railway Expresses. Cheap Fares. Tels: Onward, Deal. Phone: Deal 119 (2 lines).

NEWHAVEN
LONDON AND PARIS HOTEL – Adjoining Landing Stage for Cross-Channel Steamers. Phone: Newhaven 72.

Holborn Viaduct station in January 1938. The route indicator is blank so there is no known destination for unit No 1483. The station as seen is now closed but the Lower Level is incorporated in the new cross-city (ThamesLink) services. An interesting note is that there is no third rail on the line used by platform 3 which was used for van traffic including newspapers, all steam worked.

reveal curious and nostalgic details, such as Holborn Viaduct's old fashioned buffet with its long bar, and nearby, the secret stairs to the smoke-filled depths of the closed low level station. A visit to Holborn Viaduct on a winter evening when the place was wreathed in fog could be very worthwhile since at this time newspaper and parcels traffic was heavy and steam was much in evidence. Unfortunately no-one seems to have captured this on film.

Blackfriars, for many years the 'city' terminus for Continental services, had carved in the stonework of the frontage the names of many foreign destinations.

Epilogue

While their train services were generally more reliable than is the case today, it has to be said that with the notable exception of Waterloo and Victoria, the SR's seven London termini offered little to impress or beguile the ordinary traveller, and the often devastating attentions of the Luftwaffe hardly improved matters. Although kept well-swept and tidy, they would not be regarded as attractive by today's travelling public. But in terms of sheer traffic handled, day in day out, Waterloo, Victoria, Charing Cross and London Bridge had no equals, apart from Liverpool Street. And, as we have suggested, with their daily unfolding of the interface between the Southern and its passengers, and their varied traffics, all were rewarding for the observer of the railway and social scene. That they were at the centre of much of the nation's life there is no doubt.

The Schools: A Special Case

It is fascinating to consider what might have been the responses if the Southern's requirement for an express passenger locomotive complying with the restricted Tonbridge–Hastings loading gauge but capable of working 400 ton trains had been put to the chief mechanical engineers of the other three British railways.

Gresley might well have been optimistic that the LNER B17 Sandringham would form the basis of a solution, subject to some narrowing over the cylinders to keep within the 8ft 6½in permitted on the Hastings line and cutting down the cab and tender top. Its axleload was well within the 21 tons allowed for a multi-cylinder engine. It would have posed greater problems for Swindon; the standard two-cylinder 4–6–0 layout would have been much too wide, and the four-cylinder engines were little narrower. It might have been possible to modify a Star to fill the bill, with the outside cylinders between the bogie wheels, though the Churchward layout of valve gear and rocking levers would necessarily have been sacrificed. It would have been essential to cut down the boiler mountings, but visibility from a narrow cab past the Belpaire firebox of the No 1 boiler would have been very restricted. Fowler at Derby – or more likely Anderson, the Superintendent of Motive Power – would have looked back fondly at the Midland Compound before rejecting it on width grounds and wondering how to slim down a Patriot to pass through the Mountfield Tunnel eye of the needle.

One thing is certain; none of them would have been likely to come up with anything resembling Maunsell's three-cylinder 4–4–0 masterpiece, the Schools class of 1930.

Holcroft has said that it was the Locomotive Running Department that 'pressed for a large 4–4–0'. If this was the case it presumably had the availability of turntables in mind. A Schools could – with a very tight squeeze – turn on a 50ft table, but any 4–6–0 would have needed at least 55ft. The bigger railways would have installed 60-footers, but the Southern was not so forthcoming.

Maunsell's approach was based on the Lord Nelson of four years previously. It incorporated three of the four Nelson cylinders, and one less coupled axle, but used as much common material as possible. First thoughts were to use a shortened Nelson boiler with Belpaire firebox, but this would have caused excessive axleloads and forward vision from the cab necessarily reduced to 7ft 7in wide at the rain gutters would have been very poor, and a round-topped firebox was considered essential. A revised scheme, therefore, incorporated a shortened version of the class S15 boiler (which had wider firebox water legs than the similar King Arthur boiler) pressed to 220 lbs per sq in. Three separate valve gears were provided rather than a conjugated gear for the middle valve. The standard Nelson bogie with independent coil springing for each axlebox was

Resplendent in BR lined black livery No 30928 Stowe *sets back into Ashford shed on 26 September 1953. One of the three preserved examples of Schools class, the locomotive can now be found still in Southern territory working on the Bluebell Railway in Sussex.*

No 30934 St Lawrence *simmers on the ashpit at Dover Marine in the mid 1950s against a background of the one-time Lord Warden Hotel, while waiting her return working. A Bricklayers Arms engine, she is in lined black livery with the lining enclosing the whole tender side. Built in March 1935, the Lemaître exhaust and large chimney were fitted in May 1940. Target number 89 indicates a Bricklayers Arms duty.*

fitted. No 900 *Eton* emerged from Eastleigh works in March 1930, the first of forty.

Their success was immediate; they were regarded by many involved in their operation as the finest locomotives the Southern had produced. Furthermore, experience brought little significant modification. The fitting of smoke deflectors was perhaps natural. The bogie, which carried just over 25 tons to keep the coupled axles within the 21 tons limit, suffered frame fractures and needed strengthening, while the bogie coil springs were stiffened up to eliminate a rather bouncy ride. There were experiments with the lead of the piston valves before an optimum figure was decided. Steam sanding replaced dry trickle sanding, both to safeguard sandbox capacity and to avoid interference with track circuits. Bulleid fitted half the engines with the multiple-jet exhaust and large diameter chimney in 1939–41, but the benefit was so marginal that it was not felt worthwhile to modify the rest.

In addition to the Hastings line they were prominent on services to Ramsgate, to Dover, on the Portsmouth Direct line and to Bournemouth. It was perhaps on the latter route that they demonstrated their fullest capabilities; on sustained climbs in the 50–60mph range they could produce 1000 equivalent drawbar horsepower at the drop of a hat, and in the most skilled hands even more. At the top end of the scale was a performance in 1937 by No 925 *Cheltenham* on a down Bournemouth train loaded to fourteen coaches (55 tons over the permitted load) and grossing 485 tons. The driver was Jeans of Bournemouth shed. After reaching 63mph after Weybridge the ensuing 10½ miles to milepost 31 (before Farnborough), climbing all the way at 1 in 387/326/314 were surmounted at a minimum of 52½mph. This required a sustained average EDBHP of about 1140. Smart running with 81mph before Eastleigh brought the train into the Southampton stop just within the scheduled 87½ minutes, but excluding a signal check at Waller's Ash the net time was no more than 84½ minutes for the 79¼ miles.

After the war their heaviest work (except for that on the Hastings line) was progressively taken over by the Bulleid Pacifics and then by electric and diesel traction, and by the end of 1962 all had been withdrawn. Fortunately Nos 925, 926 and 928 live on in preservation as a testimony to Maunsell's most successful design.

Yesterday

Nine Elms was a place, a Sacred place,
Where locomotives were once born with style and
   grace,
Where men lived and loved their working lives,
In the most wonderous vocation ever devised.

Soft spoken Devon drivers, masters of their calling,
Brash, cheeky Cockney firemen their language
   appalling,
Loving the Job that bound them together,
Please God, let steam engines last forever.

Over the decades designers came,
Gooch, Beattie, Adams, were their names,
Dugald Drummond, too, that ferocious Scot,
Made sure he'd ne'er be forgot.

The engines he built, will run forever,
South of the Border and amongst the heather,
His T9s and Paddleboats, a glorious sight,
But his D15s, were my delight.

The Mighty Lord Nelson, a four cylinder giant,
At the head of a train looked resplendent,
Engines named after Legend and Public Schools,
Urie and Maunsell built them all.

A man named Bulleid, came on the scene,
And he gave birth to a Flying machine,
Channel Packet's, West Countries with steam in their
   veins,
With great ease, they'd time their trains.

But what of the men in that huge Cathedral,
Who loved their toil, were keen and able,
Hooper, Sartin and Whatley too,
Tom Smaldon and Marsh, a contented crew.

Harry Pope, John-boy-Webb,
South and Male and Golly Golly Fred,
Swain and Hooker of 'The Trials' fame,
Climbed Shap Bank, to great acclaim,

Bert Hulbert chasing as only Foreman can,
Down to the Canteen to find his missing men,
Glowering at the firemen all drinking tea,
Snaps 'Tubes and Supers you lot, then you're free'.

Little Punch Clarke with a strong right arm,
His fireman complaining about the coal they burn,
Skilful Skinner, and Conker Gee,
Shepherd, Cutting and Tancy Lee.

Frank Saunders collecting Union dues,
Turner, Poole, Coffin and Hughes,
George Newton, Master Tank driver,
Scouring the regulator 'til it looked like Silver.

Slicer Knowles and Tony Legg,
Boiler Buster Hopkins and old Bill Pegg,
The list is endless, I could go on forever,
Their faces flash past, forget them, never.

And if on a dark night you dare venture,
To Brooklands Passage, you will encounter,
A tall ghostly figure you will see,
With blackened face, aye, 'tis me.

Grubby blue overalls and polished cap,
Standing lonely vigil, by that Gap,
Army haversack on my shoulder,
Tea-can swinging from its holder.

Channel Packets wailing their mournful cry,
A Nelson's shrill scream breaks the night sky,
Up the Bank to the turntable,
Slipping, dancing to their stable.

A cry of 'ease up' rends the air,
Then 'Vacuum on mate', steady there,
Tableman's cursing, called from his break,
Snaps 'Put her in the new shed, she's out at eight'

Crashing, balancing on that huge contraption,
Turning slowly to our destination,
Up the Shed, 'put her away',
'Screw her down', it's the end of the day.

Tools in lockers, put out lights,
Sweep the floor with 'pisser' pipe,
Check the boiler, that's O.K.
Coat and hat on, I'm away.

Good-bye my beauties, I must depart,
To see you die would break my heart,
The smell, the smoke, the living steam,
Did it really happen yesterday? or was it a dream?

Jim Marsh

Above *Chelsfield station sees Schools 4–4–0 No 30920* Rugby *tackling the 1 in 120 rise on a Dover-bound boat train in May 1960. The engine is one of the twenty fitted by Bulleid with the Lemaitre multiple jet blastpipe and large diameter chimney. Apart from the first coach, a BR Mark I second, the remaining visible coaches are of Maunsell vintage.*

9
LONDON AREA STEAM WORKING

MUCH has been written and said about the bottleneck at Borough Market Junction and the benefits of transferring to another location the crossing movements essential to serve Charing Cross and Cannon Street from all routes. To accomplish this, a new layout came into operation in the summer of 1976. The crossing movements take place at Spa Road and reversible line working is now introduced at London Bridge. It is at least arguable that it was better to make the fouling movements where the adjacent Southwark Cathedral dictates a rail alignment at Borough Market Junction requiring a maximum speed of 20mph, rather than on the one piece of straight line where speeds of 60 or even 75mph might be hoped for.

However this may be, it is certain that the elimination of steam traction, the closure of Rotherhithe Road depot and Bricklayers Arms locomotive depot and the lifting of so many stops at London Bridge has given today's operators enormous advantages.

Rotherhithe Road (known as R Road) was the principal steam carriage berthing and repair depot, lying adjacent to Bricklayers Arms (B Arms or The Brick) loco and freight depots. The Brighton line depot of Willow Walk was alongside and was amalgamated with B Arms in 1931. Because B Arms was originally built as the London passenger terminal of the South Eastern Railway in 1844 the lines naturally faced towards New Cross. From and to the London Bridge direction involved a reversing movement occupying No 2 down and No 2 up lines in the busiest area.

Before the introduction of colour light signalling in the area, a permissive working operated from 9.30 to 12.30 daily whereby No 2 line from Spa Road starting signal to Southwark Park home signal became a reception siding for empty trains and light engines for R Road and B Arms. The working was controlled by a pilotman stationed at Spa Road signal box who authorised trains crews to pass Spa Road starting signal and Blue Anchor home signal at danger. Southwark Park home signal was worked for each train and was freed by Surrey Canal Junction under normal block working arrangements.

Between Surrey Canal Junction and Bricklayers Arms No 2 Junction a different system of permissive working operated with draw-ahead giving authority to enter an occupied section. There was a highly complicated system of bell codes to differentiate between empty trains and engines for the various sections of the B Arms, Willow Walk and R Road complex.

Colour light signalling and the increased electrification also forced another change in the train working arrangements at London Bridge. In the days of semaphore signalling it was regular practice for vehicles to be

---

The Train at Platform Five is For...

An *Engine Head Signals* booklet laid down a complex code of headcode discs with six possible positions – one at the chimney, one each side of the smokebox and three above the buffer beam. Excluding Royal trains, which carried four discs, they carried from one to three according to route. One code would be used for several routes which did not conflict.

For instance, Central and Eastern Sections code 17, which comprised a disc over each buffer (the express passenger indication on other railways) applied to all trains between: London Bridge (including Charing Cross, Cannon Street and Holborn Viaduct via London Bridge) or Bricklayers Arms and Tonbridge or Reading via East Croydon and Redhill; Brighton and Hove via Preston Park Spur, Three Bridges and Eridge; Victoria or Holborn and Folkestone or Dover via Orpington loop, Tonbridge and Ashford; London or Bricklayers Arms and Gillingham, Faversham, *continued overleaf*

Opposite, below *In early Southern Railway days an unidentified L class 4-4-0 approaches Orpington on an express for Ramsgate. The eight-coach train contains a Pullman car but the remainder is non-corridor ex-SECR birdcage stock. Petts Wood station platforms are in the background, and the splitting distant, before the adoption of yellow arms, is for Petts Wood Junction, routing Charing Cross or Victoria.*

continued

Ramsgate or Dover via Chislehurst loop and Chatham.

On the Western Section the same code applied to a different range of services spread between Waterloo, Oxford (GWR), Fratton and Weymouth.

Superimposed on these headcodes could be the duty numbers according to the depot providing the engine. Stewarts Lane, for instance, was allocated duty numbers 1–79 for Eastern Section turns and 501–539 for Central Section work. These numbers were shown on one of the headcode discs.

There were other 3-disc headcodes for specials, race trains, and other specified indications for trips to and from other companies' yards.

For electric trains there was a bewildering variety of numerical and letter codes, displayed in a panel in the centre of the cab front – or, in the case of the Portsmouth expresses with a gangway connection, on the right hand side (looking forward). Many passengers soon got to know the code applicable to *their* train to and from work.

With the use of modern power signal boxes with train describers showing a unique four-digit alphanumeric code for each train, these systems were abandoned as unnecessary to the operating department. This brought chagrin to many regular commuters, and after lengthy heart-searching BR has not only made provision on the new Networker electric stock to display a route code on the cab front, but has started to put these at the head of each column in the timetable.

attached to and detached from steam trains at London Bridge High Level by the shunting engine provided at London Bridge Yard. Protection was given by a 'Block Switch' provided in the inspector's office on each of the two up platforms. When the train arrived, it was the inspector's duty to unlock the case in which the switch was housed, move the switch to the 'Block' position, close and relock the case. Whenever the door was open, a warning bell rang in London Bridge 'B' Box and the movement of the switch to 'Block' locked the appropriate home signals until the switch was restored to 'Normal' and the door closed.

In 1926 electrification scheme eliminated virtually all the suburban steam trains and the consequent increase in service made the B Arms and R Road permissive working inappropriate. The loss of No 2 down line could no longer be afforded, empty electric trains were not going to R Road and the increased track occupation made it impossible to time the empty steam trains and engines to and from the B Arms branch through the bottlenecks of Borough Market and London Bridge. Likewise, the working of empty trains and engines for the evening business trains was becoming unmanageable.

The withdrawal of the permissive working was made possible by the construction of the Nunhead and Lewisham loop lines which immediately followed the 1926 electrification. These also contributed to reliable working by removing from their traditional route the cross-London freights operating between Ferme Park LNER, Brent LMS and the Southern's Eastern and Central section depots which ran via the Metropolitan Widened Lines, Holborn Low Level, Blackfriars, Metropolitan Junction, and London Bridge.

Because of the gradient from Farringdon Street to Holborn Viaduct the loads were pathetically small even with the assistance of the banking engine permanently stationed at Low Level, usually known as Snow Hill from the disused passenger station of that name beside which Holborn Low Level signal box stood. Although freight traffic was declining, there were still in the 1920s some 40 trains a day over this route and, apart from their high working costs, they did not blend with the Southern ideas of operation in the electrified area.

Drivers of the 'Midland Creepers' as they were contemptuously known to the signalmen, were very wary of the new-fangled colour light signals as well as the SR's complicated layout and treated either a double or single yellow aspect as an invitation to get down to walking pace.

The freight and empty passenger trains were almost entirely removed from the London Bridge scene when the Nunhead and Lewisham loops were opened in 1927. The loop was created by using part of the Greenwich Park line which had provided through services to North London until closed in 1917. The line was relaid between Nunhead and Lewisham Road where a new spur was constructed to Lewisham Junction.

The new line crossed the South Eastern main line at Parks Bridge by means of a steel and concrete viaduct – the flyover which was to be brought down with such devastating effect in the Lewisham disaster of 1957. A new connecting link was also laid in between Lewisham and Hither Green and when all this was done the freight marshalling yard at

Stewarts Lane was closed and the work done at Hither Green Sidings with Blackheath as a subsidiary yard to sort out the Woolwich Arsenal and North Kent line traffic.

So, as passenger traffic increased, the workings of South Eastern empty main line trains and light engines was a marvel of ingenuity – at very heavy cost.

The empty coaches of the morning business steam trains went from Cannon Street to depot via Metropolitan Junction, Ludgate Hill and the new Nunhead and Lewisham Loops. Backing-on engines were provided at Ludgate Hill since track occupation on the Holborn lines did not permit running round movements.

Because the main line steam engines were not required until the evening and were prohibited from crossing the Old River Bridge at Blackfriars, they were either holed up at Cannon Street, or queued up in the loco sidings at Ewer Street adjacent to Southwark Depot until they could make the journey to B Arms Loco via London Bridge. The country train crews were released to travel home passenger and a set of B Arms men signed on to relieve at Cannon Street, sit it out at Ewer Street, work the engine to depot and dispose.

Disposal allowance for a main line engine was around one and a half hours, later increased to over two hours for a West Country class, with

Ex-SER Q1 0–4–4T No 141 was withdrawn within a month of this view taken on 20 February 1926. The dirty paintwork of the engine (still in SE&C style) and the birdcage stock still bearing its SE&CR lettering (though barely visible) suggests that the Grove Park–Bromley North steam service was being run down: electric trains took over eight days later.

New Line
The line linking Wimbledon and
Sutton was brought into use on
Sunday 5 January 1930. Begun in
October 1927, the new railway is
5¼ miles long, and is electrified
throughout on the standard SR
direct current system, taking
current from the Wimbledon
power house and Sutton sub-
station. About four miles of the
work has been carried out by Sir
Robert McAlpine & Sons Ltd in
approximately eighteen months.

There are six new stations, of
which Wimbledon Chase and
South Merton have been opened
for some time. Then follow
Morden South, St Helier, Sutton
Common, and West Sutton.

It is at St Helier that the
London County Council have
decided to build their new town of
10,000 houses during the next ten
years, and a large goods yard has
been laid down here; the other
stations will only deal with
passenger traffic.

The new stations are all of the
island platform type, with
passimeter booking offices, whilst
the station architecture is in the
simple modern style, as adopted at
Wimbledon. The signalling is of
the two-position upper quadrant
type, and the signal posts themselves are constructed from old
steel rails.

No fewer than twenty-four over
and under bridges have been built,
including three footbridges. The
over-bridges are all of reinforced
concrete, and the under-bridges of
steel girders with concrete floors,
the longest span being that over
the London-Epsom road, which
measures 120ft. Over 500,000
tons of earth had to be excavated,
and this was used for the embankments between Wimbledon and
Morden South and between St
Helier and Sutton.

The rebuilt station at
Wimbledon has been adapted to
allow trains through to Holburn
Viaduct *via* Tooting Junction, and
continued opposite

another hour for preparation before leaving the depot. Nothing like these
allowances were normally needed. As it took an hour for men to sign on
at B Arms and get to Cannon Street it was difficult for them to manage in
their eight hours duty to bring down a country engine after the morning
peak and take another up for the evening working.

As a fast run from Ramsgate to London was only about two hours, the
engines spent more time being prepared and disposed than they did
running trains. This was even worse for the engines of the boat trains
which were similarly booked full preparation and disposal after the ninety
minute run between London and Dover.

It was permissible for empty trains to work between Charing Cross,
Cannon Street and R Road or B Arms with an engine at each end and this
method was used for the few empties off the later morning business
services and those to form the early evening departures for which precar-
ious pathways involving reversing at North Kent East Junction were
programmed.

The remainder of the empty train cavalcade for the evening trains
began leaving R Road between 14.30 and 15.00 for Blackheath or Grove
Park in order to get them out of the New Cross area and into a location
whence they could run head-on to Ludgate Hill. After a suitable interval
for running round, rest and contemplation, a forward move was made
with, possibly, a 20 or 30 minute wait between Lewisham and Nunhead
and Cambria Road Junction, hopefully dodging the foreign freights
creeping back to the familiar areas of North London, through to Ludgate
Hill where there was usually ample time for further rest before reversing
and proceeding to Metropolitan Junction home signal. The loaded train
would be leaving Cannon Street some three hours after the empty train
movement started. One minor advantage was that the trains were always
warm in winter.

Freight trains running in the London area was prohibited between 7.00
and 10.00 and between 16.00 and 19.00. The effect was felt principally by
the foreign railways cross-London services which were impounded at the
SR yard if they could not leave before a deadline. Likewise, any late
running freight presenting itself at the boundary was recessed into the first
convenient siding. The evening empty programme was the more expen-
sive. In the mornings the empty trains were nearly all on the way before
the freights commenced at 10.00, whereas during the afternoon they
shared the available paths between passenger and conditional boat trains.

After the closure of Ludgate Hill as a passenger station (principally
because it was not practicable to lengthen the platforms to take 8 car
trains) all the passenger trains for Holborn Viaduct had to work through
the one up and one down platform at Blackfriars, leaving the four tracks
behind the station free for empty train movements. Adjacent to the
passenger station were the market sidings, whence such perishable traffic
as remained was carted to Covent Garden. There were also several
bonded warehouses and Blackfriars – unique on the Southern in having a
wagon hoist until it was destroyed by bombs in 1941.

The train working in the Blackfriars area was not helped when in 1933
the London Passenger Transport Board was formed and all receipts in the

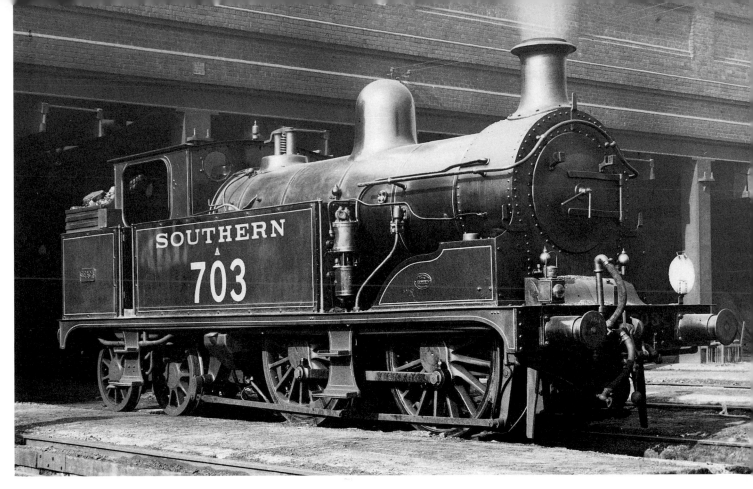

London area, less movements expenses, were pooled on the basis of passenger train miles run. Immediately, every empty electric train between Holborn and Herne Hill sidings became a passenger service. They served only Elephant and Castle but this forced them to run on the designated line and so reduced flexibility. There were rarely any passengers but the mileage qualified towards the Southern share which came to 25.5 per cent of the total. In the first years, this amounted to between £4½ and £4¾ million.

Although Cannon Street dealt with the majority of the steam hauled business trains, Charing Cross was the station for the rest of the day's standard and relief services to Ashford and Dover and most of the stopping services via the North Kent to Gillingham, Sheerness and Faversham. Charing Cross River Bridge was the subject of some locomotive restrictions whose enforcement demanded a fairly high standard of intelligence from the signalmen and drivers.

Looking towards the terminus, the seven lines carried over the Thames were styled when the restrictions were republished in 1925:-

Up West No 1	No 1 line	}	
Down West	2		West Bridge
Up West No 2	3		Between the Girders
No 2 Siding	4	}	
No 1 Siding	5		
Up Local	6		East Bridge
Down Local	7		

Slades Green shed was converted from a steam depot to house electric multiple units in 1926. On 12 September 1925 it housed R1 No A703, nicely cleaned in Southern green livery though still carrying its SE&CR plate on the bunker. Note the multi-slotted brackets on the smokebox door for destination boards.

continued

the junction at the Sutton end allows the trains to run in from the Epsom direction on to West Croydon.

The gradients are heavy, including 1 in 44 and 1 in 49 approaching the junction at Sutton. In other places they are as steep as 1 in 60.

Trains will be run every twenty minutes in business hours and every half-hour at other times. – *The Locomotive*

Rivals In Harness

It was rare in steam days to see a train double-headed by locomotives of two different companies. But in the West Country it was sometimes seen with summer relief trains from the GWR headed for coastal resorts. In August 1933, for instance, a GWR Hall working a thirteen coach Saturday extra from the Midlands to Bournemouth was photographed being piloted by an ex-LSWR Small Hopper, probably attached at Southampton. By this stage there should have been little in the way of gradients to tax the Hall; perhaps it was steaming badly with a dirty fire after a long haul.

Certainly when the attachment was made the carriage and wagon examiner would have been busy pulling the strings on all the coaches, for the Hall would have been maintaining 25in of vacuum whereas the Hopper, whose driver would be in charge of the brake, could only maintain the standard 21in. Otherwise the brakes would have been dragging until the reservoir side of the vacuum brake on each coach had leaked down to 21in – and that could take quite a time.

The East Bridge was the weak one and no two engines, whether with trains or not, were permitted to pass on adjacent lines when crossing it. This meant that if a train was moving to or from No 1 siding the up local was out of action and if an engine was standing on a train in one siding the other could not be used. Far worse was the prohibition on the simultaneous use of the up and down local lines. Much of the improved working in the Charing Cross–Metropolitan Junction area following electrification was due to the fact that the restriction did not apply to electric trains.

The Up West No 1 and Down West (now down and up through lines) operated without restriction and these were the only lines over which two engines were permitted to run coupled. Between the Girders (now middle road) had its own special restriction about the minimum distance between locomotives when standing. Markers were provided in pairs and only one engine was allowed to stand between them. When used for running movements, this line had a maximum speed restriction of 10mph.

It was the responsibility of the Charing Cross and Belvedere Road signalmen to see that these various restrictions were carried out, which was not always so easy on a dark and rainy night. The station inspector at Waterloo (Eastern) which was then called Waterloo Junction in pious memory of the connection that used to run to LSWR, was required to confirm with Charing Cross that any train arriving double-headed could be accepted to run Up West No 1. If it could not, the assisting engine had to be detached and run off separately. After the 1926 electrification, an easement was given to permit an engine to occupy No 1 siding whilst two electric trains were using the down and up local lines or an electric could use the up local with a steam engine on the down local but not vice versa.

In the 1930s and after, it was the boast of Charing Cross inspectors and staff that, on busy summer Saturdays, they could receive a loaded main line steam train, turn it round and send it out again loaded in six minutes – and they never forgot to uncouple the inwards train engine!

The PR Machine

Southern Railway's public relations are usually associated with the name of Sir John Elliot, but the LSWR had already shown the way in 1916 with signboards, posters and a film publicising the new electric trains. During the first two traumatic years of the SR's existence the lesson had been forgotten and the new company had acquired a bad reputation with press and public.

The recruitment of John Elliot from Fleet Street in January 1925 coincided with a gathering of civic leaders at which Sir Herbert Walker outlined what the company was trying to achieve, despite its problems of inadequate ex-SECR infrastructure and the need to withdraw rolling stock for conversion to electric traction. Later in the year, the operating officers met the press to explain the new summer timetable; in 1924 major changes had been sprung on the public without warning. One of the benefits of having a journalist in a key position at Waterloo was to create a better understanding by railwaymen of the needs of the press.

When Elliot's appointment was confirmed in November 1925, he was given the title of assistant to the general manager for public relations and advertising. He claimed in his autobiography that this was the first use on this side of the Atlantic of the phrase 'Public Relations'. His appointment certainly established the reputation of this profession for lavish rewards, as his salary of £2,500 was equal to those of senior officers with a lifetime's railway service. Besides the press (there was no other media in 1925), the railway needed to keep its passengers informed and the SR produced a quarterly magazine, *Over the Points*, which was

This is the original photograph taken by Charles Brown and used for one of the most successful posters put out by the Southern. The text for the poster came from the small boy's mouth: 'I'm taking an early holiday 'cos I know summer comes early in the South.' The hand-coloured print actually used for the poster is somewhat touched up but the whole, including the photographer's original idea, is a mark of genius.

During the summer of 1937 the Southern staged two attractive scenic model railway displays of their new London and Portsmouth main line electric service for which they sponsored in conjunction with Trix Twin Railways a very attractive Portsmouth electric train set. The first exhibition was at Waterloo, next door to the cinema, the second was at Charing Cross Underground booking hall. During November a revised version was displayed both at Waterloo and Portsmouth. The set box was in SR green and carried an end label explaining that it was an official SR model.

sent free to those influential figures, the first class season ticket holders.

Elliot developed other ideas to improve the image of the Southern; a competition was held which found the name Atlantic Coast Express for the 11.00am from Waterloo, to be followed by the introduction of the Golden Arrow and Bournemouth Limited named trains. The new 4–6–0s for service on the main lines to the West of England were given names associated with the court of King Arthur and these were followed by the Lord Nelson class, with their names appropriate for a line serving Plymouth, Portsmouth and Chatham. While it was difficult to arrange naming ceremonies for (perhaps mythical) warriors or long-dead admirals, the advent of the Schools 4–4–0s provided opportunities for future members of the ruling class to scramble all over a steam locomotive.

The use of engine names for publicity reached its climax during and after the war, when Bulleid's large Pacifics, regarded with some suspicion by the Ministries of Transport and Labour, could be associated with the sacrifices being made by the seamen of the Merchant Navy. The subsequent light Pacifics found their way to every accessible city or town in the West Country for the unveiling of a nameplate and crest by the local mayor or council chairman. The succeeding Battle of Britain series enabled RAF squadrons and airfields, wartime commanders, air aces and government ministers to take part in naming cere-

monies, all of which brought publicity to the railway.

The inspired use of a snapshot of a small boy gazing up at the driver of a Urie N15 4–6–0 below the old 'A' box at Waterloo created one of the most famous of railway posters, which appeared year after year with various slogans based on the theme of 'South for Sunshine'. This message was also delivered by that benign railway character, 'Sunny South Sam'. The author, S.P.B. Mais, was employed to write little guide books for ramblers and holidaymakers. A substantial booklet *Southern Homes* was produced giving details of housing and local amenities in the Southern's suburban area, but it was noticeable that its coverage concentrated on the electrified routes where the company was anxious to create traffic to pay for the cost of conversion. Slogans used were 'Live in Surrey free from

worry' and 'Live in Kent and be content'. The publicity department does not seem to have found a suitable slogan for Sussex!

Publicity for the SR's docks at Southampton was encouraged by sightseeing tours, usually including a visit to a liner, while railway enthusiasts could go round Eastleigh works. The company's steamer services were featured on some very attractive posters by such artists as Norman Wilkinson. Southern trains in their dark green livery had a rather sombre appearance until Bulleid introduced his startling malachite green shade. Even the public timetable was brightened by a colourful sunshine design for the summer issue of 1939. In conjunction with the Locomotive Publishing Company the SR published picture postcards and illustrated booklets featuring its steam engines and trains. John Elliot's pioneer publicity work was continued by Cuthbert Grasemann during the 1930s, while F.V. Milton's editorship of the *Southern Railway Magazine* has provided a mine of information for SR historians.

Engine Working and Train Identification Numbers

The Southern was unique in having its steam locomotives display the route of the train rather than its own classification. White painted discs were of course used, singly or in combination at varying positions like lamps on other railways, each position and combination denoting a different route.

On at least one of such discs it was usual to find a number formed by one or more printed labels. This was the engine duty number and indicated that the engine carrying it was engaged on that particular roster. There were two main series of numbers: one for the Western Section starting with Nine Elms and concluding with

Plymouth Friary, and another for the Eastern and Central Sections commencing with Stewarts Lane and finishing with Fratton. The Isle of Wight maintained its own series. Not every number in each block would necessarily be used (see list below).

Each duty would encompass a period of up to 24 hours. Some duties might just be for one journey (such as the once a week Union Castle Ocean Liner Express from Waterloo to Southampton Docks) although it was more usual to find an out and back working (say London to Dover and return) or a series of return workings on a branch line such as Seaton Junction to Seaton. Others would be more complicated in working several trains in an area within the period.

161

To coincide with the introduction of the summer and winter timetables, engine workings books were issued in at least two volumes (weekdays and Sundays), sometimes three, the weekdays section being divided into Mondays to Fridays and Saturdays. Printed amendments would be made during the currency of the books and alterations at short notice would be catered for by the issue of a stencil notice (typewritten and duplicated). Special workings were prefixed SPL and were one off jobs. To prevent the books being too cumbersome, they were divided into four issuing areas: London West and Southern, Eastern, Central and Western.

Workings for weekdays and Sundays would be entirely separate so that duty 301 on a Sunday would have no relation to the same number during the week. While the majority of weekday workings would be for every weekday, exceptions abounded for Saturdays (when there was not a separate book for them), Mondays and even odd couplings such as Tuesdays and Thursdays. One year's duty numbers would by no means relate to another's, particularly in the case of high season Saturday dated trains. What might be 497 one year could be 515 the next. Within each season, one duty number might relate to different trains on various dates.

However, having said all this there were a large number of standard workings which carried the same number for years. The Night Ferry was duty 430 for nearly 20 years without change. The observer had to be wary of pitfalls. For example, if one of the labels peeled off, it could give a false message — so that Bournemouth duty 383 might appear to be Nine Elms 33, 38 or 83. Sometimes two distinct numbers might appear and one would be left to ponder which, if either, was correct or a disc with the wrong number might be attached. At least 89 could not be put on upside down to read 68 because the discs could only be affixed one way.

Quite distinct from the engine working numbers were the train identification numbers in the shape of head-boards carrying large numbers which were attached to the locomotive smokebox door. These were used on summer Saturdays, at Bank Holidays and for special events which required quick and easy identification of the train by the staff. West of Salisbury and Bournemouth, the traffic density was not such as to warrant their use. At one period these numbers were promulgated in the special traffic notices for each Saturday, but later this was amended to detailing the numbers at the start of the summer season and keeping to the list throughout.

The train identification numbers had no more relation to the engine working numbers than did those to the engine numbers, although it must be conceded that when St Leonards shed had its duty numbers starting at 400 and an allocation of Schools class engines starting at 30900 there was some sort of effort to send out 30900 on duty 400, 30901 on 401 and so on. But it could not be sustained.

Duty Numbers for Southern Region Sheds
Weekdays 1951

WESTERN SECTION

Nine Elms numbers commencing 1

Feltham	102
Reading	181
Guildford	201
Basingstoke	251
Andover Junction	266
Eastleigh	271
Lymington	346
Fratton	350
Gosport	367
Bournemouth	380
Swanage	414
Hamworthy Junction	415
Dorchester	418
Weymouth	424
Salisbury	430
Yeovil	480
Lyme Regis	492
Seaton Junction	493
Exmouth Junction	494
Exmouth	568
Barnstaple	572
Torrington	588
Ilfracombe	592
Okehampton	593
Bude	601
Wadebridge	602
Callington	610
Plymouth Friary	614

EASTERN SECTION

Stewarts Lane	1
Bricklayers Arms	80
Hither Green	170
Gillingham	225
Faversham	260
Tonbridge	290
Ashford	340
St Leonards	395
Folkestone	415
Dover	421
Ramsgate	465

CENTRAL SECTION

Stewarts Lane	501
Bricklayers Arms	531
Norwood Junction	580
Redhill	620
Tunbridge Wells West	655
Three Bridges	675
Horsham	700
Brighton	735
Newhaven	780
Eastbourne	795
Fratton	810

10
SALISBURY TO EXETER

ONE of Britain's most exhilarating railway journeys was by express from Salisbury to Exeter. The pace was considerable, the geography superb, and the railway interest outstanding.

For a start it was all quality main line, in the best thousand or so miles in Britain. Curves there were in plenty, but gentle; gradients were pretty continuous, mainly taken in high-speed stride, but with a vicious climb going west through Honiton tunnel and station, every bit a summer Saturday bottleneck as the GWR's more publicised Wellington bank. But what really made this route was the almost complete absence of towns. Even in SR days people spoke of an overcrowded South of England, but in just under ninety miles you passed through nowhere larger than a modest market town, and not many of them.

Eastbound from Salisbury 1951. An up troop special behind West Country Class Pacific No 34038 Lynton on 28 July 1951. The sharp curve with its mandatory speed restriction is evident. The Great Western station (closed 12 September 1932) is to the right of the picture. The type of reporting number displayed on the locomotive smokebox was used by all regions for troop trains and the top figures indicated the day of the month.

Battle of Britain class 4–6–2 No 34050 Royal Observer Corps *standing under the footbridge at the London end of Salisbury station about 1949. The locomotive is still in malachite green with yellow bands but carries its BR number.*

King Arthur *himself; Salisbury (72B) based N15 class No 30453 (Eastleigh, February 1925–July 1961) works a short parcels train from Yeovil Town (LSWR/GWR joint) to Pen Mill (GWR) in the mid 1950s. The line to the left is the Great Western to Weymouth. The GWR loco shed is in the V of the junction.*

Two factors combined to ensure that this was so. The first was the unusual wisdom of the promoters of the Salisbury & Yeovil Railway. Unlike most companies seduced by mythical traffic prospects, the S&Y men instantly realised that a railway was not automatically a railway but had to be given its own special character. They opted for the main line, their eyes on the trunk traffic to Exeter and beyond, and blow what the locals said. In particular they ignored the repeated pleas to serve Shaftsbury; it was better commerce to ignore it. Only about a single mile of branch line was built by the S&Y at Templecombe, though the end of its main line into Yeovil Town rapidly in effect became branch. Wise men they were and they reaped a rich reward when the time came for the South Western to buy them out.

The South Western itself built the continuation on to Exeter again to high standards and serving pretty well nowhere, though geography here was tougher and dictated taking the line in a loop surprisingly close to the sea, and since there were more junctions than market towns, most of them were deep out in the country. In fact only at Axminster did main-line trains combine substantial local business with branch-line connections. Crewkerne and Honiton were country towns on the main line generally with a much poorer service than Seaton Junction and Sidmouth Junction away from population. At the extremes, Chard Junction seldom showed much sign of life except when the daily milk train was shunting, while of course Exeter Central was an extremely lively place almost as interested in the Exmouth branch as the main line.

Holiday trains. A scene at Axminster on 13 August 1954. Salisbury (72B) based class S15 No 30829 (7/27–11/63) is just leaving with an Exeter Central train, having detached the through coach for Lyme Regis. (13 August was a Friday and the only Monday–Friday through coach was the one detached from the 1.00pm from Waterloo at Templecombe and then coupled to the 3.36pm ex Templecombe, arrive Axminster 4.30pm — depart Axminster 4.43pm — arrive Lyme Regis 5.04pm.) This will shortly be picked up by Adams 4–4–2 tank No 30583, seen standing in the up platform, and attached to the brake third in the bay platform out of sight on the left of the photograph. Three of these small tanks, once used on the London suburban services outlived their sisters by many years due to the tight curvature and light axle loading on the Lyme branch. Judging by the evidence of the lamp on the right the station is still gas lit. Note the pull wire hanging down from the valve.

Salisbury, Templecombe for the Somerset & Dorset, Yeovil Junction for Yeovil Town (and if you changed again at Pen Mill for Weymouth), Chard Junction for Chard (and if you had all day Taunton), Axminster sensibly for Lyme Regis (except you still had to walk the last mile), Seaton Junction for Seaton, Sidmouth Junction for Sidmouth (and change again at Tipton St John's for Budleigh Salterton and one way to Exmouth) and Exeter Central for the busier way to Exmouth.

It was great for the through expresses, pretty miserable otherwise. Because there was no obvious pattern for local traffic, stoppers terminated and started at an amazing number of different points, while nearly everybody knows about the single through coaches carried by the Atlantic Coast Express for the resorts down branch lines.

It has often been said that the railway made South Devon's fortunes and lost that of North and East Devon. Brunel's broad gauge had the great merit of serving population. Not merely did the Salisbury–Exeter trunk route bypass most people, but with the notable exception of Exeter–Exmouth the branches were steeply-graded and difficult to work. Geography was again largely responsible. Seen from the platform at Tipton St John's, the Sidmouth line looked as though it belonged more in

Lyme Regis station on Thursday 22 August 1957. Adams 4–4–2T BR No 30582 has worked the two coach branch train from Axminster. Two locomotives were considered insufficient, so in 1946 the SR purchased for £800 LSWR No 0488 which had been sold in 1917 to the Ministry of Munitions and after World War 1 to the East Kent Railway. It became BR No 30583 in 1949.

Switzerland than Devon, while Sidmouth's shingle beach encouraged exclusiveness that resulted in the railway being welcome no closer than a mile to the sea. Exeter's crowds went for the sand at Exmouth, Dawlish Warren, Teignmouth and Paignton.

Nowhere in the country was the contrast between the expresses and local trains greater. The writer recalls with relish afternoon tea on high-speed runs from Yeovil Junction to Exeter, and with equal relish the leisurely extremes of railway travel such as from Honiton to Budleigh Salterton, requiring two changes.

But it has to be said it all worked with admirable precision. Except at summer weekends, late running was indeed a surprising rarity. Even with the locals, station work was done at that Southern speed (electric and steam alike) that struck the GWR enthusiast as almost indecent. This applied even on the branches, at Tipton St John's for example the Exmouth engine running smartly round its train off the running tracks in the yard while the up and down Sidmouths came and went smartly.

Though as already said the contrast between the expresses and locals could hardly have been greater, and there was equal contrast between ordinary and high-summer weekend days, yet the East Devon system

With her BR power classification (6F) neatly above the cabside numerals S15 class No 30845 (10/36–7/63) drifts down from Honiton tunnel with an Exmouth Junction to Nine Elms freight on 3 August 1955. She is allocated to Exmouth Junction (72A). Note the large flat sided tender carrying 5,000 gallons of water; the LSWR main line — as with all SR lines — had no water troughs. These later engines were originally destined for the Central Section with 4,000 gallon tenders off the King Arthurs, but as the new engines had slightly smaller cab side cut outs which resulted in differing handrail heights this was not found to be practical. Nos 833/4/5/6/7 received these tenders.

Class N No 31834 (7/24–9/64) of Exmouth Junction (72A) lifts a train of empty ballast hoppers bound for Meldon Quarry up Honiton incline on 3 August 1955. The position of the discs confirm the route – West of England main line. The quarry at Meldon still provides ballast for BR.

certainly did not lack variety. The daily Waterloo through coaches added one touch; the cross-country Brighton to Plymouth (in many timetables without a single branch connection between Salisbury and Exeter other than at Yeovil) another. Freight was never heavy but you could see a Mogul shunting for an hour or so even at Budleigh Salterton, while Seaton Junction like Chard Junction sported a busy creamery.

Freight was of course heavier west than east of Templecombe thanks to the contribution of the S&D, which on summer Saturdays included the exotic of exotica, the Cleethorpes to Sidmouth and Exmouth, which divided at Tipton St John's. Sidmouth had several through trains to Exeter and in term time a school special ran from Honiton to Ottery St Mary (first station out on the branch) requiring reversal at Sidmouth Junction. The timetable was as stable as it was ingenious, giving sharp branch-line connections in both directions at many junction stations such as Seaton Junction. It was possible to get from Exeter to Seaton in about an hour which seemed incredibly quick. Though the timetable was stable, it was not unchanged, one post-war improvement being the running of a 6.30am as well as 7.30am from Exeter to Waterloo; they both arrived in London far earlier than anything the Western could offer.

Ancient tank engines consorting with Bulleid Pacifics, those dreaded Bulleid tavern cars you could not see out of, as well as luxury sit-down meals in proper restaurant cars, different destination boards on every coach of some trains, expresses that ran with whole empty coaches in February but hardly had a spare seat when divided into five sections on

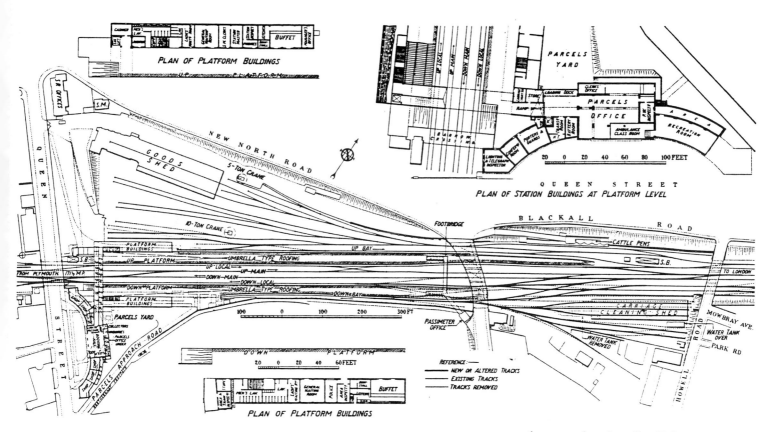

General layout, showing platforms, new buildings and carriage-cleaning shed, New Exeter Central Station, Southern railway

An unusual station pilot. Z class 0–8–0 No 30954 is the carriage pilot at Exeter Central on 30 July 1960. Note the very 1930s Southern platform extension to No 3 in reinforced concrete.

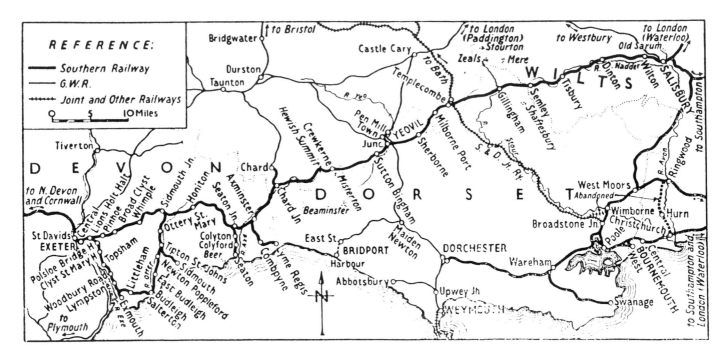

Map of the Salisbury and Exeter line

A goods off the Southern rolls into Exeter St David's station behind N class 2–6–0 No 31832 (July 1924–January 1964) of Exmouth Junction (72A) on 23 June 1950. On the left is an M7 class 0–4–4 tank which may well be waiting at the ground signal ready to act as banker for the steep climb round twisting curves to Exeter Central. All Southern trains running to North Devon and Cornwall used Western metals to Cowley Bridge Junction running in opposite directions to their hosts. No 31832 has yet to be fitted with a shed plate and carries neither lettering nor device on its tender.

One of the ex-LBSCR E1/R class 0–6–2 tanks No 32124 carrying a white disc as light engine headcode moves up to bank an Exeter Central bound freight which has come in from Barnstaple. The scene is Exeter St David's (GWR) where all SR passenger trains hd to make a compulsory stop. The E1/R class was also used for trains (usually mixed) on the North Devon & Cornwall Junction Light Railway linking Halwill Junction with Torrington.

summer Saturdays, locals from Exmouth Central to Broad Clyst, Honiton, Topsham and Budleigh Salterton via Exmouth, long strings of non-corridor coaches disgorging hundreds of Exmouth commuters at Exeter Central, the daily through coach to Waterloo in the bay platforms at Seaton and Sidmouth, the summer Saturday Cleethorpes in the refuge siding at Littleham, and an extra Waterloo set in one of the four platforms at Exmouth for the entire week, and above all the speed (even of many stoppers) and spaciousness of the countryside... here was a distinctive world. And that is without mentioning the Adams 4–4–2 tanks that made the Lyme Regis branch a living museum, the evening express that ran non stop to Exmouth three minutes before a stopping train, and the large Exmouth Junction complex of locomotive shed with an esprit de corps as strong as anything St David's had to offer, marshalling yard and the railway's own concrete works.

Much was the sorrow when the route was 'Westernised', its surviving freight diverted, and the two-hourly expresses slowed to stop at nearly all the remaining stations. Now they race through the abandoned junctions instead. Once proclaimed as the eighth busiest InterCity route in Britain, it is however run by Network SouthEast, but instead of being electrified is to be the domain of a new breed of diesel multiple units. Exmouth, with a restored half-hourly service much of the day, is now Devon's fastest-growing town, but the rest of East Devon, especially away from the coast, develops lazily, Shaftesbury still slips down the economic league, and those in a hurry to get from Crewkerne to London drive to join an HST for Paddington. In fact joining someone returning from London to Crewkerne in the restaurant car at Westbury was a passenger bound from Southampton to Devon; both were saving time making a substantial deviation north from the direct route, a sad commentary indeed on what has happened to the South Western's showpiece.

Two Junctions
Barnstaple Junction

All of the Southern's many junctions in the west were characterised by short periods of intensive activity between long siestas. This was true even on the main line at places like Seaton and Sidmouth Junctions, where up and down branch-line workings dovetailed into a time-honoured pattern of up and down main-line departures, a through carriage or van perhaps being transferred.

Halwill somehow managed more sustained periods of activity, with extensive goods shunting, especially for the

cattle trade, between bursts of passenger activity when trains from three or four different directions arrived in rapid succession and expresses from Waterloo were usually divided for the last time.

Exeter Central saw intensive shunting when expresses were being made up or separated, sometimes simultaneously. One train from Waterloo usually proceeded as two down to Exeter St David's and beyond, while the restaurant car was terminated and connections from and to Exmouth provided – and maybe a Meldon ballast train came noisily up from St David's with two Victorian tank engines performing well as bankers. Meldon, Southern owned, developed considerably as the whole Southern went over to using its excellent stone, the reballasting of the SE&C section giving an especial boost. The ballast business added considerably to activity at Okehampton, another junction station where sometimes it seemed perpetual Sabbath and others that the layout was far too small.

But if there was one junction that epitomised the Southern in the West it was Barnstaple. Though Barnstaple Junction was the original broad-gauge station

Barnstaple Junction shed on 1 September 1949 with ex-LSWR 0–4–4T still carrying its very early BR number variation S42 (so numbered 28 February 1948 renumbered to 30042 4 April 1952). This class was used for the branch service to Torrington and locals to Exeter Central. The column to the left of the line is typical LSWR with wheel controlling the water valve in the column itself. Note the simple but effective form of mechanical coaling (though it looks more like slack than coal).

of the North Devon Railway, Waterloo ultimately won premier position in North Devon. Admittedly much of the line from Exeter remained single, the crossing stations with inadequate loops, but there was no feeling of Southern inferiority at Barnstaple Junction. It was the GW, coming into the station at the end of its long undulating (if better signalled) branch from Taunton down a steeply-inclined bridge you could see from the platform, that played second fiddle.

The variety of trains and movements was immense. The cycle in the up direction normally began with a single coach plus perhaps a van or some milk tanks arriving from Torrington, the engine running round using the middle siding and pulling it back toward Torrington to allow the Ilfracombe train to screech its way round the sharp curve from Barnstaple Town. But there were local trains from Torrington and Ilfracombe that terminated at Barnstaple, as there was a morning local from South Molton Road and often a Waterloo train that went no further.

During most of the Southern Railway's history, the GW trains – usually three coaches, one by popular demand a corridor coach for passengers with weak bladders – terminated at either side of the down island platform and were shunted into a siding on the Torrington side to await their chance to use the up platform at the start of their return trip. But there were always, even in the war, several summer Saturday through GW trains to Ilfracombe, and later through Taunton–Torrington running became the norm to save shunting, green coaches and Maunsell moguls reaching Taunton.

Traffic wise, Ilfracombe was very much the 'main line', with double if hideously-graded track beyond Barnstaple Town, but signalling – and what an array of lofty brackets! – still reflected that pre-1926 Torrington had been regarded as main, the major portion of Waterloo trains terminated there. Down trains to Ilfracombe could hardly have had a worse start. It was always fascinating to watch them bear sharp right over the diamonds as the signalman who had walked to the end of his little platform handed the token for the single line, sharply curved before and on the bridge over the estuary, to beyond Barnstaple Town – a real bottleneck on busy Saturdays.

Tail-end traffic, reflecting the district's agrarian economy, resulted in constant movements around Barnstaple Junction: horse boxes, milk tanks from Torrington, cattle wagons still regularly attached to many passenger workings until after the war, gas vehicles, parcels vans, GW as well as Southern.

Over a dozen freight workings left Junction daily, for Exmouth Junction, Bideford and Torrington, Ilfracombe, with local trip workings to Rolle Quay, Fremington Quay (where all the locomotive coal was brought in) and Barnstaple GW. Even when there were no passenger carriages needing the attention of window cleaners and wheel tappers, there was bound to be coaling, watering or cleaning of engines – mainly an aged breed excellently

maintained – at the depot close by the down platform; and goods shunting in the extensive yard continued even when the station's refreshment room was catering only to railway staff enjoying a lull.

Even the blind could have found Barnstaple Junction an entertaining place: the screech of wheels round the sharp curve to Ilfracombe, the constant escape of steam and short bursts of power needed in shunting movements, attaching and detaching, luggage trolleys pushed over to the down island platform, the patter of feet on the wooden booking hall floor, the clanging of bells in the two signalboxes, and much more produced a continuous symphony of the country railway junction.

Over the years the pattern changed, away from intensive local traffic with school children and shoppers en masse, to the long-distance holiday business. Local trains in winter then steadily resembled empty stock. Freight reached a peak during World War II, when thousands of American troops under General Eisenhower were stationed in North Devon, and declined sharply after 1950. The first economy was the closure of the GW station, Victoria Road, which had of course maintained its separate locomotive depot, freight and other facilities. Once after that a visit by the Queen brought local trains mainly carrying school children into Junction from all four directions. But steadily Barnstaple Junction or just Barnstaple became the end of a dieselised branch from Exeter, even its future under threat.

Once Junction employed much of the cream of the local labour force, and standing on its platforms you could gauge the time of year and state of the local agriculture and industry. But few local people ever rode the Atlantic Coast Express to Waterloo, generally viewed as a distant slightly mysterious place only reached after crossing the GW at Exeter. Even the all-Devon Ilfracombe and Torrington to Exeter Central trains were beyond the scope of most.

Tonbridge

'Tonbridge . . . This is Tonbridge', came the announcement. 'The train at platform three for Margate, calling at Headcorn, Ashford, Sandling Junction and all stations . . . change here and remain on this platform for the 12.10 to Maidstone West, also for the Hawkhurst branch. Change here for High Brooms and Tunbridge Wells West, which will be the second train at platform 3. For Lyghe Halt, Penshurst, Edenbridge, Godstone, Nutfield, Redhill and stations to Reading, cross over the bridge to platform 1 . . .'

That was just one of the many connectional permutations that could be made at Tonbridge, major junction on the former South Eastern main line, in steam days. Some survive even today. There were main-line express services from London to Ashford and beyond (some running via Dover, others via Canterbury West to Ramsgate and Margate), and the main-line stopping services, some through from London, others starting at

Sevenoaks or Tonbridge. The Hastings line, with express and stopping services, diverged just east of Tonbridge (to climb right from the junction to Somerhill tunnel and Tunbridge Wells Central) and also carried trains from Tonbridge running through to Brighton, Eastbourne, or Oxted – the latter diverging at Grove Junction to run round to Tunbridge Wells West and on to Groombridge.

At Paddock Wood, the next station five miles down the Dover main line two more branches diverged, to the left to Maidstone West and to the right to Hawkhurst, the former with either through services or connections from Tonbridge and the latter with connections, usually from bays behind the through platforms.

Back at Tonbridge yet another junction: this time to the west, taking the cross-country line to Redhill and on to Guildford and Reading. This was the original SER main line from London, via Redhill, which accounts for the fact that it is on a straight alignment with the line on to Ashford, while the present main-line from London via Orpington approaches Tonbridge on a sharp steeply-canted check-railed curve, which brought the speed of the mightiest expresses down to 50mph as they turned from south to east or vice versa.

Tonbridge station itself has five through tracks, a down platform line, down and up lines in the centre without platforms and two up platform lines astride the up island platform, the outer track often used for Redhill line trains to give cross platform interchange with an up London service or as an independent arrival platform from the Hastings line, allowing a parallel move with an up stopping service from the Ashford main line. Behind the down through platform is a dead end bay facing from London or Redhill (the Redhill connection crossing the entire layout) used by terminating trains from the West. After unloading they set back into carriage sidings adjoining the London main line without fouling the through running lines to await their next working, which in steam days would often be an onwards service to Ashford or beyond, or to Hastings, Eastbourne, or Brighton. In the reverse direction trains would arrive at Tonbridge from those starting points and after a short wait would continue to Redhill or even Reading, sometimes designated in the working timetable as a through train, for example from Eastbourne to Reading, even if they were not so shown in the public timetables.

Tonbridge shed was situated on the up side at the Ashford end of the station just on the country side of the junction with the Hastings line. With many trains starting or finishing at Tonbridge, there were frequent engine movements between the shed and the carriage sidings or platforms, and to the goods yard, Tonbridge West Yard, adjoining the Redhill line, for freight trains.

Signalling in Tonbridge station area was from two mechanical boxes, which lasted almost until the 1961 electrification, one at the west end in the fork of the Redhill line and the curve of the London line via Orpington, the other at the east end controlling the Hastings line junction with the main line. The latter was perched high up on stilts, giving a good view of the east end of the station although not (because of the limited view through the single arches – each wide enough for just one line – of the bridge carrying the road and the modern booking office entrance) of the tracks through the station. Because of the close spacing of the two station signalboxes, there were outer and inner distant signals, the latter carried under the stop signals approaching the station from each end, including a down splitting distant for the Hastings line.

During the last years of steam, Tonbridge normally handled over eighty passenger trains daily on Mondays to Fridays calling at one or other of its four platforms, mostly between 5am and midnight, plus the numerous services that passed through non-stop, mainly boat trains between Victoria and Folkestone or Dover, and the morning and evening commuter expresses running non-stop between Hastings line stations or Ashford and London. Except for the Hastings line, the coastal expresses and boat trains had the latest coaching stock and the SR's most modern locomotive classes: the Schools 4-4-0s (on most Hastings line expresses but also on a few main-line ordinary and boat trains), Bulleid Pacifics (exclusively on the main line), and BR Class 4 2-6-4Ts, 4-6-0s and 2-6-0s (on some of the cross-country trains). Virtually all the many other services were run by the Southern's rolling museum of pre-Grouping locomotives and stock, and continued to be right up to the end of steam in 1961. There were the H class 0-4-4Ts on pull-push trains of low-roof antiquities originating from all three of the Southern's constituents on the Westerham branch from Dunton Green (which was worked by Tonbridge-based engines), the Maidstone West, Hawkhurst and Oxted routes, while the stopping trains along the main line and the Hastings route were often in the hands of SEC 4-4-0s trailing three-coach birdcage sets. On the Eastbourne, Brighton and Redhill/Reading services there could be almost anything: pre-Grouping locomotives and stock, BR standard Class 4s or SR Moguls, with birdcage sets or the SR's straight sided 8ft 6in wide corridor coaches of the mid 1920s. Nothing more modern would go through the tunnels at Tunbridge Wells.

On summer Saturdays and bank holidays out came the special-traffic sets for reliefs to booked services, excursions, and extra trains to unusual destinations – perhaps a through train from Charing Cross to one of the branches to replace the two-coach push-pull train normally working from Tonbridge. Maidstone West often had one of these, serving the picturesque halts along the Medway. Usually it was formed with an SEC 4-4-0 and a long set of pre-Grouping non-corridors, with birdcages and the odd lavatory carriage, all by the 1950s a good forty years old, a few well over the half century. Because of the close departures of branch connections from the down platform at Tonbridge after the departure of a down London service to Hastings or Folkestone, two trains coupled together would sometimes emerge from the down

sidings, perhaps an 0-4-4T with a push-pull set and a Class C 0-6-0 and four-coach corridor set for Eastbourne, which would be split as they stood in the platform.

Often on bank holidays the normal train service was replaced by a special timetable which used the paths of weekday morning and evening business trains for the extras and excursions. Excursions ran not only from the London termini to the coastal resorts but also from surburban starting stations such as New Cross. There were also some unusual resort-to-resort workings, particularly before World War II, such as excursions from Margate to Brighton and vice versa. One unusual through working at Tonbridge on Whit Monday 5 June 1933 was an excursion from Gillingham to Brighton which ran up the Medway valley through Maidstone West to Paddock Wood, and along the main line to Tonbridge, where the train ran forward on to the Redhill line before setting back into the down platform where another engine took over. It then continued down the Hastings line to Tunbridge Wells and the usual route via Eridge and Lewes.

On bank holidays and on summer Saturdays most of

Tonbridge station in the first year of BR on 28 August 1948. The train is the stock for the 4.10pm to Paddock Wood with train engine class L 4–4–0 No 1785 and an SEC three coach birdcage set. The other two locos, class R 0–4–4T No 1671 and class O1 0–6–0 No 1109, would be for other trains starting from Paddock Wood and were sent attached to the passenger train to save a block section. This was a daily working circa 1948. The factory of T. Ives & Son, cricket ball manufacturers, is behind the class O1.

the engines on longer-distance trains carried duty numbers on a board hung from the top lamp bracket so that signalmen could identify the train. On that 1933 Whit Monday Tonbridge passed no fewer than sixty up trains alone between 4pm and midnight, many of them booked excursions, and several from Hastings not going up the main line via Orpington to London but routed instead via the Redhill line to Edenbridge then Crowhurst Junction to Oxted and the Mid Kent line from Sanderstead through New Beckenham to emerge on the main line again at Parks Bridge Junction. The Southern's bank holiday programme was ever full of interest.

175

11
ON THE ROAD WITH PADDLEBOX AND SPAMCAN

IT is the autumn of 1924 and the Southern Railway has not yet cut its teeth, let alone become anything of an entity. Maunsell is in overall charge but on the South Western Drummond and Urie are still the names to contend with.

Nine Elms shed has some of Drummond's less likeable legacies, the Paddlebox 4–6–0s, not the worst engines on the line but bad enough; every fireman fears he will get one sooner or later, if lucky to be told by the time-keeper: 'You could be worse off. You're only going to Salisbury. Be glad it isn't Bournemouth.'

This is a Saturday working and the young fireman is spare; the driver does not look best pleased to find he has not got his regular mate; he is no more pleased when he learns that the newcomer has never fired a Paddlebox or any other four cylinder engine. His words of greeting are 'Well you have a good chance of learning something today, something you can't learn anywhere else!' All the tools are locked up on the engine so the fireman goes over to the stores for the keys, taking the oil bottles with him to get their quota. The engine is newly painted in Southern livery, all cleaned and polished as if the cleaners think she is the finest thing on wheels and they had never heard any fireman say anything about Paddleboxes.

Once in the cab and after checking the water in the boiler and the tender tank the driver kicks the coal in disgust as it's Welsh and someone has given them the dust from the bottom of the wagon. The fireman mentions that it should 'cauliflower' (swell as it gets really hot) but the driver only glares at him. 'The first thing for *you* to do is to get underneath and make sure that ash-pan is empty – at least you can make a clean start. Then get your fire going. Build it up flat to the bottom of the hole but put plenty up at the front, then oil up round the tender. You must have had one of these damned eight-wheelers before. The bloody shed's full of 'em!'

The fireman is not amused. Whoever designed the ash-pan on a Paddlebox had never tried to empty one in his life. With the firebox sitting low over the driving and leading axles, the pan is very shallow, made worse by a firebar bearer across it. He gets the driver to move the engine to set the inside cranks on the top quarters; that way he can get the pricker in through the front damper, though the front ledge is inaccessible. He then takes a long rake to the rear part of the pan, which is not quite so difficult. Five minutes of hard, filthy labour and he is satisfied.

The fire is burning but needs brisking up with the blower and the fireman puts a good round on as best he can. It is not so easy as it sounds; the South Westerns' style of fire hole, part blocked by the inward-opening

T14 class No E460 waits to back out of Waterloo station in 1927: she has recently been shopped. Note the glass 'porthole' in the enormous splasher. Waterloo A signal box in the background.

Gloss Finish

When Eastleigh works built the D15 class 4–4–0s in 1912, they went into the paint shop to receive seven coats of paint and three coats of varnish, with filling between undercoats and rubbing down with pumice between all. The result was magnificent, and depots made certain that the finish was kept sparkling.

Eastleigh was reorganised in 1931 in order to reduce the time that locomotives were out of traffic. After that, painting was done in the erecting shop while fitting staff were putting the finishing touches to their work. Any dirty finger marks on wet paint had to be touched up afterwards. The painting process for passenger engines was filler, one undercoat, one top coat and one or two coats of varnish. While some engines in service were kept creditably clean, in other cases it might be hard to see the colour under a layer of grime.

No 461 was the last T14 to be superheated in 1918. The fireman has a nonchalant air as the engine moves out of Waterloo to set back on to a West of England train waiting in an adjacent platform.

door which formed a baffle plate, is hard enough on small engines with deep fireboxes but it needs a good swing to get anything to the front of the level, shallow grate. This done he gets down to oil the tender axle boxes and curses every one of them. Most tenders have outside boxes but not these Drummond bogie contraptions; here there are eight inside oil boxes to feed between the spokes, check the trimmings are in place, and hope that no water has got in. But this is a Paddlebox, four cylinders where two would do, a grate too long and awkward to fire and a self-choking ash-pan. And an express train to run.

When they are ready to leave the shed the fireman sets the sight feed lubricators until he is satisfied with the interval drops. They potter to Waterloo to pick up the train; by the time they are hooked on the guard has come for the driver's name and his ticket and has told them they have nine on for 253 tons. Steam is coming up to the red mark on the gauge with plenty of water showing in the glass.

The driver looks at the fire. 'As we go by Vauxhall give her a good sprinkle round the sides then get plenty on at the front before we get running too fast. That's where she will burn most of it. You can leave the injector till then. We've only got a T9 load and you won't need to fire heavily.' By Clapham the coals are good and bright, the safety valve blowing off and they have half a glass of water.

For the next fifteen minutes or so the fireman keeps sprinkling the coal, firing mainly to the front but elsewhere when it is white and the steam keeps pretty close to the red mark. After Esher the driver looks at the

A 'Paddlebox' rebuild in full cry. T14 class No 459 is passing Byfleet with a down Bournemouth express about 1938. Maunsell rebuilt her in January 1931, removing the enormous splashers and taking the platform up clear of the motion. The profile of the cylinders blending to the smokebox makes it self-evident why enginemen bestowed the alternative nickname of 'Double Breasters'.

gauges and the fire. 'There you are, she'll steam fine if you go the right way about it. Thicken it up a bit as we go past Weybridge. It's a pull from there but not far really, another 33 miles gets us over Oakley then she'll run herself most of the way to Salisbury. These Paddleboxes are not bad downhill.'

By the bottom of the dip they are running at sixty-five to seventy and the driver sets her to pull harder. The fireman thanks his Maker that he has listened and has a good thick fire as he knows he has to keep hard at it until they are by Farnborough. But in the last mile or two the steam drops some 20 pounds below the red line and does not come up again until the driver eases up on the reverser on the level and the fireman can briefly shut off the injector. By the time the train passes Hook the steam is just below the red mark. The driver looks at the fire again. 'That's alright. A couple of thick rounds and you'll be right down to Andover.' It works and there is nothing to do for another twenty miles but watch the water and the road. After Red Post Junction the fireman looks at the fire, puts a couple of rounds and guesses that this will take them over Grateley even

The cab of the Merchant Navy contained more piping than most! Prominent in the centre the Ajax steam operated butterfly firedoors: the foot pedal is just off the picture. The two Klinger water gauges above are flanked by the vacuum and steam chest pressure gauges (on the left) and boiler pressure gauge on the right. Below these are two lubricating oil gauges for the oil bath and carriage heating gauges. The vacuum brake valve and ejectors in front of the driver largely obscure the front window. The pendant regulator handle is alongside. The large oilboxes fed the coupled axleboxes and other points.

179

The L1s – An Appreciation

The Southern L1 class inside cylinder 4–4–0s had a lovely action, closely akin to the Holden 4–6–0s of the Great Eastern; no hesitation or jerkiness, they just moved smoothly away. Known as the 'Glasshouses' by enginemen, they were all attached to the South Eastern Division and appearance of the class at Nine Elms was virtually unknown until electrification of the Kent Coast lines in 1959. Several of them came to Nine Elms and stood over in the 'old shed', out of work. Occasionally one would be lit up and put into service.

The only occasion I had charge of one was when I received instructions to go Light Engine to Surbiton, shunt the yard and work a freight train to Nine Elms Goods, calling in at Wimbledon West Yard to pick up more wagons. It was a humdrum job by any standards but made interesting by the fact that I was breaking new ground with an L1. We went tender first to Surbiton so that I could have the shunter on my side and also to work the train engine first. I was struck by the buoyant 'feel' of the engine, a comfortable ride and the Stirling steam reverser was a boon during shunting operations. Apart from being somewhat wary of the braking power available it was hard to believe that it was a passenger locomotive.

I would have loved to have it (I think it was 31786) on one of the semi-fast services to Basingstoke from Waterloo, or even a moderately loaded Ocean Liner Special to Southampton Docks; it was a splendid engine and not deserving of the scrap heap. – A.E. Hooker.

with four miles of fairly steep up hill and hopes he is right. They stop just on a minute early and the fireman wonders why his mates make such a fuss about Paddleboxes. They unhook and get away as quickly as they can to the shed.

After they have turned on the table and got water there is still over half an hour before they are back to the station. The driver shuts the fire door and both dampers and goes to the front. He opens the smokebox and fiddles for a moment inside it, and comes back. 'Whenever an engine has steamed well I have a look in the smokebox and I nearly always find something in the blast pipe.' He takes the fireman round and sure enough there is a 'jimmy', a piece of thick wire in the form of a cross in a ring with three short bent prongs and a long one. 'When we get back we may as well keep it', he says. 'It may come in useful some other time.'

A quarter of a century on and the Southern Railway has gone but these are early days of Nationalisation and the Southern Region still reads SR. Bulleid has reigned at Waterloo since 1937 and has more than made his mark with his Pacifics and Q1s. The Spam-cans are really something – not all good to the engineman, but most of it alright.

As soon as you get on the footplate you notice that there is a filler hole for the tender tank at each side, more convenient than the one in the usual position at the back with that climb up over the coal or up the back steps. But to the practical man there are disadvantages. If the leather hose leaks (and many of them do) there is a jet of water to soak you which can be nasty in winter. Another thing, if you have to brake sharpish with a tenderful of water a couple of torrents come out like Niagara. Oil boxes for axle-boxes are in the cab and that is handy. All the valve gear and the inside crosshead and connecting rod are in a big box under the boiler so you do not have to oil the joints one by one and there is a good seat for the driver, though if he uses it he cannot see ahead through the front window as the vacuum brake valve and ejector are in the way. The engines ride splendidly, too, but that is after you get going as they are terrors for slipping and that 280lb/sq in pressure does not help. Keeping it down to about 200 in the boiler solves some of the problems for some drivers. The steam operated firedoor is just a gadget (though if properly adjusted, and you have the knack, it can be a help) and so is the steam reversing gear but more so. On most Spam-cans you have rather tenuous control over what the reverser does, so if it stops anywhere near what you want you leave it at that and get the pull you need by setting the regulator. In fact for an SR crew used to the more staid South Western engines there is plenty of interest on a Spam-can.

The 2.30pm from Exeter Central (12.15 from Ilfracombe) gets into Salisbury at 4.45 just in time for the driver to book off and nip home to make a deal over those boiling fowl which have finished laying, so he intends to make good time today; the fireman is his regular mate and both know the new Pacifics as well as most. Nothing to make anyone feel uneasy: twelve on for 370 tons, and the firebox only has to catch sight of the shovel for the needle to go up to the red line. Mind you the fireman is a '210 man' so that should help with getting away smoothly.

With a big hot fire it is not easy to stop No 21C9 *Shaw Savill's* pressure from getting into the two hundreds as they stand in the station but the fireman has left room for more water in the boiler and is able to keep things in check with the injectors and they start without slipping.

She goes up to Exmouth Junction with a fine rasping crackle at the chimney, then away down past Pinhoe and 21C9 is doing seventy by Broad Clyst giving them a flying start so that she hardly notices the climb up to Whimple. By the time the driver has juggled the reverser to drop her down on the lever to get over the next knob it's time to shut off for Sidmouth Junction and they stop a bit ahead of time. They are away again without slipping with plenty of fire as the train goes down into the dip before one of the hardest climbs on the whole trip, four and a half miles up to Honiton Tunnel, first at 1 in 100 and finally at 1 in 90. No problems here today as it is good and dry, nor would there be with any Spam-can in

On a hot summer's day in the last year of the Southern, Merchant Navy class 4–6–2 No 21C2 Union Castle *begins the ascent of Honiton bank. The driver views the extent of the burning lineside grass while his fireman is kept busy with the shovel! The locomotive is in malachite green (applied June 1946), has modified cowling, circular builder's plate on smokebox door, cast number plates and a cast Southern tender plate.*

Merchant Navy Pacific No 21C6 Peninsular & Oriental SN Co *(the longest name in the class) is hard at work on a West of England express. (The name was rendered in small letters to fit the standard circular plate.) Built in 1941 and rebuilt in October 1959 she was withdrawn in August 1964. Another distinction was that she was the only engine of the class to remain at one shed (Salisbury) throughout her life. This view dates from about 1947 as 21C6 was repainted malachite green in September 1946.*

decent order provided the sanding gear works. Sometimes it does and sometimes it does not; you just have to hope.

They get over the top nicely and dive into the blackness of Honiton Tunnel. The turbo-generator is humming away below the cab and the gauges come to life with a ghostly, luminous glow. The driver gives her plenty of blower and shuts the regulator, setting her at what might be called thirty-five per cent cut-off for drifting down into Axminster. For seven miles she runs herself, riding easily on the curves and picking up speed to nearly eighty with the driver opening the regulator bit by bit after they pass the bottom of the dip, pulling up the reverser for the start of the rise to Hewish. Then trouble strikes.

When the Spam-can is really moving and you start juggling with the reversing gear funny things can happen and today is no exception. The indicator seems reluctant to move then starts rapidly in the wrong direc-

tion and lands in full forward gear. *Shaw Savill* starts roaring from her chimney and running as if she is on a ploughed field.

At the speed they are going the blast will lift all the fire out of her with a big regulator. The driver shuts down fast until he can get the cut-off back to something sensible. But he cannot. Then he realises that there is a steam blow from under the brake casing that was not there before. Probably the steam pipe to the reverser has fractured. One of his mates had this happen a month or two ago. Now she is stuck in full forward gear. The driver pulls a face; the last thing he wants today is trouble as the chap who is coming about those boiling hens is only calling in on his way elsewhere. Can they cope with it, just using more steam and coal? He tells the fireman to get down to it and build up a good thick fire. There are over ten miles of steep climbing ahead of them and that will give them time to think what is to be done once they are over the top. Perhaps a new engine at Templecombe, the next booked stop – if there is anything suitable there – and they can get there. But if they do send a message to the shed and the driver decides on another engine it means a delay. So no message is dropped. Even if she stops with the cranks in an awkward position, it is an easy start out of Templecombe and they will be very unlucky if they cannot get away in full forward gear.

With that settled, the driver concentrates on fine tuning the regulator opening to keep them going up the bank at something like the right speed without throwing too much fire out of the chimney. They do quite well and as soon as half of the train is over the top he shuts off for the steep drop down into Crewkerne. There on four miles of climbing, a dip past Yeovil Junction, a climb to Sherborne and Milborne Port and a drop down into Templecombe where the driver sends a note to Salisbury shed that they cannot get the engine into backward gear and a replacement will be needed. Not only that, yet another engine will have to get them back into the shed and he makes sure that they do not send the message before they are away – or else there might be one back pronto telling them not to start.

The fireman runs down the platform to give the note to one of the staff. As he gets back the driver gets the right away from the guard, blows off the brake, eases the regulator open and they hold their breath. She moves very slowly but after she has gone a yard or two they know all is well.

In a steep downhill mile and another on the level she is up to sixty or so with no trouble getting through Buckhorn Weston tunnel, running fast through Gillingham and up the bank to Semley. After that, with 18 miles of downhill, it is easy. They roll into Salisbury nicely on time and no one could have guessed there was anything wrong.

But they cannot unscrew the coupling behind the tender. It is too tight and they are not able to set the engine back to slacken it. The tank that the shed has sent has a bit of a struggle, but by first pulling forward and then reversing with steam on he manages to buffer up hard enough for the fireman to move the bar of the screw coupling. After they hook off the train the tank goes forward easily enough but in setting back on to the shed, the Pacific fights every inch of the way despite the cylinder drain cocks being open. As the driver says, there is entertainment in every can.

Excursions on the Footplate
On Sunday 23 April the Southern took the remarkable step of offering a footplate ride to participants in a special excursion for railway enthusiasts. The ride took place on a tank engine between Brookwood and Bisley, and was included in the fare of 7s 6d for the excursion proper between Waterloo and Brookwood.

The Bisley branch, which witnessed this relaxation of official caution, is hardly the place in which to expect anything in the way of high-speed running, and though one of the drivers declared to his small and dutifully-impressed audience that 70mph was easily attainable by his steed, such magnificent progress was debarred by the 10mph restriction. The two Drummond 0-4-4 tanks, coupled back to back, proceeded gravely down to Bisley and with becoming austerity, back to the funereal neighbourhood of Brookwood, conveying a lively and appreciative cargo of all ages and both sexes. In all over 100 were carried.

Every handle that could be turned on a Lord Nelson locomotive placed on view in Brookwood station (which proved to be No 864 *Sir Martin Frobisher* fitted with a Lemaître blastpipe and high-sided tender) was made to perform its allotted task over and over again. A small exhibition of photographs, prints, and models was examined with great interest and, though the weather failed to clear, the excellent meals obtainable in the dining cars specially parked at the station more than made up this deficiency. – *Railway Magazine* 1939.

Southern Railway, Goodbye

When, in March 1945 S.W. Smart was appointed super-intendent of operation in succession to W.J. England, he determined on a quick return to Southern Railway standards of efficiency both in train service planning and daily performance with the passenger services paramount.

Using the train supervision network (Control was a word which S.W.S. refused to recognise and which was never uttered in his hearing) he instituted the 10am telephone conference – known to the Divisions as the inquisition – which he frequently took himself and castigated the divisional superintendent in person on the shortcomings of the previous day's performance and that morning's business period workings. The ammunition was prepared for him by Jim Crowe who had been appointed to take charge of the train supervision office at Waterloo to which the HQ staff had returned from the rustic and cavernous delights of Deepdene.

But S.W.S.'s chief weapon was the monthly trains conference. Here he would sit, unlit cigarette twirling round his mouth, undisputedly the Top Man, and take his divisional officers through specific details of train and locomotive performance, always probing with the significant question and making his displeasure very clear if he did not get the right answer. If he was not fully satisfied, the Division would be required to submit a written report, the bones of which would be picked clean by 'The Bird of Ill Omen'.

He also instituted a series of trains meetings at which a divisional assistant met members of all grades of operating staff to go through an agenda which was partly a 'pep talk' and partly designed to give an opportunity to discuss suggestions for improvement. Each division was required to hold at least three such meetings at different locations each month. These served a very useful purpose at the time as there were many wartime legacies that needed to be dealt with as no longer being appropriate. Since it was known that S.W.S. read the notes of these meetings, quick remedial action was assured. The trains meetings, however, carried on after they had outlived their usefulness. The agenda became stereotyped and the whole thing time wasting. As the staff shortages increased it became more difficult and less sensible to release traincrews to attend the meetings.

From the time of his appointment S.W. Smart impressed the weight of his personality and power on the Southern operating performance with the result that the average late arrival of passenger trains was brought down from five minutes to one minute in a year. This was not achieved, as happens so frequently today, by adding recovery time which was unknown on the Southern except for the five per cent built into the electric train schedules. There was nothing for steam except for the occasional minute or two for crossing purposes at flat junctions.

Similar pressure was exerted for the repair of war damaged facilities so that full passenger services could be restored at pre-war speeds. There was a real need for this as business firms had returned to London and all the evac-uees were home. All this put a heavy strain on public transport as there was still little if any petrol for other than official private motoring. Overcrowding, particularly on the London East business services, was becoming insupportable.

Services were gradually improved. Already, some civilian boat trains were running. The Golden Arrow was restored for the summer of 1946 although foreign travel was still difficult. Then, S.W.S. decided that the full pre-war business services were to be restored for the following year in all Divisions in order to alleviate the overcrowding.

This proved to be a difficult and complicated job. The chief civil engineer had imposed a 60mph maximum speed throughout the inner London area due to deferred maintenance and this upset the schedules of all the fast steam trains and those of the electrics which missed some stations. In fact, so energetic were the 'civils' that this restriction was allowed to last for almost twenty years.

All sorts of unstandard items had been built into the timetables during the war years to cater for local needs which in many cases still existed and could not be ignored. But they did not blend with the pre-war timetable structure. And not all of the operating facilities had been restored.

In January 1947, the country was swept by exceptionally severe snowstorms, gales and bitter cold that went on for some weeks. Roads were impassible over wide areas and rail movement ground to spasmodic halts with slow starts. On 7 February, Mr Shinwell as Minister of Fuel, had to tell the country that, with immediate effect, there would not be any electricity available for offices and 'non-essential' industries and no domestic supplies for five hours a day. The train services had to be cut drastically and a chilly weekend was spent at Waterloo doing this. It was typical of S.W. Smart that he appeared in the office on Saturday, kept himself informed of all that was being done – and took us all out to supper.

Ever since the disastrous freeze of 1940 the CM&EE had been experimenting with means of inhibiting the formation of ice on the conductor rail. By 1947 there were nine coaches each fitted with five tanks holding 750 gallons of low grade oil which was dribbled out on to the conductor rail through nozzles and spread with a following brush to make a thin film. The treatment was reasonably successful with ice but not so much so with snow. When the temperature was only a degree or two below freezing this tended to form an oily mush which the collector shoes impacted into a hard lump between shoe and rail, causing heavy flashovers and eventually either isolated the shoes or caused burnt out armatures. The CM&EE then designed scrapers for fitting to conductor shoes and to the locomotives of snow ploughs and a few others. Despite all this, there were monumental delays followed by severe rolling stock shortages resulting from the burn-outs. With the eventual thaw came lashing rains and widespread flooding. Chalk falls in the Dover area repeated the 1940 pattern and closed the line beyond Folkestone.

THE RAILWAY EXECUTIVE
SOUTHERN REGION

JOHN ELLIOT,
CHIEF REGIONAL OFFICER
Telephone: WATerloo 5151

HEADQUARTERS,
WATERLOO STATION,
LONDON, S.E.1

To all men and women of the

SOUTHERN REGION

To-day the railways of Great Britain pass into the ownership of the State. which means all of us—those who work on the railways and those who use them.

I know that every one of us who was yesterday a member of the Southern Railway staff, will carry into the future the long and honourable traditions of public service which our old Company built up. and. as a member of our new Southern Region. will strive with might and main to serve the public—not merely as well as in the past. but even better.

We have been a happy family of railway folk. and "S.R." has meant a lot to us. We are now members of a larger family, so let us keep our team spirit. working loyally together with pride in our service and for the public good.

As Chief Regional Officer. I send you my sincere greetings and best wishes for your future well-being and happiness as a member of the staff of the BRITISH RAILWAYS.

January 1st. 1948.

The Parliamentary Bill to nationalise the railways published in December may have uplifted the hearts of the faithful but it did nothing to ease the shortage of coal which had become as critical as the shortage of food. Much of the coal that did come through was totally unsuited to locomotive needs. Briquettes of coal dust bound together with cement and opencast coal known euphemistically as 'nutty slack' were just the thing for steaming locomotives built for anthracite! A programme was prepared to convert over a thousand steam locomotives to oil burning to save a million tons of coal a year. It was never completed.

The success of S.W. Smart in restoring the pre-war train service as early as 1947 and, even more, his victory against heavy odds in the battle for punctuality and the way this was achieved, set the seal on his overlordship of the Southern operating for a decade. Nobody would argue with him – including the general manager.

One of his firm policies was that every movement that occurred regularly should be shown in the timetable and have rolling stock and crew allocated. To this end he directed that all conditional and special pathways used more than four times a year should be included in the permanent workings and dated. These were incorporated in the 1948 timetable. One unforeseen effect was that, as freight trains were timed clear of all 'conditional' paths, they wasted much time in sidings waiting for non-running trains to pass.

It was also directed that all booked light engines which passed through a signalling section were to be timed and

Tickets

Sorting tickets was a twice weekly job. Singles, outward halves and return halves were sorted alphabetically and then numerically. The whole lot was then despatched to the audit accountant's office where some 200 girls spent their working lives checking them.

This checking was a deterrent to a classic booking office fraud – issuing a rarely used ticket out of order from the ticket tube. This allowed an unscrupulous clerk (or, more often, a relief clerk) to pocket the money since there would be no debit until that particular ticket came to be issued, perhaps several months later. This was, of course, long before the days of cash registers and one-piece tickets now standard in all booking offices.

The girls were also vigilant in comparing the destination on all hand written 'blank' tickets with what was afterwards shown on the monthly accounts. All blank tickets issued to stations on other company's systems were returned to the issuing company for this to be done since accounting for a blank ticket to a nearer destination was also an obvious opportunity for fraud.

The station clerks knew that this audit office existed and attempted frauds were very rare indeed. Your job was at stake. Probably the most useful product was the maintenance in work of girl clerks in an era of high unemployment, although this charitable object was unlikely to have been in the mind of the audit accountant.

the timings published. Although this caused a lot of work since there were some 3,000 light engine runs in the London East Division alone, it was a worthwhile exercise since it proved that, in many cases, there was no possible pathway available in the 'notional' time off-shed published in the engine workings so that quite a number of alterations had to be made. It was another of S.W.S.'s practices to obtain first hand background reports from his own staff on any subject on which he was taking or contemplating action. This greatly helped his reputation for never asking an awkward question to which he did not know the answer.

As part of the campaign for improving timekeeping, Ivor Marshall and one or two others were encouraged to go out and about seeing what there was to see. Noticing a shunting engine standing idle at Chatham, Ivor's enquiries established that it stood there for 24 hours a day, seven days a week and had been provided as a wartime requirement but had no apparent peacetime use. It seemed that nobody had questioned the need and the local station master had come to regard it as part of the scenery. A scathing letter from HQ demanded that coaching (which was the term for passenger) shunting provision elsewhere in the Division should be critically examined. It was a routine part of trying to get back to pre-war efficiency when every shunting provision had to be justified and sanctioned.

The Chatham engine episode touched S.W.S. on a sore spot. He was justifiably proud of his mastery of Southern operating and, perhaps, a little contemptuous of a general manager who had joined the Southern from the *Daily Express*. He was, therefore, highly incensed that J.B. Elliot had recently drawn his attention to a statistical increase in the number of coaching shunting miles for which there was no explanation readily available. There was still working at Waterloo and also left over from the war years the elderly Father Dyer – close on seventy years old and the sole survivor of a famous pre-war economy commission for train crew economies. He was asked to investigate but did not find much of consequence.

In the autumn of 1947 a new training school was opened at Clapham Junction. For the first time in SR history, new entrants to the clerical and uniform grades would be taught on a full time basis by experienced instructors and not left to fend for themselves at stations. At a higher level, Woking College was opened with courses for established staff in railway accounts, shipping and continental work and traffic control, the last being organised and lectured by Jim Crowe. It was, of course, called train supervision instruction. But in the last months before nationalisation there was still a 'Is Your Journey Really Necessary?' attitude to public demand and a stilted civil service cum socialist mentality which, in the interest of fair shares for all, prevented the Southern from offering 'Evening Cheaps' on existing services from London to Brighton because the LMS could not offer the same facility to Blackpool!

It was a fairly sparse Christmas with food and clothes still severely rationed. Then, on 1 January 1948, all woke up to find that the Southern Railway Company had passed peacefully away.

For all its despotism (more or less benevolent and in accord with the times) its frugality and cheeseparing, it was a highly viable and lively business, well managed and pursuing known, sensible and realiseable objectives. Its policy decisions were taken by directors who had their money in the business – and there is no public ownership substitute for that discipline.

Low Closure Score

These were the passenger lines the Southern closed during its life.

Near Dumpton Park to Ramsgate Harbour	2 July 1926	Replaced by new line – Dumpton Park to Ramsgate and new station at Ramsgate.
Ramsgate Town to Margate Sands	2 July 1926	
Tooting Junction to Merton Park via Merton Abbey	4 March 1929	
Canterbury to Whitstable	1 January 1931	
Fort Brockhurst to Lee-on-the-Solent	1 January 1931	
Hythe to Sandgate	1 April 1931	
Hurstbourne to Fullerton	6 July 1931	
Basingstoke to Alton	12 September 1932	
Brighton to Kemp Town	2 Janaury 1933	
Botley to Bishop's Waltham	2 January 1933	
Chichester to Midhurst	8 July 1935	
Christchurch to Ringwood	30 September 1935	
Lynton to Barnstaple (1ft 11½in gauge)	30 September 1935	
New Romney Junction to Dungeness	5 July 1937	Replaced in part by new line with stations at Lydd on Sea and Greatstone on Sea using old terminus at New Romney
Part of New Romney branch	5 July 1937	
Ash Junction to Farnham Junction	5 July 1937	
Dyke Junction to The Dyke	1 January 1939	
Kew East Junction to New Kew Junction	12 September 1940	LMS Trains
Lyminge to Harbledown Junction (Canterbury)	2 December 1940	Elham Valley line
Lyminge to Cheriton Junction (Folkestone)	3 May 1943	
re-opened	7 October 1946	
finally closed	16 June 1947	

The Southern Railway's territory was then, more prosperous than the rest of the country and this is reflected in the number of passenger services withdrawn between 1923 and 1947, a total of 17 including two which were replaced by new lines. (Ramsgate and New Romney)

The corresponding figures for the other three groups were GW 51, LNER 80 and LMS 102. Even allowing for much greater route mileage the proportions of closures was much higher. Many of the lines in the South East have been closed by BR but again the proportion is lower than the rest of the country.

Deptford

The London East Division was the heaviest of the Southern managerial areas for volume of traffic. It was also the most complicated geographically with its maze of inner suburban lines, its five London termini – Charing Cross, Cannon Street, Victoria Eastern, Holborn Viaduct and St Pauls, the last being renamed in 1936 when Post Office station on the London Transport Central Line took the name St Pauls and the SR station became Blackfriars.

Probably the heaviest line in the 1930s was the North Kent, one arm of which ran through Deptford with its notorious Creek Bridge, the other snaking through Lewisham Junction and Blackheath, joining up with the Deptford branch at Charlton.

For many years, a running battle was fought between the Southern and the Deptford Wharf frontagers. The railway was under statutory obligation to lift the Deptford Creek bridge at any hour, day or night, at ten minutes notice to permit the passage of ships without moveable masts. The station master at Deptford knew a thing or two about ships and refused to open the bridge to ships whose moveable masts were temporarily immobilised by a clutter of deck cargo. This led to complaints, fist fights and the threat of legal action. But the railway always stood firm.

From Charlton the freight line to Angerstein's Wharf was kept busy with imported railway sleepers which were unloaded from ships, pickled in creosote and sent away by the trainload all over the Southern. There were also the United Glass Bottle and other wharfingers who brought much business to the railway. One feature of Angerstein's wharf was a delapidated four compartment SER coach built around 1865 which was in use as a shunter's lobby.

A little further down, Woolwich Arsenal was still in being and turning out much or little armament according to the political climate. Below Plumstead was a succession of private sidings, the largest being William Cory's North End coal wharf at Erith whence numerous trains ran daily to supply Lower Sydenham, Croydon and Tongham (Aldershot) gas plants. On the marshes near Abbey Wood was a colony of gypsies whose children and horses alike had a predilection for wandering on the electric railway. As the horses had the usual metal shoes, they rarely survived. The children, being usually unshod, had a better survival rate.

From the electrical rolling stock depot at Slades Green (now only one Slade) the line ran into the triangle joining the Bexleyheath line or straight down to the bottleneck of Dartford. Between Dartford and Gravesend Central was cement country with Northfleet and Greenhithe as its grey eminences. On the one up and one down running line with no passing facilities were intermediate sidings at Kent Works, Ingress Park and Johnson's, all generating several trainloads daily and covering the roofs of the surrounding area with a fine grey dust that settled everywhere.

Between Gravesend and Strood the railway ran through the two Higham tunnels, originally constructed as a canal to join up with Strood Dock. From Strood to Maidstone West was given over to cement and paper mills. Reed's, Holborough, New Hythe and Brookgate were its centres. Just beyond Maidstone West was another paper mill at Tovil, whence the line ran through hop growing country to Paddock Wood.

But this money-spinning line never had any money spent on it. It was worked by a variety of ancient signalling systems. At Dartford, the signal boxes at either end of the station were worked by Walker's block, in which the most reliable safeguards against conflicting movements were the reliability and coolness of the signalmen. The interlocking was minimal.

Before its postwar rebuilding, Dartford had one up and two down platforms, the latter being used to terminate electric services as well as for through traffic. The working there was so complicated that the whole timetable and carriage workings for the North Kent, Bexleyheath and Dartford Loop lines were built around the practicability of the Dartford station working.

The open countryside along these lines rapidly vanished as speculative builders filled every available space with 'desirable homesteads' at prices ranging from around £850 to £450 freehold. At least one estate got down to £399 houses with three bedrooms and bathroom.

Since almost all of these houses were brought by people working in London, the overcrowding during the peak periods built up to almost intolerable levels. As trains for all suburban lines ran to and from both Charing Cross and Cannon Street there was a tremendous interchange at London Bridge, aggravated by the thousands fighting their way up and down the steps and along the overbridge to and from the Central Section against a contra-flow making its way between the Underground and the South Eastern side.

The narrow platform 1 and 2 at London Bridge where the evening action was, presented a scene of ordered chaos and no little danger. The platform faces were crowded to the edges.

187

12
THREE 1950s JOURNEYS

Exmouth–Bournemouth

A steady trickle of travellers arrive at Exmouth's red-brick 1920s station, a handsome Southern rebuilding, and all four platforms are in use. The 9.42 and 9.49 arrivals from Tipton St John's and Exeter Central have disgorged shoppers and day trippers, we are due away at 9.52 and four minutes later there is a departure for Central. We had been tempted to take the latter to enjoy the run along the Exe and it actually gives the shorter time to up-country, but we settle for the daily Waterloo through coach. The scene is dominated by those ex-LBSC tanks whose shrill whistles frighten passengers at Exeter St David's and still feel out of place in this part of the world.

Ours is a standard Maunsell coach, half full; the two ex-LSWR coaches only have a couple of passengers between them. Though this is the only through train to anywhere except on summer Saturdays, there is no departure ceremony, but the tank engine works hard crossing the long red-brick viaduct and climbs until we are almost on the cliffs at Littleham. The long rake of the summer Saturdays Cleethorpes–Exmouth service rests in the refuge siding.

Climbing again on one of the last pieces of railway to be built in Devon, we reach the summit and drop through a deep cutting into Budleigh Salterton, where we cross a down train and where the Mogul of the daily goods is shunting. Rush hour! Two very Budleigh Salterton ladies claim their reserved seats, talking plummily without acknowledging our existence. Over a tall viaduct and we are in the Otter Valley, the next station being East Budleigh though it is actually Otterton. The LSWR had too many stations beginning OTT, so it was said, but caused total confusion by first calling this Budleigh and naming Budleigh Salterton just Salterton.

Four minutes smart running brings us to Newton Poppleford, served by all ten daily stoppers each way but missed by occasional summer Saturday extras, including a Waterloo service that starts at Littleham for the campers. Now Tipton St John's and a daily ritual that is always enjoyable. Normally the Exmouth train goes into the yard so the locomotive can run round free of the running lines, but our engine leaves us in the up platform. We look out and see the Sidmouth train descending almost mountain-rail style before we are pulled back the way we came. The Sidmouth train takes our place, we are attached to it, and the engine we have just given up shunts the other two coaches into the down platform to form a local to Sidmouth.

Ottery St Mary, whose locals have a choice of two through coaches to

188

Waterloo, is our only stop before we abandon the Otter for a run across the fields to Sidmouth Junction, arrive 10.45, 16¼ miles so far.

Thoughts have already been given to the origins of the train we are about to be joined to. It should have left Central 10.30, a few minutes after the arrival of the Exmouth train that left after us, and have through coaches from Torrington and Ilfracombe (joined at Barnstaple Junction) and Plymouth, its refreshment car – we fear it will be a Bulleid Tavern job you cannot see out of – added as the Plymouth and North Devon sections were put together at Central with precision timing. The service offers a huge range of journey options. Torrington and Ilfracombe coaches both started at 8.10, a Bude–Okehampton connection into the Plymouth section will have started, almost before we were up, at 7.58; a third 8.10 departure was the single coach Launceston–Halwill connection into this – while the Plymouth section set off from Friary only five minutes later at 8.15. And running ahead of us up the main line to Templecombe and serving all but one of the intermediate stations will be the 9.33 stopper from Central carrying the through carriage from Seaton we will eventually

Last farewells are said to passengers on the two coach train for Sidmouth Junction as 30323 waits to depart from Tipton St John's with the 2.04pm from Sidmouth Junction to Sidmouth on 3 July 1956. Most trains from Exmouth connected at Tipton St Johns with the Sidmouth to Sidmouth Junction trains. M7 class 0–4–4T No 30323 was one of the class without the smokebox wing plates and forward sand box incorporated into the splasher. Note the long clinker shovel wedged behind the hand rail and the disconnected steam heating connection. Set 447 was part of the Atlantic Coast Express the 11.00am from Waterloo affording one of the many through services to Southern-served resorts.

continued opposite

Unappreciated Bargain

'Fancy a short trip into the countryside'? asked the 1927 enthusiast. 'Only if we're back by ten and we don't spend too long getting there,' replied his loving wife.

His itinerary was a mere 47 miles in less than three and a half hours. What he did not tell her was that it meant eight different trains, though to be sure they could sit tight for six of them rolled into... but if she complained he had a super alternative.

They set out from Ashford (however often you used the train there the interest in the stock beside the works was tremendous) at 12.40... almost exactly half way between the two express departures on the line to Hastings (Dover to Brighton and Plymouth and Margate [actually Holborn Viaduct] to Brighton).

At Appledore they of course changed, into the branch train to New Romney via Lydd. She wanted to explore New Romney and he encouraged her saying he would be back to pick her up in just under two hours. 'But I want to be with you, love.' So she endured the whole of the 'short' trip whose exact timings were:

Ashford dep 12.40
Appledore arr 1.3 dep 1.10
New Romney arr 1.15 dep 2.3
Lydd arr 2.11 dep 2.17
Dungeness arr 2.20 dep 2.30
Lydd arr 2.48 dep 2.55
New Romney arr 3.2 dep 3.8
Appledore arr 3.32 dep 3.43
Ashford arr 4.0

She never wanted to see a train, leave alone Lydd, ever again, and was utterly enthusiastic about the fact that the Southern economised by sending the same train down different branch lines one after the other.

If you said you wanted to go to Dungeness (very few people did and later only New Romney had passenger trains, other of course

pick up. It all runs like clockwork daily, an intricate system of through coaches and locals, every one of which has to perform to avoid delaying the vital London service. Only on summer Saturdays do things sometimes go awry.

A Merchant Navy pulls short into the up platform punctually at 10.48. It is allowed five minutes to pull forward, cross the down main to pick us up in the bay and take us over to be the first two coaches of a lengthy train. It is done smartly but unfussily, and people from all over the West Country who have endured frequent stops and shunts relax in the knowledge that smooth high-speed travel is about to begin – seven minutes before the Atlantic Coast Express that detaches the Sidmouth and Exmouth daily through coaches leaves Waterloo: we imagine the scene [as portrayed on the jacket]. There is great contrast between locals that utterly reflect the deep countryside they serve and carry for more short than long-distance passengers and the great expresses that hurtle through the land filled with a fascinating collection of minorities skilfully brought together.

We have three minutes less than an hour for our next 63 miles. The route is far from level, or straight, but it is well laid out and we have the power we need – though our Merchant Navy slips as we get started – and the second steward visits the extended front of the train inviting us to coffee and proffering luncheon tickets. We decide to miss that and the Tavern car with its mock brick and sit back. Through Honiton and its tunnel and down its bank at 85mph, through the centre road at a deserted Seaton Junction, and on we go... Axminster, Yeovil Junction where a handful of people are on the down platform waiting for the arrival of the day's first express from Waterloo, and then up and down beautiful, unspoilt landscape. We are now going through but are scarcely of the countryside and, after we brake sharply down downhill and come to a standstill at Templecombe; the stop is all about connections and not the local life.

We alight, see the Seaton coach added, and reflect that the Lyme Regis and Yeovil Town ones are on a following train that will call here in an hour or so, to be added at salisbury to the up Atlantic Coast Express which will itself dash through on a non-stop run from Sidmouth Junction (with Sidmouth and Exmouth connections but not through coaches) to Salisbury. Though our journey is well into nationalisation, the routine has changed little over the years: there were wartime curtailments and shavings while Bulleid's Pacifics enable heavier loads to be carried at slightly higher speeds than during the 1930s. Oh, and there is now a 6.30 as well as 7.30am express from Exeter Central to Waterloo. More people seem to go on day trips to London and start earlier.

Fifty or so passengers who have arrived on the Somerset & Dorset Highbridge, Bristol and Sturminster Newton trains (the latter giving a connection off the Pines Express from Bournemouth) join the Waterloo-bound train, but of the similar number getting off, three-quarters are young lads going to report for national service at Blandford. Since the Bristol–Bournemouth left ten minutes ago (connections from the West to Bournemouth are traditionally bad), we have to wait for 12.32 all stations except Corfe Mullen Halt to Bournemouth West, first seeing off the noon to Bristol headed by one of those famous S&D 2–8–0 freight engines that often fill in time on gentler duties and the 12.01 to Yeovil Town hauled by a mogul.

We of course back out, a 4–4–0 at each end and reverse before going south. We have a Southern coach and generally this southern part of the route has become Southernised but (the train almost empty after losing the conscripts who alight with their noise at Blandford Forum) we do not regain pure SR metals until Broadstone. High tide makes it an enjoyable ride onto Poole, picking up three mothers with prams at Creekmoor Halt, and then we pass a succession of expresses and locals through Bournemouth's rich western suburbs before bearing right and dropping into Bournemouth West. Four hours 13 minutes, everything on time, great contrasts of scenery, trains and speed. Our final thought is why Bournemouth has such a ramshackle terminus, making Exmouth's feel very civilised?

Plymouth–Gunnislake

The Withered Arm they may call it, but there are excellent journeys to be savoured on the Southern in the West. Over the gradients to Mortehoe

continued
than on the miniature RH&D) you were allowed to stay on board free for the trip down the other line before and after. What a bargain down the Southern's 'Road to Sunshine', always remembering 'It's safer and quicker by Rail'.

Calstock Viaduct from the south side of the river Tamar on 4 August 1960 with ex-LSWR 02 class No 30225 hauling the 4.23pm Callington to Bere Alston train. Calstock station can be seen at the far end of the viaduct which has twelve arches each of 60ft span and stands 120ft above the river.

Okehampton

While most junctions on the Withered Arm instantly gave the impression they were only linked by single tracks, Okehampton at least occasionally felt as though it were main line.

Full-length trains arrived in various forms: the through Plymouth–Brighton was a time-honoured daily, while extra cattle trains and empties ran through, sometimes non-stop, as did the frequent Meldon quarry trains of hopper wagons supplying the whole Southern with ballast. (Strange to think that the fortunes of the quarrymen living in villages on the Dartmoor foothills depended on how much electrification was currently being completed in the South East.) Then there were numerous military specials and after World War 2 the summer car carrier from Surbiton to Okehampton itself and, of course, the Plymouth section of the Devon Belle.

It all added variety to the routine junction business of dividing and joining trains, though for some hours on summer Saturdays this was abandoned as all trains were strengthened and ran to single destinations, some with restaurant cars.

On summer Saturdays there was indeed a true main-line feeling and one imagined what Okehampton's role might have been had the original trunk route to the far West gone down through the middle of the peninsula, as once seemed likely under the Whig
continued on page 194

The crew of Class O2 No 30225 assist each other to take water at Calstock whilst working the 3.15pm from Bere Alston to Callington on 31 August 1960. The train composed a two coach corridor set No 24 and two four wheeled vans for the important fruit and vegetable business that sometimes meant adding a dozen or more vans.

and down the curves with excellent views of the Atlantic to Ilfracombe's high-above-the-town terminus; along the Torridge past the Southern's own busy port of Fremington to Bideford; along the Camel into Padstow, if you are lucky behind a T9 which always seems at home here and makes a magnificent spectacle when being turned in the evening sunlight. [The Torridge and Camel lines have been restored as excellent walks still with some railway hardware.] Then there is the grandly named North Devon & North Cornwall Junction Light Railway where you will probably enjoy the very rural ride in solitary state as passengers at least south of Petrockstow are rare.

But for sheer idiosyncracy take the 5.0pm from Plymouth Friary to Gunnislake. In 1 hour 21 minutes you will traverse 18¼ miles and apparently travel in equal amounts heading east, north, south and west. And [this in the 1950s] you still do in a pair of LSWR auto cars with open platforms protected by wrought iron gates.

Friary is already on the way out. The Turnchapel branch has been closed and no longer does the railway make any pretence of carrying suburban traffic. We leave as almost the only passengers. There is the usual queue through Mutley and as usual we are late into North Road, and glad to be off the Western at Devonport Junction. Passenger numbers double at Devonport King's Road, the original LSWR Plymouth terminus, again at Ford. The train's purpose is now clear. It carries dockyard workers home. No business at St Budeaux and we miss Tamerton Foliot, but after we cross the Tavy estuary and enjoy the last of many glimpses of the Royal Albert Bridge we do brisk business at Bere Ferrers – where in World War I dozens of young New Zealand soldiers lost their lives as a down express mowed into them. (They had been told they would be fed at the first stop out of Plymouth but that at Bere Ferrers was by signal and they got out on the wrong side.) And at Bere Alston business positively booms, as it does a few minutes later when the following Tavistock-bound train arrives. Geography protects the railway. Even the Brighton–Plymouth stops here and we pick up a few who have transferred from it as well as some dozens from the Tavistock-bound service which gives a faster connection from Plymouth to Gunnislake than our one daily through service. Indeed for the second time in this chapter we learn that through trains may be convenient but are not necessarily the fastest. Our engine has meanwhile run round for these ancient LSWR auto cars are no longer used for push and pull.

We zig-zag down the bends that heavy trains carrying the Tamar Valley's strawberries struggle even double headed coming up, and then have a magnificent view of the Tamar going into its gorge as we cross Calstock viaduct. We squeal into Calstock station, cramped and amazingly busy, and then get down to hard work. It is less than three miles to Gunnislake but the slog and the whistling at the open level crossings (for this is a Light Railway) takes all of the 14 minutes allowed. As we climb the view it becomes ever wider, but for the one daily train terminating at Gunnislake – the rest go over the moor to Callington – it seems positively wasteful to have to go high up above the town when most of the thirty or forty passengers immediately walk off down to it.

continued

support that went on to create the South Western. But it has to be said that even on the busiest of days the local patronage at Okehampton's station, a stiff walk up the hill from the town centre, in the Southern's later days a prime congestion point on the holiday road to Cornwall, was pretty sparse.

One other kind of train remains to be mentioned: the all-stations Plymouth Friary to Exeter Central which habitually followed a few minutes after the two-hourly expresses. Even business men travelling between Devon's two cities regarded the expresses as potentially useful if there were no GWR train. The stoppers (one of them handled by a GWR mogul as a Southern 'West Country' went via Newton Abbot so that drivers remained familiar with the alternative routes around Dartmoor) were strictly for locals, most of whom travelled in solitary state in ex LSW non-corridor stock with lavatories between a few compartments. Though passengers were never numerous and were mainly quickly lost to road competition, the snail's-pace climb up hills was between leisurely station stops for heavy parcels and perishable traffic, including rabbits that sometimes overflowed the guard's van into an adjoining compartment.

Explosion

Merchant Navy Pacific No 21C16 *Elders Fyffes* went new into traffic in March 1945, and was officially named at Waterloo with due ceremony on 5 July. Just twenty days later it was in Eastleigh works, reported as having suffered from 'an oil bath which had exploded after running hot'.

Forty seven years on it is not known in what circumstances this happened. The only bearing
continued opposite

The tank engine leaves its auto cars in the siding and goes to the shed only it occupies. As we stand on the island platform we recall the great mineral wealth of the Tamar valley and the collapse of mining and the emigration that led to Cunard maintaining an office in Gunnislake. The newly opened railway was a godsend, and since Devonport Dockyard did not yet have electricity the times of trains changed weekly in spring and autumn to maximise daylight working hours. [Even today, dockyard workers struggle up the hill to catch the morning train, Plymouth–Gunnislake surviving as single-line branch with reversal at Bere Alston because the Tavy and Tamar bridges give the railway a much shorter route than the road.]

Folkstone–Charing Cross

In the early 1950s, the Kent Coast still feels a long way from London, especially on Sunday, even in summer, when there are huge gaps in the through service and only one express in the whole day offers refreshments. But this is still the era of solid Saturday-to-Saturday bookings, and Folkstone (still largely a holiday town) is obviously choc-o-bloc as we drive through it to the Junction station [the one that survives today].

We catch the end of the symphony of a train heaving itself up the Harbour branch as we dash along one of the two island platforms: too late to identify the two tank engines in the front, but an R1 from the Canterbury & Whitstable section, an 0–6–0 with cut-down cab and boiler mountings, and to a Western enthusiast a bit of a museum piece. But we shall be seeing many of *them* today. [Pannier tanks were just about to be brought in for the Harbour branch but this was not known and had it been would have caused considerable surprise for in the early 1950s the former Big Four still kept themselves very much to themselves.]

Then we have to buy singles to Sandling Junction, so to the booking office and back to find much activity, most of it purely local. Trains on the opposite island include a well-filled excursion. Our 2.36 from Margate arrives a few minutes late, just after 4.15; we are alarmed by the number of passengers on board, but most again on local journeys alight, and we leave the Kent Coast only moderately full, though a full five hours have elapsed since the previous Charing Cross service, the one with refreshments.

Coming from the Western, again we are not over the moon about having only a 4–4–0 to take us all the way to London. The squat-looking School looks a bit like a compressed Lord Nelson, but we have heard the class is not only powerful but that that power is flexibly available and often gives fine performances over the switch-back route to the capital. We certainly make a brisk start, and though we are all stations to Ashford certainly do not hang about. Our coaches, by the way, are a mixture of Maunsell and Bulleid, more Maunsell and since dad's work has gone well we are in its first-class version with a splendid distance between the seats. There is, of course, the ever-pervading special Southern smell; they must use oceans of their disinfectant or whatever it is.

Through the tunnel and first stop at the curved platform of Sandling Junction where we alighted on the down journey. The word Junction brings pangs of regret. We see that the track of the Hythe branch has already been removed. While most pre-war holidays were at Hythe, dad always switched us to the private bus that took you to any part of town, no doubt a lot more efficient than being dumped up the hill where the branch train terminated. We used to watch the progress of its steam and smoke from the seafront. The closer attraction of Romney, Hythe & Dymchurch station always beat a determination to walk up that hill one day. But mother remembered how the guard of the businessmen's morning departure would tick off his regulars to make sure they were all present. Even when an inspector ordered him to start, he refused to do so until the last of the bunch dashed in a minute late.

A rural ride to Ashford, always the highlight. In pre-war days as now there were lines of ancient tenders and locomotives some presumably waiting for the next world. Today's bunch includes numerous SE&C 4–4–0s plus a couple of H class 0–4–4 tanks. But then the engines of the other trains we have seen or passed are nearly all pre-Southern, and while Bulleid's Pacifics dominate Exeter Central they are conspicuous by their absence in Kent this summer Sunday. There are some ancient coaches of six wheels waiting their valhalla at Ashford, too. But we always dash past the works too quickly and come to what one friend called a 'stopping finish' ie brakes on hard, at Ashford station, a busy and welcoming junction affair. Though we are much closer to London than where we live, it still seems in a different world.

The disappointment of this route is always that the dead straight section from Ashford to Tonbridge is not the racing ground the map suggests. It is a fascinating piece, up hill and down, in cuttings and on embankments, truly through the Garden of England, many fields alive

continued

within the oil bath likely to run hot enough to cause an explosion of the oil mist around it was the centre big end – the very bearing whose wellbeing led Bulleid to provide the oil bath in the first place.

Crankcase explosions have long been a problem with large diesel engines when big ends or pistons become overheated, and for many years the fitting of large pressure relief doors on the crankcase sides has been mandatory. But Bulleid's oil bath was of such flimsy construction that such doors would have been ineffective, and would probably have been a source of even greater oil leakage!

Doing the job she was designed for, No 30916 Whitgift *is working hard on the 1 in 122 of Hildenborough bank with a late afternoon Dover to Charing Cross via Tonbridge express in the early 1950s. She is in black livery with LNWR lining and carries a Ramsgate shed plate. The train is Maunsell corridor stock with separate doors to each compartment.*

Broadstone

It is one of those August Saturdays that do more to encourage Spanish tourism than anything the Spaniards achieve. A couple of enthusiasts huddle under their macs at the north end of Broadstone station's most westerly platform.

They have seen a string of lengthy trains set off on the Somerset & Dorset for Bath, and a few locals come and go from Brockenhurst and Salisbury by the line to the east, still sometimes nicknamed Castleman's Corkscrew after the founder of the route from Southampton to Weymouth and its propensity to wander around the countryside. It came this inland way since Bournemouth had not then been invented.

Now a late S&D train is threading its way round the curve to the most westerly of the four platforms. The enthusiasts glance at their watches and exchange glances. Will the road be clear in time?

No sooner is the tail of the S&D train on the straight into the platform, where it will halt briefly without doing any business before going on to Poole and Bournemouth, than the signalman throws levers around and the road is set and signalled for a train cutting diagonally across the S&D's path.

First faintly between the gusts of wind and then roaring above them is the sound of a rebuilt Merchant Navy pulling what is obviously a heavy load up the single track from the Weymouth direction. Though the rails are greasy, it is sure footed, and the driver has to ease her over the junction. Several hundred returning holidaymakers are on board, some finishing a cold lunch in the restaurant car. Hardly any of them aware that they are taking an historic route now rarely used.

On summer Saturdays two
continued opposite

with Sunday workers, the hops beginning to swell, the oast houses plonked neatly into the scene as though by design; but the miles pass slowly. Smart station work (amazing how the Southern manages that even on Sundays) means we left sharp at 4.47, but are allowed until 5.50 for the $26\frac{1}{2}$ miles... and that's in theory.

It soon becomes clear that our ten coaches are quite a challenge for our School going up hill, speed varying sharply according to the grade. 'Bad coal,' dad remarks; there is indeed a filthy exhaust when we climb, making the game of counting the oast houses quite difficult. We are twelve minutes late into Tonbridge, where many more passengers join but a malaise sets in, even the station work being a touch slapdash. Now our School finds the climbing really hard going. No longer on that dead straight route (on whose continuation by cross-country trains to Reading pre-war progress was also disappointingly slow, if compensated for by the complexity of through-coach and connection arrangements) we head north polluting the landscape and raising an ineffective noise. Plenty of time to stop, but we part with occasional slipping (there is now light rain) until peering out the window we can see the signals off for our journey through Sevenoaks Tunnel. But the slightest touch on the brakes brings us to a stop at the starting signal, just short of the tunnel entrance. The driver alights with oil can, the fireman climbs his coal heap no doubt in search of more combustible material.

Silence. A few passengers poke their head out of the window but return to snooze or read the *Sunday Times* in which 'Spectator' is no doubt warning of the dangers of war with Russia. This post-war land is not all we had expected it to be.

Another School flashes past us on the down line, followed a few minutes later by a King Arthur in full splendour with as long a train as we have seen on this route. Only a gentle hiss from our School... but eventually the safety valve blows off, the signalman who returned the starter to danger after our halt again lowers it, and we are off... uncertainly at first, but then surely, if forty or so minutes late. The guard walks quickly along the corridor checking that all windows have been reclosed. Enough sulphur comes into our compartment even with it and our door tightly shut. We seem to be underground for ever, though the lights that only feebly flickered at first steadily make it possible to read again.

Thank goodness for that; we are out in daylight, albeit gloomy daylight, and we cut quite a dash through Sevenoaks where the platform is crowded with people no doubt returning to London after the weekend... as many of our passengers are. 'Sorry about that,' says the ticket collector, accepting personal responsibility for the delay. 'Coal isn't what it used to be, and instead of running an extra train they will give us two bogies too many.'

Now we are in those approaches to London where you always see trains, electric and steam, passing, crossing, starting and stopping, like a huge but somehow uninteresting model railway system. We reflect how we wait for hours to see two trains cross at a characterful passing station on the Withered Arm yet here, where there are trains, trains and more trains, there is such lack of our understanding as to what it all means and does and how it fits together, that we merely gape. Yet every mile has its intricasies, and certainly the driver cannot rush ahead mindless of the numerous curves and junctions. It is a challenging but not a comfy way to approach London. Much of the surroundings are positively hideous.

Many passengers get off (and more surprisingly quite a few join us; how long have they been waiting?) at the grand muddle of London Bridge and at the less glamorous part of Waterloo. We start crossing the Thames about thirty five minutes late, noticing the abandoned Festival of Britain site and after a minor check take our place at number five platform. Charing Cross has been familiar since early childhood, and unlike its approaches it is fully understandable: one of London's smallest but by no means quietest termini, where when things go well, which means normally, the platforms are seldom empty more than a couple of minutes and drivers and guards of steam and electrics alike seem to play a game with just as much intensity as teams in the Cup Final.

Though we are in the front part of the train, we are not surprised that our School is already unhooked and the fireman combing through his coal again as we pass. Dad and the driver exchange wry glances such as to say better coal will surely be available one day, and if not, God help us. The rest of the family want to push straight ahead through the crowd to start queuing for a taxi, but the writer is anxious to take the scene in. Platforms 5 and 6 spelt many early holidays on that very different railway, the Southern, where they did so much with precision, where there seemed to be such goodwill and common sense, yet such backwardness… and again slowness just where you'd expect to move fastest. And there, as always, people are having to queue until the last moment (or so it seems) before being allowed to join one of the Kent Coast trains at platform 5 or 6. Somehow the more trains, the less significant. You never felt anyone special getting on at Charing Cross like you did at Paddington or a wayside branch line station or even on one of those great northern cathedrals of steam. And the lack of a refreshment car today: was not that serious since most Southern cars, even when the staff wore Pullman uniform and the sugar lumps were Pullman wrapped, offered pretty ordinary fare with service that was polite but no more?

Yet even on Sunday, the number of people, the number of trains coming and going, make Charing Cross feel the centre of the universe. The taxi queue stretches half way round the station square overlooked by that most glamorous of Southern institutions, the Charing Cross Hotel, even if its roof had once fallen in (obviously not built by Brunel). So ten minutes' freedom are allowed for a further look round. Astonishingly, the train we had only just seemed to get off has finished loading passengers and the ticket collector has closed the gate… that beastly gate that prevents you getting on early or at the last minute and which the ticket collector seems positively to enjoy using as a weapon. Perhaps necessary here but shocking; the Southern does the same thing at Exmouth. Yet how would the Great Western cope with Charing Cross with only two thirds of the platforms of Newton Abbot?

continued

Weymouth to Waterloo expresses run this way, avoiding the congestion in Bournemouth. They do not have down countparts. Otherwise there is only a single third-class only early morning Salisbury to Weymouth (obviously mainly for parcels) and a summer Salisbury to Weymouth and back for day trippers. The latter is favourite choice for those 'doing' this steeply-graded link so they can ink it in on the map.

Though a railway crossroads, windswept Broadstone on the edge of Hardy's Egdon Heath seldom sees passengers changing trains, any connections there are being accidental. For the most part it is a matter of stoppers from Brockenhurst (on the main line between Southampton and Southampton) and Salisbury simply joining the S&D's trains round the curve to Poole and on to Bournemouth.

But there are plenty of oddities, like almost simultaneous evening departures from Bournemouth going round the circle in opposite directions, of Broadstone's few passengers wanting to catch the Pines Express to the North having to go to Poole and then travel back through Broadstone non stop. Throughout the Southern's history (and well beyond) Brockenhurst-Broadstone remains double, though carrying many fewer people and freight than the single-track S&D.

Originally indeed the S&D went into Wimborne, where its trains for Bournemouth had to reverse. Having seen the Waterloo on its way, and wondering what will come off the S&D next, the two enthusiasts recall with laughter how Wimborne, now a scantly-used wayside station, was once described as the key to Dorset's railway geography. They wonder when Broadstone's crossroads and four platforms will seem equally odd and perhaps be bulldozed out of existence.

The Indian Summer of Steam

Who could have realised, on entering the No 3B link at Nine Elms in late 1958, that within ten years the great depot would be no more? But promotion brought 'seventh heaven' with rostered main line work. The days of 'copping' a trip to Southampton Docks, Bournemouth or Salisbury were over. There had of course been the occasional Salisbury job on a summer Saturday when every engine and crew was utilised... and men were even borrowed from other depots to cover the work.

Now a couple of drivers had retired from No 1 link, and one had gained appointment at Waterloo as running

Nine Elms was to become the last steam depot in London and conditions there had changed little over the last two decades. Amid the grime in July 1964, Battle of Britain class No 34082 615 Squadron receives an ample supply of coal for its next turn of duty which with the unusual combination of white disc and headlamp would indicate the Bournemouth line, the last route for high speed steam running in Britain. The whole site was cleared after the Bournemouth electrification and is now London's fruit and vegetable market transferred from Covent Garden.

foreman with his office at the country end of No 11 platform, the mecca of an ever increasing band of engine spotters. Promotion for several men at once.

'Road refreshers' were chosen with drivers likely to offer the regulator. Like on the 8.30 to Bournemouth, first stop Southampton, with a modified West Country. A great trip, helped perhaps by reading the Worting Junction home before the driver. The distant was always on for the Bournemouth line turnout, albeit a 60mph one, but on a rising gradient. Catching the home at the first possible second was vital. Saving valuable moments and the respect it gained led to being asked to take over the unmodified West Country on our return.

Next was a chance to try a BR Class 5 4–6–0 mixed traffic engine. What a noise up the chimney! But the 5s bark was worse than their bite... and at least one could see where one was going as the exhaust shot up out of the way instead of flopping along the top of the boiler casing and down around the cab as it did, spoiling the outlook from the Bulleids. The BR 5s thrived on a thrashing and could make a reasonable job of any Elms turn, providing the driver and his mate worked hard. They were fine on fitted freights and van trains where the graduated steam brake

Bournemouth Central just under two years before the end of steam. Rebuilt West Country class 4–6–2 No 34018 Axminster is leaving with the 9.32am to Waterloo on 5 September 1965. The all-over roof is complete and the two middle roads are still in use.

was a boon – especially to freight guards. But they were cold, draughty engines; the best thing was for the driver to sit with his feet surrounded with newspapers in a cardboard box to keep them warm. The tenders were a disappointment with the short shovelling plate; it should have been eight or nine inches longer so that the coal remained in its quarters and did not fall onto the floorboards. GWR men were used to that, but Southern ones were spoilt with the Maunsell and Bulleid tenders with good shovelling plates almost on the same level as the bottom of the firehole door. Firing the Standards was no sinecure. Essentially they were hard coal engines, and with our second class Welsh coal it was difficult to get them in 'the palm of your hand' as firemen could so easily do with Bulleids and Arthurs.

As at all big depots, the footplate fraternity at Nine Elms ranged from the conscientious to those who preferred to leave some details of preparation and disposal to the next chap... from the men who wanted running work to those who were prepared to let others get on with it. Some drivers hated going fast enough; they regarded passing times shown in the working timetable as tiresome marks best ignored. Their mates knew they were usually in for a hammering, preparing a big fire in readiness.

On a thirteen coach boat train to Southampton Docks, with a West Country in its original condition, the fireman had built up his fire expecting the worse. Approaching Woking on time, still busy with the shovel, he called out 'I

ain't used to this, fire ain't burning'. It was obvious he had overdone it. 'Sit down and enjoy the scenery.' He did not need to add more coal all the way to the Docks, nearly sixty miles, where arrival was still on time. A lot of coal was consumed unnecessarily, usually when the boiler optimum rate had been exceeded.

There is no doubt that the Bulleid Pacifics saved the day in the general running of the main line in the sixties until the final closure in July 1967. Had the Nelsons still been on top jobs, the 'Indian Summer of Steam' would have been a misnomer. For a start, quality of coal so necessary on the long, narrow fireboxes of the pre-nationalisation 4–6–0s was not available, and while a few firemen would have coped, unfortunately the general run would have failed to rise to the challenge, mainly of course through lack of experience. After all, Nelsons were never everyone's engines, even with the right coal.

An excellent fireman was Alan Newman. The hour from 6.55am to prepare Merchant Navy No 35007 *Aberdeen Commonwealth*, simply raced, and ten minutes before starting from Waterloo at 8.30, only calling at Southampton before Bournemouth, everything was in

Above *The Southern Region was very helpful to enthusiast organisations when special trains were requested and many interesting itineraries were formulated. Here Battle of Britain class 4–6–2 No 34079 141 Squadron crosses the river Hamble at Bursledon with a special from London Broad Street to Southampton which it had hauled from Fareham. The train comprising one of the last rakes of ex-LMS stock was chartered by the Home Counties Railway Society on 6 December 1964. During the electrification of the Bournemouth main line a number of services went this way.*

Left *One of the many specials run in connection with the end of steam, the Dorset Limited is seen between Litchfield tunnel and Worting Junction on 3 June 1967 hauled by Merchant Navy class 4–6–2 No 35030 Elder Dempster Lines.*

Opposite page *By 1966 Southern steam was, sadly, scruffy in appearance though still efficient in fact. One year before the end, West Country Pacific No 34009 Lyme Regis waits at Waterloo with a Southampton train of Bulleid stock.*

apple pie order. The backhead shone with an oily gleam, the gauge glasses were clean, the water level healthy. The footplate and coal had been slacked down, and there was time for a cup of tea when a man climbed aboard and introduced himself as Mr Sands, assistant to our motive power chief. 'Will you get us to Southampton right time, driver?' he enquired. 'We'll be right time to Eastleigh where I'll be surprised to get the road; why don't you ride with us.' 'I don't wish to get dirty, besides I have two colleagues to look after in the train.' He was, of course, assured he would not get dirty, and he looked at the clean footplate with approval, and 'right then, I'll nip back and tell my colleagues I'll see them in Southampton'. While he was doing so we agreed to show what could be done.

No 35007 was kept on the red line, very little smoke (photographers would not have approved!), no dust on the footplate... everything running splendidly until Eastleigh was approached. As usual, the outer distant under Allbrook stop signal was a caution, meaning a heavy brake application, down to about 25mph when Eastleigh East and West boxes permitted us through (ironically, for years there was a large sign in Eastleigh yard on the down side instructing drivers to 'shut off steam') so we arrived at Southampton three minutes down. The distant signals never seemed to be off at Eastleigh around this time, lending weight to the rumour that the East and West box staff were at loggerheads. Colour light signalling did not replace the pair of boxes until after the demise of steam. It transpired that Geoff Sands had served his apprenticeship at Crewe works and after this trip to Southampton he brought a few colleagues to share the pleasure of a footplate trip on a real express while it could still be enjoyed. After retirement he gave valuable help at Bressingham and reciprocated by offering a footplate trip on a Krupps on the 15in gauge.

One of the most satisfactory alterations made to the Bulleids was the fitting of the Giesl oblong injector on Battle of Britain No 34064 *Fighter Command*. The free running character was still there, but the exhaust now went up out of the way and fire throwing was almost non existent. What an improvement... but fifteen years too late. If only all the engines had been fitted. It was on a Sunday morning on the 9.00 to Salisbury that fireman Robin Bell, a most capable man, discovered that No 34064 was not happy with a normal 'light Pacific' fire, one well banked up under the door and back corners, thin across the front of the grate, which would virtually feed itself with coal rolling down off the heap under the door. Robin had to allow the fire at the back end to burn away and feed some coal across the front, producing a more uniform, level fire... and then the power available was a treat, and one had to be careful to observe the 85mph line limit. Only occasionally did we break it, like on the A4 *Mallard* in February 1963. When we were approaching Andover, the senior King's Cross inspector called out 'What's your road speed?' Being told it was 85, he pointed to the speedometer showing 93. 'Speedometer is wrong,' he was assured, but of course it was not. The LNER Pacific rode superbly, the A4s running the Merchant Navys very close in performance.

The final year or two at Nine Elms were grim, the engines generally filthy, though if one was earmarked for a special tour it was cleaned... and not normally by the usual cleaner waiting his promotion.

The two Merchant Navys marked up for the 2 July 1967 'farewell to steam' specials were a good example. But, generally, any locomotive developing a major defect, such as needing a hoist for hot boxes, would be withdrawn on the spot. An example of this was with BR Standard No 73155. The enormous rivets which held the brackets supporting the right slide bars and attached to the main frames had worked loose, creating a shiny spot on them about two inches high. When the examining fitter saw this on arrival at Nine Elms, the locomotive was instantly withdrawn from service, languishing at the bottom of No 12 road for weeks until painted by David Shepherd in his famous 'Last hours at Nine Elms'. The whole shed, with lines of silent engines, seemed to exude gloom, and every trip on a steam locomotive — at the very end usually because a diesel had failed — became a challenge. In those days a cancelled train was still unheard of. The end happened quickly. Long after steam was of very secondary importance if it survived at all elsewhere on BR, Bulleids were giving a fine overall performance on the Bournemouth and Weymouth road. And then it was clear that even here it was all downhill.

The writer's final steam trip out of Waterloo was on 26 June 1967 on the 8.10 Weymouth boat train, with Battle of Britain 34060 *25 Squadron*... a vastly different machine from that we knew some thirty years earlier as 21C160. It was locomotives like this that allowed SR steam to go out with a bang on the South Western Division. Though the relaying of the Bournemouth section meant frequent speed restrictions, quite a few drivers were determined to leave their mark... encouraged by the zealous band of train spotters. Indeed, a friendly rivalry sprang up between a few drivers, and high speeds became accepted in unlikely places, and happily officialdom looked the other way. How about 20 mins 12 seconds from MP51 at Worting Junction and MP 81 (near Tunnel Junction) on the Salisbury road: 30 miles at an average of 89.8mph, 101 recorded at Andover, and 99 at Porton. The engine? Merchant Navy 35023 *Holland Afrika Line*, with eight coaches, an special in aid of the SR Woking Homes. That was on 15 October 1966. What memories... and of Merchant Navy 35009 *Shaw Savill* leaving Waterloo eight minutes late on a Sunday trip to Salisbury. 'MP 31 in even time?' The fireman accepted the challenge. With only nine coaches, the MP was passed nicely within 31 minutes, the arrears of the late start all won back... and then she had to be eased or Basingstoke would have been reached too early. Happy days and miles... and what job satisfaction.

Overlord to victory

The special traffic section had a sub-section to deal with military freight trains conveying 'stores' for the D Day build-up, exceptional loads of guns and tanks, ballast trains and special vehicles on both passenger and freight trains.

The progress of military stores trains built up to a crescendo. Staplehurst, a quiet country station between Tonbridge and Ashford with two unloading sidings, was the site for an enormous Army munitions and stores dump operated by the US Army and a similar but smaller depot at Hothfield Halt was used by the American Air Force. Station master at Staplehurst was Pat Harvey, an ex-relief signalman of quite exceptional ability who seemed to be quite happy to accept an unending flow of trains provided that they arrived an hour apart. They came off the LMS and LNER via the West London line and their time-keeping offered no evidence whatever of the ability of these Companies to act as exemplars in the efficient handling of freight traffic or of the benefits of train control as expounded by them. Arrivals could be anything from two to three hours before time to ten hours late. The running from Scotland and from Liverpool was so erratic that Tim Hall, head of the engine working section refused to send his engines and men to relieve until he was advised that the train was actually approaching the West London line or arriving at Willesden. Although sensible, this arrangement meant that the whole of the pre-arranged special traffic engine workings and men's duties were prepared for nothing and the work had to be covered at the time. Likewise with all the timings which were carefully worked out in theory. In the end, the 'non control' train supervision office had to ad-hoc pathways, engines and crew duties through the most intensive suburban area in the world.

Hothfield was run by a cheerful RTO evidently from somewhere deep in Texas. Whatever the size of the programme given him when he telephoned each evening, the only answer was a lovely, drawling 'O.S.Sirr. And good night to you.'

Pat Harvey's system was equally simple. He was out by six am, counted up the previous day's wagons side-tracked at Tonbridge or Paddock Wood because of late running, added those known to be on the SR and wrote the total on a piece of paper. At 6.15 the US Army major arrived, gave Pat a cigar and translated the figures into terms of lorries and men, strode out to his jeep and communicated his needs back to base by despatch rider. There was never any shortage of men or transport. Work started at 6.30am and went on until dark or finish.

From 1943 restriction on the movement of fresh fruit was lifted and the Kent crop flowed all over Britain. There was no petrol allocated to its haulage by road and in the busiest three months the Southern moved 66,000 tons in 20,000 vanloads. Almost all the soft fruit went by passenger train but much of the apple and pear crop was by freight. Most of the passenger-rated soft fruit came from Rainham, Newington, Sittingbourne and Teynham

and the small country station at Rainham turned into a miniature marshalling yard. A direct train ran from Rainham to Willesden, later extended through to Manchester and another to Kings Cross. Other trains ran to Chislehurst Goods where they were joined up with the 30 to 40 vans form the Paddock Wood area. Fruit on passenger account reached a peak of some 150 vans per day.

There was always trouble with the LMS who received the bulk of the traffic because of the rough formation of the trains. Each station would set out the loading sidings in the morning so that vans for the principal stations to which the growers said they were loading were grouped together. In the early afternoon they would find out that the price was 2d more in Liverpool than in Manchester and the price somewhere else was 2d more than that. They would work out the difference in the rail charge and relabel the lot to ensure the maximum net revenue.

There was a permanent shortage of box wagons and it was laid down by the Railway Executive and reiterated before every fruit season that, because of the importance of the freight business to the war effort, box wagons were not to be used in place of passenger vans which were in even shorter supply to carry the passenger rated fruit. Of course, they always were.

By the autumn of 1943, the possibility of invasion had virtually disappeared and thousands of London families came back from Kent for their customary hop picking holiday.

As stated in the introduction, each Sunday, the hoppers were visited by their 'friends'. There were literally thousands of these and a programme of some thirty to forty special trains was operated. It was a poor 'friend' who did not come home with a sack of apples, another of vegetables and a chicken or rabbit together with a bellyful of good Kentish ale.

The 'special traffic' proper – and they regarded the hoi-polloi of the sub-section as being slightly improper inasmuch as it dealt in such mundane items as freight trains – were known as the 'Military'. They dealt with nothing but services personnel and their impedimenta. Their trains ran in great numbers. By the end of 1943, the Southern had run 20,000 military special trains. In the build-up to D Day another 10,000 were run shifting 5½ million troops.

In charge of the whole room was 'Gentleman George' Dutnall whose speciality was looking after the two trains of super heavy batteries which were used to shell the French coast. These used to run about the Ashford-Hastings area, potting away from time to time. He also looked after the wanderings of the two 'patrol' trains which consisted of armour plated trucks with machine guns and runner wagons. Their occasional excursions from their camouflaged nests must have been for exercise only since there were no enemy troops within machine gun range and not likely to be.

Also in the special traffic room – actually, a wooden pre-fabricated hut – was an ex-patriate rolling stock

Assault craft loaded in a variety of wagons probably at Hither Green in the build up to D Day (6 June 1944). It was only possible to load one vessel in five plank open wagons but two or more could be accommodated on flat wagons. There is a line of US Army four-wheel box cars on the left.

section from Headquarters consisting of two HQ staff in exile and two ex-station clerks as assistants. The senior was a very eager beaver and spent much time poking around the Military papers for advance information of operations exercises which he would transmit quietly over the phone to his superiors at Deepdene to impress them with his zeal. The Military men cured this by making a file of an imaginary 'Operation Nosey' with a list of trains required as well as a number of elephant trucks, which were duly gathered from other railways in anticipation. When nothing happened, the penny dropped.

At last on 6 June 1944 the announcement that the Allied invasion of Europe had begun showed that 'Exercise Overlord' was the real thing. A few weeks earlier, there had been a large scale exercise, 'Spartan' hurriedly arranged over the telephone during the weekend which was obviously a dress rehearsal and designed to test, amongst other military matters, just how the railway could cope.

Then, just a week after D Day, the V1 flying bombs started. The first consignment came over during the night of 13 June. The raucous roar of the primitive engines and the yard long tails of flame gave them a fearsome appearance. Their detonation on landing was spectacular.

Their arrival caused the last and least organised evacuation of the war. As the nightly raids had long since ended, many parents brought their children back home. The new danger sent people fleeing not only form London but also from the areas of Kent over which the bombs flew and were so frequently brought down. The RAF fighters operated from the Channel to the Sevenoaks area with a particularly daring wing of Polish pilots stationed at Tonbridge. These pilots discovered that it was possible to fly exactly alongside the bombs and, by tipping one's own wing, to nudge them into a descent course in open

country. After Sevenoaks, there was a network of barrage balloons in the Chelsfield area and those few V1 bombs which passed through these were targets for the experienced London area anti-aircraft gunners.

Although blind flying, the V1 bombs did a great deal of damage and, indeed, reached targets other bombs could not reach. On Sunday morning, 17 June, one scored a direct hit on the piers of Charing Cross Hungerford Bridge – something that the Luftwaffe had tried in vain to to. Anther fell on Cow Lane Bridge at Peckham Rye and demolished it. These two incidents caused as much disruption to the train services as any aimed bombs had done. Unluckily, one V1 shot down at Rainham in Kent swung round and fell on to the line where it exploded in the face of an oncoming train. The locomotive fell into the cavity and several passengers died.

Railwaymen were just getting used to the blessed quiet when, on 2 September, the air was shaken by several large and unexplained explosions. The V2 rockets had arrived.

More tension, more damage, but 'Overlord' was going well. For the first month or so, it made little difference to the special traffic workload. Then it was decided that it was safe to reopen Dover and Folkestone, and the freight poured into the division.

In the months before 'Overlord' several mysterious special trains had conveyed huge electric transformers to Dungeness siding on Romney Marsh. These were highly secret, running only at night and to be cancelled if an air raid warning was received. They were propelled from Lydd Town to a point beyond which railway staff were not allowed and pushed by the military to the underground pumping station constructed for 'Pluto' – the pipeline under the ocean to supply the invading forces with fuel. One of the most imaginative of wartime projects, the pipeline was constructed to run from Milford Haven to Dungeness, thence by flexible pipe laid on the ocean bed across the Channel. Despite 'Pluto' there were still ample petrol trains to the Channel ports.

In January 1945 leave trains began running for the British Liberation Army as it was styled. Since the leave was short, BLA trains took priority. They ran during the night from and to Dover on 24 hours notice from the War Office. As the workings had to be produced during the night for distribution to the line early next morning the military men were required to work round the clock.

In May 1945 the Germans surrendered and the war in Europe was over. Alas, victory brought no improvement in the civilian standard of living. On the contrary, rationing and general austerity got worse. Not surprisingly, perhaps to forget their woes, Britons flocked to the seaside in unprecedented numbers. The Southern ran over two hundred trains during the August Bank Holiday period, mostly to the Kent coast and the Isle of Wight. Victoria and Waterloo were besieged. Allhallows enjoyed a boom. The enormous demand for weekend and holiday travel to the Kent Coast stretched the Eastern Section resources of engines, coaches and train crew to the limit and there were some notable engine failures.

Although the Southern had lost only one locomotive to enemy action, fourteen more had been badly damaged. The effect of this, coupled with age, incessant heavy service duty and restricted maintenance caused increasing availability problems, particularly amongst the older classes. To combat this, the allocation was overhauled and a new list issued with effect from 1 January 1947 whereby many machines found themselves in unfamiliar territory – many of them to spend their last days before nationalisation hauling heavy loads with indifferent fuel.

A Southern Career

In this (as in the uniform volumes) there are many contributions from people who knew the subject first hand. One of a diminishing band of those who had a varied and active career on the Southern is Francis Knight, responsible for the chapter on the London Area Steam Working and the two features (with much fascinating detail) on the Southern at war among other contributions. He witnessed first hand the tremendous changes wrought under the management of Sir Herbert Walker. Nowhere was this modernisation more impressive than on the South Eastern Section which still suffered for the constructional shortcomings of the impecunious South Eastern and LC&D Companies and their disastrous feuding.

When he started as a station clerk at Sole Street two weeks before the General Strike of 1926 the electrification went no further than Orpington and Dartford and the first ever 'light signals' had just been installed in the London area. Like most country station clerks, he spent much of the spare time between trains working the signal box (when the stationmaster was out of the way) so learning the intricacies of the Sykes Lock & Block and the movements for detaching 'double headers' needed for the stiff Sole Street bank. Communication with the outside world was by the single needle instrument so the morse code had to be learned and practised. Only the larger stations had PO phones.

After some time as a relief clerk he came into the London East Divisional superintendent's office in 1930 and to headquarters in 1938 to get his first timetable experience with the Maidstone and Gillingham electrification project. The war saw him as passenger train controller in Orpington Control through the days of Dunkirk and the blitz after which, he says, any subsequent derailments and incidents were an anti-climax.

His interest in engine workings prompted the S.W. Smart (the last of the operating Czars) to appoint him to tour the SR as a one-man engine economy commission which gave him unrivalled geographical knowledge, before going to the South Western as deputy head of trains, then back to HQ to become head of electrification and planning a few months before the 1955 modernisation programme which put him in the forefront of the Kent Coast Electrification where he was a firm supporter of the electro-diesel concept as a sensible alternative to 'spending £50 million on electrification and £20 million on building a fleet of young power stations which do not use traction current'.

Nationalisation began to destroy the family feel of the Southern as officers moved between regions. Francis Knight went for a spell with that railway genius Gerry Fiennes before finishing a non-untypical but distinguished career back at Southern HQ as movements planning officer.

ACKNOWLEDGEMENTS

This book is the product of teamwork which takes advantage of deep personal experience of the Southern. In particular we wish to acknowledge the contributions from Francis Knight (see above) and Patrick Stevenson. The latter's anecdotes on his life as a cadet remind us that 'The Railway' was paternal and human. Alan Warren has again produced some fascinating locomotive profiles while the joint authors have been able to delve into their experiences of Southern holidays and travel back to pre-war days. Much of the technical work has come from John Powell's pen while the piece on Paddlebox and Spamcan owes much to the late Professor W.A. Tuplin, always one to stir the imagination. The consultancy team led by Patrick Whitehouse has been the same as for *The Great Days of the GWR*: John Powell, John Edgington and David Johnson. Without this pool of knowledge it would have been impossible to produce this broad-based book.

Some line drawings have come from copies of the *Railway Magazine* and we thank both John Slater and Peter Kelly for their courtesy. Again we would like to thank the photographers whose work has helped so much to bring the book to life. The principle contributors include P.M. Alexander, Hugh Ballantyne, C.R.L. Coles, R.K. Evans, R.C. Riley and P.B. Whitehouse.

The main chapters are based on material supplies as follows: David St John Thomas (This was the Southern, Salisbury to Exeter, Three 1950s Journeys); Patrick Whitehouse (On the Road with Paddlebox and Spamcan); John Powell (The 4–4–0s and their Work, An Engineer's View From the Bridge, Maunsell and Bulleid, A Comparison); John Gilkes (Having a Flutter on the Southern); J.N. Faulkner (An Observer Remembers); Alan Warren (Profile on Tanks); Alan Jackson (Bustle and Variety,

The London Termini); Francis Knight (London Area Steam Working).

'Fillers' between chapters were provided by Patrick Stevenson (How I Became a Cadet); Geoffrey Kichenside (Famous Bottleneck); Patrick Whitehouse (Preservation, Holiday at Bexhill); J.B. Snell (A New Boy's Impression of the Last Year); John Edgington (The Belles); John Powell (The Schools: A Special Case); Francis Knight (Overlord to Victory, Southern Railway Goodbye); Bert Hooker (Indian Summer of Steam).

The authors gratefully acknowledge illustrations as follows. Black and white photographs: P.M. Alexander/Millbrook House Collection (19 lower, 21 lower, 25, 43, 45 lower, 65, 85 lower, 86, 87 upper, 87 middle, 112, 119 lower, 121 lower, 128 both, 138, 171 lower, 172, 175); J. Ashman (131); H. Ballantyne (21 upper, 34, 35, 53, 189, 191, 201 both); C. Brown (159); H.C. Casserley (12 lower, 40 upper, 79, 155, 157); C.R.L. Coles (16 both, 23, 78, 80, 124 lower, 178); D. Cross (72 lower, 152 upper, 47); A.G.S. Davies (61); T.J. Edgington (29 upper, 199); T.J. Edgington Collection (60, 88 both, 91, 93, 116, 135); R.K. Evans FRPS (24, 26 lower, 32, 49, 75, 121 upper, 129, 145 upper, 163); J.N. Faulkner (58); J.C. Flemmons (133, 143); A.W. Flowers (176 both); G.F. Heiron (123, 164 upper); P.J. Howard (70); D.A. Johnson (160, 193); L&GRP (12 upper, 64, 182); P.J. Lynch (50, 52 both, 139 upper, 166); Millbrook House Collection (33, 40 lower, 42 upper, 85 upper, 126, 146, 152 lower, 164 lower, 204); O.J. Morris (8, 9, 113); S.C. Nash (109, 119 upper, 136 upper, 137); National Railway Museum (22 upper, 96, 179); K. Nunn/LCGB (94); C.F.H. Oldham (171 upper); P. Ransome-Wallis (17, 22 lower, 29 lower, 72 upper, 87 lower, 134, 142, 145 lower); W.J. Probert/Millbrook House Collection (169); R.C. Riley (27, 28, 31 lower, 76, 115 lower, 136 lower, 139 lower, 140 upper); R.F. Roberts (18, 37, 54, 148); J. Robertson/Colour Rail (165, 167, 168, 181); R. Russell (66); E. Treacy/Millbrook House Collection (4, 45 upper, 82, 101, 115 upper, 127, 132, 140 lower, 150, 195, 198); R.E. Vincent (149); P.H. Wells (124 upper); C.M. Whitehouse (68/69); P.B. Whitehouse ARPS (19 upper, 26 upper, 46 lower, 200); D.W. Winkworth (31 upper).

Colour photographs: P.M. Alexander/Millbrook House Collection (6 both, 7 both); Colour Rail (98 both, 99 upper, 107 both); D. Cross (14 lower); J.G. Dewing (14 upper); T.J. Edgington (110 lower); N. Glover (15 both); P.J. Howard (111 lower); Millbrook House Collection (99 lower); B. Swain (110 upper); P.B. Whitehouse ARPS (111 upper).

INDEX